T0304850

Brendan Cooper has published widely in the fields of literature and sport. His most recent book, *Deep Pockets: Snooker and the Meaning of Life*, was published by Constable in 2023.

ECHOING GREENS

How Cricket Shaped the English Imagination

BRENDAN COOPER

CONSTABLE

CONSTABLE

First published in Great Britain in 2024 by Constable

3 5 7 9 10 8 6 4 2

Copyright © Brendan Cooper, 2024

A CIP catalogue record for this book
is available from the British Library.

ISBN: 978-1-40871-944-2

Typeset in Electra by Hewer Text UK Ltd, Edinburgh
Printed and bound in Great Britain by Clays Ltd, Elcograf, S.p.A.

Papers used by Constable are from well-managed forests and other responsible sources.

MIX
Paper | Supporting
responsible forestry
FSC
www.fsc.org   FSC® C104740

Constable
An imprint of
Little, Brown Book Group
Carmelite House
50 Victoria Embankment
London EC4Y 0DZ

An Hachette UK Company
www.hachette.co.uk

www.littlebrown.co.uk

For Nouska

CONTENTS

Opener: Standards to Uphold

In many ways, 20 June 2023 was a typically English summer's day – mild and mellow, not exactly hot, but not cold either, an occasional hint of blue emerging from behind long spools of silver cloud. The kind of day that would have had club cricketers, up and down the country, trying to decide if the short or the long-sleeved jumper would suit best. Rain had been around that morning – thin rain, English rain, a light persistent drizzle. It had been enough to delay the start of the final day's play at Edgbaston, in the first Ashes test.

But at just after 6 p.m. that evening – in the darkening light – England were two wickets away from a dramatic victory.

Australia needed fifty-four to win. They had no specialist batsmen left. All their dwindling hopes seemed to rest on captain Pat Cummins – a dangerous customer, in the agricultural style, but who only had two test half-centuries to his name. At the other end was Nathan Lyon, who had never made any. It was England's game. Their brash declaration on day one – with fewer than four hundred on the board – had been widely criticised as foolish, evidence that their hyper-aggressive 'Bazball' philosophy lacked balance and sense. But it looked like it was going to pay off.

Ball by ball, though, the Aussie batsmen chipped away at the total. With the situation so precarious, some presumed they would play it safe and block out for the draw. But defence was not the plan. Cummins clubbed two Joe Root half-volleys over mid-off for six. Lyon nurdled, swung, and rode his luck. One top-edged pull flew out to Ben Stokes at deep square leg – who dived backwards, jabbed at it with one hand, juggled it, and watched it flop to the ground. It was a tough chance – but for someone of Stokes' superhuman prowess, something of a surprise mistake.

As things went down to the wire, echoes surfaced of the famed finale at the same ground, eighteen years before. On that occasion, England had managed to snaffle victory with two runs to spare. But this time round, they were losing control. The bowling grew more erratic. Even Lyon found some confidence, smiting Stuart Broad for two imperious fours – an improbably elegant off-drive and a lofted thump over mid-wicket. When a thick edge from Cummins oozed down to the third man boundary, it was all over. Lyon was being hoisted by his captain in a triumphant bearhug. England had lost.

The brilliance of the match, though, had deeper implications. The whole thing had been an explosive justification of test cricket's pre-eminence. At a time of unprecedented paranoia about the speed of cricket – and the need for newer, faster forms of the game – the nerve-shredding finish to the first Ashes test showed that no other format could begin to match such levels of theatre. Social media was immediately awash with exhilarated responses from pundits and players. 'Test cricket is best cricket,' affirmed legendary India batsman Virender Sehwag. 'If this is the cricket we will get this summer, then yes please,' wrote former England fast bowler Alex Tudor. 'Kids at school asking for the score every five mins . . . trust me, test cricket [is] still No.1'.

The English summer of 2023 was developing a special kind of significance, in a reclamation of test cricket as the sport's untouchable pinnacle. A fortnight later, Ben Stokes was at the crease on the final day of the second test. He had taken England from a hopeless position – 190 for 6, chasing 371 – past three hundred with the kind of innings he had made his signature; a defence-minded initial phase, sprouting into a transcendent atom bomb of attacking batsmanship under the most extreme pressure. A total of nine sixes were hammered into the Lord's stands. But just as he was beginning to look invincible, and an impossible victory inevitable, he botched a drive high into the air and was caught. England would fall just short – this time by forty-three runs. In a series of tiny margins, with neither side deserving to lose, England had lost again.

The drama of the second test, though, had a very different feel. By this point a miasma of hostility had fallen between the two teams. The match had been electrified by some of the most controversial incidents in Ashes history – incidents that raised fascinating, complicated questions about patriotic loyalty, national character and the so-called 'spirit of the game'.

The first happened close to the end of day four. Ben Duckett – fifty not out – gave himself some room, Bazball-style, for an audacious lofted flick to third man. But there was extra bounce from hulking all-rounder Cameron Green and the ball found the top edge. It swirled down towards fine leg and the dependable dinner-plate hands of Mitchell Starc – who took the catch comfortably, moving to his left, before skidding along the turf and pumping his fists in triumph.

The umpires, though, were not sure about something. Replays showed that after taking the ball, Starc had slid it along the grass, as if trying to wipe it clean. There was no question that the ball had touched the ground – but had he been in control of his body at the time? After some consultation, the big screen at Lord's showed the third umpire's verdict: NOT OUT.

To say the very least, the Australians were not happy.

'That is the biggest load of rubbish I have ever seen,' raged Glenn McGrath in the commentary box. 'If that is not out, then every other catch that has ever been taken should not be out.' And it was followed by an even more pointed claim. 'If that's *England* taking the catch, that's out' ... the implication was clear. It was not a fair contest. Corruption was at work.

Starc's disputed catch had brought acrimonious spice to the fray – but in the end, it turned out to be nothing more than an *amuse bouche* ahead of one of the most controversial cricketing incidents of the twenty-first century. The next day, as lunch approached, Jonny Bairstow was at the crease alongside Ben Stokes. England were 193 for 5 – on the back foot, still nearly two hundred adrift, but just about in the game. A lot depended on this particular partnership between the last two recognised batsmen.

The final ball of Green's eighth over was a tired-looking bouncer that Bairstow easily ducked. It would, in truth, have been a forgettable piece of cricket, if it were not for what happened in the moments that followed.

Bairstow looked down at the crease and – in an *apparent* acknowledgment that the over had ended – marked his ground with the spikes of his boot, before ambling up the pitch. But over had not been called. Carey threw the ball straight at the stumps. The Aussies appealed, and Bairstow was given out.

The boos from the crowd boomed round the ground for the rest of the day. The customary, decorous hum of Lord's had gone; in its place was a riot of ill-feeling. But the real astonishments happened in the Long Room itself. As the Australians came through for lunch, a mob of members stood waiting. There were boos, jeers, chants of 'Cheats!' and 'Shame on you!' Usman Khawaja was upset enough to offer a few words back in response; David Warner had to be restrained by some attendants.

'Do I contradict myself?' Walt Whitman once wrote. 'Very well then, I contradict myself. (I am large, I contain multitudes.)' Well, there was certainly contradiction at Lord's that day, amid the blazers, jackets and ties. Because what those members were claiming – as they bayed for Australian blood in such unseemly fashion – was the moral high ground.

There was no doubt at all that the stumping of Jonny Bairstow was within the laws of the game. The point of contention was murkier: was such a sneaky move consistent with the *ethics* of the game?

In his book *Spirit of Cricket*, former England captain Mike Brearley explains, 'What falls under spirit is harder to pin down than what is prescribed or proscribed by law ... Virtue and grace in life raise deeper questions than doing one's duty. We need clear rules, but we also need to question them. Spirit is broader than simply obeying the letter of the law.' The laws and the spirit of cricket are connected – but they are not the same. Had Australia contravened the 'virtue' and 'grace' that should underpin all cricketing action?

Former England opener Geoffrey Boycott certainly thought so. 'If you want to win at all costs,' he claimed, 'then cricket should not be for you. We want people to play hard and fair – but surely there are standards to uphold? When batsmen are not trying to take an advantage then you should not follow the letter of the law.' Even journalist and presenter Piers Morgan weighed in on the matter, arguing that the stumping – while 'perfectly within the laws of cricket' – was 'also entirely against the spirit of the game'.

The summer was no longer just an advert for test cricket; it was a battleground for cricket's honour. Perceptions of national character were under scrutiny. Old xenophobic stereotypes wormed their way into the mentality of England fans: 'Same old Aussies, always cheating!' had been the words ringing round Lord's that fateful day. Pat Cummins was unrepentant. Ben Stokes, meanwhile, was tersely aggrieved ('Would I want to win a game in that manner?' he said on *Test Match Special*. 'The answer for me is "No"'). Amazingly, even Prime Minister Rishi Sunak felt the need to comment. 'The PM agrees with Ben Stokes,' explained Sunak's official spokesperson. 'He said he simply wouldn't want to win a game in the manner Australia did.'

The hypocrisy written into the English stance of moral superiority was easy enough to see. The boorish chanting of fans was hardly an example of civilised respect for a visiting team. And the ugly scene in the Lord's Long Room – ultimately resulting in a member being banned for life – was hardly an example of refined conduct at the home of cricket. England, one might say, was showing itself to be what it always had been – a meeting place of truth and fiction, where lofty ideals of cricketing integrity collide with a much more defective, down-to-earth reality.

In this way, the Jonny Bairstow stumping was just the most recent example of an old English claim, a claim as enduring as it is fanciful – that it is England where cricket really belongs, where its spirit is protected and kept alive. As journalist Jonathan Liew observed,

> There is a common thread running through England's new vibes-based style of cricket and the piqued outrage that has greeted Bairstow's stumping. Both, ultimately, are grounded in an idea of impunity and presumption: an assertion that England and England alone gets to adjudicate on what is good for the game. We get to say what constitutes entertainment. We get to decide how Test cricket must be saved. And, by extension, we get to judge what is sporting and fair, the norms of behaviour that our opponents will be expected to follow. You can keep your silly rules. We stand for more.

For hundreds of years, in fact, the English have claimed ownership of cricket in such fashion. As an expression of noble conduct – so the argument goes – cricket is also an expression of England.

However outlandish it might be, it is a belief that sits at the heart of the relationship between cricket and the English imagination. No other game has enchanted artists and writers like cricket has and no other game has been so wrapped up in that most treasured and tenuous of dreams, the dream of the precious stone set in the silver sea, the blessed plot of England.

'There can be no summer in this land,' wrote Neville Cardus, 'without cricket.'

It is, perhaps, the most famous line from the most celebrated cricket writer in history. Evidently, it is a grand claim to make

– but it is not the only time he argued such a thing. 'A wonderfully English game is cricket,' he wrote in 1929, before going further:

> The fact is, cricket is more than a game. For one thing, it is part of summer. How many of us have gone home after watching cricket and taken with us no impression more likeable than that we have seen during the day the sun climb up the sky, pause over us for a while in beneficent noon heat, and then descend towards evening while the field turned a softer and softer green?

Cricket, for Cardus, is interwoven with its surroundings – so much so that it becomes indistinguishable from the colour and light of the day itself, the warmth and movement of the sun. Cricket does not just happen on a summer's day: it is a summer's day.

For all its lyricism, this is a view open to critique, even to ridicule. Is it not, in fact, a sanitised picture – a dishonest fantasy, detached from the reality of English life? Maybe so. But Cardus was far from alone in harbouring a belief that there is an essential quality to cricket in England.

According to his son Tom, J. B. Priestley 'thought cricket was a part of England and part of English character. Losing it would have diminished England somehow.' Poet and novelist Edmund Blunden wrote of 'cricket, that ever changeful, changeless game which some even among the English view as the prime English eccentricity'. John Major claimed, 'Cricket is an English invention – an export as potent as the English language itself.' Michael Henderson, in his elegiac lament *That Will Be England Gone*, wrote, 'An English landscape without cricket on the green between April and September is inconceivable.'

The persistence of such claims show that something is at work: a dense web of associations, links and memories. Throughout the ages, the aesthetics of cricket have been as vital to the English landscape as the hills and meadows immortalised in the art of Gainsborough, Constable and Turner. The game has inspired a library of literature so vast it dwarfs that of any other sport; according to historian Benny Green, 'It is almost as though the game itself would not exist at all until written about.' Cricket, in other words, has flourished not just in history, but in the fires of the imagination. In every direction – visual art, poetry, fiction, drama, film, television, photography and music – it has played a part in the story of English creative endeavour.

This is a book about cricket and the art it has inspired; but it is also a book about England – about the disorderly workings of the English imagination, its visions and ideals as well as its vexed relationship with the blunt reality of life.

And for models of English spirit, there is no better place to start than with two icons of English cricketing greatness. In many ways, they can be thought of as parallel figures in cricket history – a hundred years apart, but nevertheless somehow linked, heroes of the English cultural imagination who were often seen not so much as real people than as transcendent stars of myth and fable.

I
ICONS

Lord's. June 1984.

For Ian Botham, the media scandals had been punishing. The recent tour to New Zealand had been blighted by allegations of louche behaviour. One story claimed that Botham, along with Allan Lamb, had holed himself up in a hotel room with girls and bags of cocaine. Another alleged that Botham and others had been smoking pot in the middle of a test match, stuffing towels at the bottom of their hotel doors to contain the fumes. Tales abounded of players boozing in bars until the early hours; debauched parties had been reported with Elton John and his entourage. It was to go down in history as the sex, drugs and rock 'n' roll tour.

No one, not even Botham, could remain unaffected by such trials. Many observers felt that, at the age of twenty-eight, his best days were already past. But amidst the chaos, a gift for inspiration remained.

It was the second test of the summer, against a formidable West Indies side that had not lost a test match for over two and a half years. And against a line-up stuffed with legends, Botham produced something sensational – a virtuoso display of swing and seam bowling, burning his way through the opposition more or less on his own. He took all the first six wickets, and eight in total. It was vintage stuff, Botham moving the ball both ways in the air and off the seam at will, a conjurer of confusion and surrender.

He seemed able, somehow, to conduct the script entirely to his liking, magically manipulating events like a cricketing Merlin or Prospero. One minute he was charging in mightily with the ball; the next he was blowing kisses to the Lord's crowd. Even his great friend Viv Richards succumbed to the spell – Botham smilingly goading him after a bouncer skimmed his cap, before trapping him l.b.w. Everything, including Botham's bad balls, seemed fated for success: a tame leg-side long hop was top-edged by Jeffrey Dujon straight to mid-wicket. It was a reminder of something special and precious about the man – something numinous, a rare instinct for miracles . . .

. . . Lord's. July 1867.

W. G. Grace, just nineteen years old, had already been tagged as the finest player in England. The previous summer, he had averaged over fifty with the bat – including an innings of 224 not out, the highest first-class score for nearly half a century – as well as taking thirty-one wickets at an average of fourteen.

But this had been a tough season, to say the least. Throughout May and June, he had been laid up with an ankle injury before suffering a bout of scarlet fever. His batting had been badly compromised. But in the 'Gentlemen v. Players' fixture, he produced some brilliance with the ball – taking eight wickets for twenty-five runs in the second innings. His teammate Alfred Lubbock marvelled at the feat – wondering how Grace's deliveries, while 'never above what might be called a modest medium pace', were so destructive. Grace's bowling, he noted, seemed to 'puzzle them entirely'. It was as if there was something else about the man, some kind of inexplicable magic – perhaps even something numinous, a rare instinct for miracles . . .

1

'THERE HAS NEVER BEEN THE EQUAL': IMAGES OF W. G.

The gaze is intense, searching. Fires of white light burn in the heart of the eyes. The beard, of course, is magnificent, a vast expanse of chocolate brown that sits somewhere between unruly and coiffured – the edges wild, but the moustache and sideburns carefully shaped and oiled. The body is nothing but a giant sea of white, giving the impression not just of physical size, but of other-worldliness, as if this particular individual is something beyond the human. On the top of the head, the cap flaunts the familiar egg-and-bacon stripes of the MCC.

The painting of Victorian England's most famous man, by Archibald Stuart-Wortley, was made between 1885 and 1905 and hangs in the National Portrait Gallery. It is far from the only image of W. G. Grace that emphasises his larger-than-life qualities. In 1877, the following picture appeared in *Vanity Fair*:

It is signed by 'Spy' – the *nom de plume* of Sir Leslie Ward, who worked for the magazine for over thirty years. The image is a hybrid mix of orthodox portrait and caricature. Grace gazes at the viewer, face fixed in a confident grin. He is padded up, gloves in his hands – ready to go out to bat. But the torso is oversized, the arms bloated with bulging muscle – affording him the look more of a strongman or a bodybuilder than a cricketer. The padded legs look pencil-thin beneath the heft of brawn.

Even more dramatically, in a famous sketch of 1895, Max Beerbohm presents Grace as a towering giant:

It is certainly true that, by this time, Grace was a hefty physical specimen, not far off twenty stone. But Beerbohm's sketch puts less emphasis on flab and more on muscle, giving Grace massive forearms and thick biceps that appear to be on the verge of bursting through the rolled-up sleeves of his shirt. Once again, everything here is designed to suggest something superhuman. The feet are enormous. The torso is an engorged globe, the face veiled beneath a rich jungle of beard. In one hulking hand, he grips a bat between his fingers as if it were a teaspoon or a toothpick.

In the top corner of the image, the text reads 'Portrait of dear old W.G. – to the left is the Grand Stand, to the right, the funeral of one of his patients.' The twin undertakings of his life, cricket and medicine, are thus presented, though the depiction of a patient's funeral hints at which lay closer to his heart. In his right hand, he grips a cheque – a nod towards a thirst for money-making for which he had become notorious. It bears the name of Edward Lawson, editor of the *Daily Telegraph*, who in 1895 organised a trio of testimonials for W. G. to celebrate him scoring a thousand runs in May. The fund brought Grace a cool ten thousand pounds – in today's money, about £800,000.

Images such as these reveal how Grace was seen not simply as a cricketer, but as a transcendent being – an English cricketing god. And it must be said that the facts of his career make this a pretty understandable conclusion.

His achievements were astonishing. In an era of lethal wickets – when bowlers ruled, batting was perilous and big totals were rare – Grace redefined what was possible. When he reached his fiftieth first-class century, in 1875, only 109 other centuries had been made in the entire history of first-class cricket. He had made over 30 per cent of the total number; the tally of the next *thirteen* top centurions was needed in order to equal him. In the middle of one of his greatest summers, that of 1876, he made 344 (a first-class record), 177 and 318 not out in three consecutive innings – a total of 839 runs at an average of 419.5. He finished that season with over 2,500 runs, at an average of 62 – twice the runs and twice the average of any other player.

He was not only prolific – he was a visionary. Grace spectacularly transformed the art of batting, introducing undreamt of sophistication and range. Before him, players developed restricted techniques to suit their strengths. There would be 'back players' or those who batted in the 'forward style'. Grace cast all this into the fire. He would play forward or back as it suited him, with equal comfort and skill. He would attack or defend, depending on the circumstances or the state of the pitch. He could advance down the wicket and belt the ball out of the ground – or he could block vigilantly, surviving on pitches where the ball might fly at your head or at your toes within the same over. A famous story tells of the Lord's crowd rising to their feet in order to applaud his masterful blocking of four 'shooters' in a row. 'W. G. discovered batting,' wrote K.S. Ranjitsinhji, one of the greatest batsmen of the generation that followed. 'He turned its many narrow straight channels into one great winding river . . . Those who follow may or may not get within measurable distance of him, but it was he who pioneered and made the road.'

And that is just his batting, the aspect that gets the most attention. He also took nearly three thousand wickets, at an average of less than eighteen. On a total of ten occasions, he took over a hundred wickets in a season. No other cricketer in history, besides Donald Bradman, has gone so dramatically beyond the achievements of his rivals. Grace was not just the world's best cricketer; he was a miracle, who had somehow made the impossible real.

Victorian writing on Grace invariably seeks to capture this mythical quality about him. In 1872, R. A. Fitzgerald captained a pioneering MCC tour of North America; the following year, he wrote a memoir about the trip called *Wickets in the West: Or, the Twelve in America*. The touring party included some fine cricketers, such as A. N. Hornby, Lord Harris and Arthur Appleby, but there was no doubt that Grace was the star of the show. Fitzgerald characterises him as a kind of omnipotent folk hero, capable of godlike feats. At the end of their torrid transatlantic voyage, the author casts himself in the third person, struggling his way into a sleep that is peppered with Gracean dreams: 'The Captain was the last to sleep, as he revolved in his mind the various chances of the game, but he fell asleep at last like his less thoughtful comrades; and dreamed that W. G. was not out, 1,000, he couldn't tell where, but he awoke refreshed.'

Fitzgerald refers to Grace via a range of monikers – 'The Mammoth', 'Gilbert the Great' – to stress his superhero status. Without the star quality of Grace, the North American tour may well have not happened at all. It was, after all, Grace that people came to see. Many turned up purely to witness the genius at work:

It is admitted by the oldest admirers of the game that for patience and judgment, for strength of play, and precision of placing the ball, there has never been the equal of Mr W. G. Grace. He has arisen as a phenomenon in the game. Against all bowling, and on all grounds, he has left his mark. All who are acquainted with our metropolitan grounds cannot have failed to notice the anxiety of the public on its arrival on the ground to ascertain which side had won the toss. On learning that Mr. Grace's side is going to the wicket, the public to a man remain; should it be otherwise, a large majority apply for their 'pass', and return some hours later on the chance of seeing the 'Leviathan'.

Here was Grace, cricketer as leviathan, a mythological being brought to life. Watching him was like being given the chance to watch Achilles or Heracles, a figure from the realm of the imagination who had somehow entered into the world of men.

Unsurprisingly, Grace became a hero to boys across the land. The *Boy's Own Paper* of 1880 delivered an affectionate profile that highlighted his achievements. 'England has no more popular game than cricket,' it begins, 'and cricket has had no greater exponent than William Gilbert Grace. For the last seventeen years his position in the cricket world has been unique ... few bowlers have surpassed him, few fields have equalled him, no batsman has approached him.' And then, with a familiar touch: 'He is the very leviathan of scoring.'

But the profile goes on to stress other things – an integrity and a strength of character – that existed as an example to all. 'Let all our readers remember that if a thing is worth doing it is worth doing well; in work or in play earnestness is never wasted. The secret of Dr Grace's excellence has been his thoroughness.' Former cricketer and Whig politician, Lord Charles Russell, is then quoted: 'Looking at Mr Grace's playing, I have never been able to tell whether that gentleman is playing a winning or losing game ... just as he plays one ball so he plays the game; he is heart and soul in it.' Grace, in other words, was not just a great cricketer – he was a living embodiment of Victorian English virtue. Hard-working, dedicated and motivated by noble instincts, he was a moral as well as a sporting paragon.

It has now been amply documented that this romanticised view of Grace is some distance from the truth. The statistical transcendence of his career is undeniable; the numbers speak for themselves. But other elements of the man sit less well with the caricatured superman image. Even his imposing physical size, so suggestive of hypermasculine power, does not quite tell the whole story. As his biographer Simon Rae noted, 'For so large and so obviously virile a man,' his voice 'was remarkably high-pitched.' It was the source of self-consciousness and some embarrassment for the great man. On one occasion, he had a proposal of marriage rejected 'because of his high, squeaky voice'.

Beneath the simplified vision of Grace as folk hero lies a much more complex story, one that is tangled up with the intricacies of Victorian England's class struggles. Notoriously, he operated as an amateur whilst happily pocketing fees dwarfing those of any professional. It was a hypocrisy lampooned by illustrator Alfred Bryan, in an 1883 edition of the *Entr'acte* theatrical review:

BOBBY ABEL, TO W. G.:—"LOOK HERE, WE PLAYERS INTEND TO BE SUFFICIENTLY PAID, AS WELL AS THE SO-CALLED GENTLEMEN!"

Surrey and England batsman Bobby Abel makes a plea on behalf of his fellow professionals: 'Look here, we players intend to be sufficiently paid, as well as the so-called gentlemen!' In real life, Abel was a diminutive figure – just five feet four inches – but here he is absurdly tiny, a mere child or cricketing homunculus. The half-closed eyes may allude to his dodgy eyesight, which prematurely ended his international career; but it looks more like he is wincing, unable to look directly at the chilling figure of Grace looming above him. W. G., like the Colossus of Rhodes, stands with hands in his pockets, supremely unconcerned as he frowns down at his foe. The comical David and Goliath mismatch makes the balance of power perfectly clear.

A doctor, and the son of a doctor, Grace's middle-class West Country origins were an iffy fit for the aristocratic clique of the MCC. But once he was made a member in 1869 – on the strength of his already formidable reputation, at the age of twenty – he remained the club's loyal servant. In fact, his relationship to the professionals he played against and alongside was often fractious. And nowhere was this more apparent than on the inaugural 1873 tour of English players to Australia.

The three-month trip was beset with problems. Travelling conditions were grim, and the Australian pitches often unplayable (Grace later recalled in disbelief how, on a Stawell pitch recently converted from a ploughed field, one ball jammed in the dust and never made it to the batsman). But most striking of all was the ill-feeling that developed between the England party and their Australian hosts. The team was greeted with excited cheers and large crowds upon their arrival in Melbourne; but the positivity did not last.

In particular, the Australian public were shocked by some of the snobbery they witnessed. A light was suddenly cast on England's class divides – and it uncovered some ugly truths. 'In the colonies,' ran a column in the *Sydney Mail*, 'I have always been led to believe that the cricket-field levels all social distinctions, but in England . . . a line is drawn between gentlemen and professionals, and in many cases the latter are made to feel their social position somewhat acutely.' Another columnist was more withering:

> The gentlemen cricketers . . . trading on the professional cricketers of the team and endeavouring to secure for their genteel selves as much of the three thousand five hundred pounds of colonial money as they can . . . They will not even lodge at the same hotel with them! . . . The consequence of all this is what might be expected – insubordination in the ranks, a divided team, and humiliating defeats. We were not prepared to find such wretched specimens of snobbery as these amongst British gentlemen cricketers.

The writer concluded by denouncing 'the vulgar pretentious species of gentility set up as the Grace standard'. So-called 'Victorian English values' were nothing more than a sham – a veil for nastiness and arrogance. Before the tour, Grace had claimed that his team would have a duty 'to uphold the high character of English cricketers'. Instead – as both captain and their greatest player – Grace was being pinned as the figurehead of English hypocrisy, an incarnation of Perfidious Albion.

And there were even darker accusations in the mix. Rumours circulated that the English team were throwing games in a ploy coordinated by Grace himself. The *Sydney Mail* avowed that 'the play of Grace and his team is looked upon with the utmost distrust, and even when they score an easy victory the public think they have all the more reason for saying that previous performances, where they were less fortunate, were not fair and above board'.

Grace had arrived on Australian soil as an idol and a legend. But by the tour's end, things had turned sour in astonishing fashion. He was now pilloried as a puppet-master of sleaze and trickery. 'Instead of his brilliant and skilful play being remembered with profit and pleasure,' explained the *Sydney Morning Herald*, 'his name will become a synonym for mean cunning and systematic fraud.'

Such stories as these give Grace the great Victorian an awkward, double-edged quality. Heroic feats and underhand tactics sit alongside each other, in a doubtful mixture of light and dark. In *Beyond a Boundary*, C. L. R. James explored the way in which, in Grace, honour and skulduggery coexisted:

> It would be idle to discount the reputation he gained for trying to diddle umpires, and even on occasions disputing with them. He is credited with inducing a batsman to look up at the sun to see a fictitious flight of birds and then calling on the bowler to send down a fast one while the victim's eyes were still hazy. Yet I think there is evidence to show that his face would have become grave and he would have pulled at his beard if a wicket turned out to be prepared in a way that was unfair to his opponents.

There were also, of course, occasions when the gamesmanship of Grace backfired. None is more famous than the moment when, in the 1882 test match at the Oval, Australian batsman Sam Jones wandered down the wicket to pad some divots, thinking the ball was dead. To the horror of the Australians, Grace whipped off the bails and ran him out. The echoes of the Jonny Bairstow stumping incident of 2023 are hard to ignore – but on this occasion, it was the great icon of English cricket visibly failing to uphold the spirit of the game. 'In strict cricket no doubt Jones was out,' reflected Australian batsman Thomas Horan, before adding, 'I do not think it redounds much to any man's credit to endeavour to win a match by resorting to what might not inaptly be termed "sharp practice".'

What followed now sits at the summit of cricketing legend. An enraged Spofforth steamed in to take 7 for 44, winning the match for Australia by seven runs and motivating a journalist at the *Sporting Times* to create a nugget of immortal satire involving the cremated body of English cricket. As Grace's biographer Richard Tomlinson notes, 'Grace's "cheating" was the flame that lit the bail and created the "Ashes", the greatest – and often the most rancorous – of all international sporting series.'

The attributes of Grace the man might for ever remain the source of conflicting views – but the revolutionary brilliance of his batting can never be disputed. And it is as a batsman that he is appears in the most famous of all Gracean portraits. In 1890, Archibald Stuart-Wortley depicted him poised at the crease:

For all its fame, though, it is a surprisingly wooden image. Grace looks stiff, even bored. 'At first glance,' laments Tomlinson, 'he looks in danger of toppling backwards on to the stumps.' Grace had been reluctant to sacrifice much of his time for the project. The fact that he was having to pose contributed to his awkward, leaden stance. And it has to be said, too, that his substantial physical bulk, by this point in his life, gave him a rather unathletic air.

The dynamic nature of Grace's technique comes more vividly to life in portraits that show him in the act of mid-match batting. A memorable example is S. T. Dadd's sketch of Grace playing against Australia at Lord's in 1896:

It is true that there is an element of the idealised here – what we might, in modern times, call airbrushing; Grace's unfeasibly slender frame implies that Dadd was less interested in accuracy than in recalling an earlier phase of his career. Nevertheless, it is a portrait of technical batting excellence that transcends changes in technique across the ages and could easily be taken from a much more contemporary coaching manual; the great man watchfully plays a forward defensive with the flawless orthodoxy of a Geoffrey Boycott, Rahul Dravid or Virat Kohli.

Only a single, brief film of Grace's batting survives. It was made in 1901; by this time, he was in his fifties and well past his best.

The footage shows him practising in the nets. As he waits for each ball, his front foot is cocked, toes in the air; a hint of this technical quirk is visible in Stuart-Wortley's painting. But as the ball approaches, his lifts the bat with a wiggle, and his body comes alive; he is seen playing a front-foot drive, then a back-foot push through the covers, then a flick to mid-wicket. The stroke play all looks rather casual – oddly so, as if he is not paying full attention and not worried about where the ball might go. It is hard, though, to come to any firm conclusions. The images are bleached and blurry; the unfamiliar frame rate makes the movements seem warped and alien.

But it does not matter. These few hazy seconds of an ageing W. G. are just as compelling as any cricket that has ever been captured on film. It is a tantalising window into a lost age; a momentary glimpse of a mercurial genius who still, to this day, might well be the greatest English cricketer of all.

2

'A VERY ENGLISH HERO': IMAGES OF BEEFY

The body is huge – swollen well beyond normal proportions. In this respect, it uncannily resembles the Victorian images of W. G. Grace – a picture not of a human being, but of a titan, a giant. It was made by John Bellany in 1985 – right in the heart of the action-movie decade – and the jumper-busting torso conjures the heft of Arnold Schwarzenegger. But it is the eyes that are the real heart of the image: strong, searching, fierce crystals full of fire. The eyes – above everything else – show that this is a competitor of rare intensity.

Ian Terence Botham was born with a level of self-belief that is alien to most people. It is, in fact, the very first thing that he mentions in his autobiography:

> Two of my distinguishing features were evident almost from the day I was born. I weighed in at an eye-watering ten pounds one ounce – Beefy from the start – and from my youngest days I had an unshakeable self-confidence and belief in my own abilities ... though others might have found less flattering ways to describe it.

For Botham, confidence was not something he had to learn. It was just there from the beginning, as in-built as hair colour or skin complexion. There was something very unusual in his DNA – something that went well beyond the kind of self-assurance we might commonly find in a person. It was more like actual knowledge – a prophetic sense that he was destined for transcendent things. When he was seven, his mother stumbled upon him writing his name again and again on a piece of paper. 'What on earth are you doing?' she asked. 'Well, people are going to be asking me for my autograph one day,' was the reply. 'So I'm just practising it.'

And the story of his career was sprinkled with a unique kind of magic dust – playing itself out like the incomparable caperings of a comic-book hero, a cricketing Roy of the Rovers. A five-wicket haul on test debut; sixty-six test-match wickets in the following calendar year, at an average of eighteen; the fastest man ever to reach the double of a hundred wickets and a thousand runs; and at the heart of it all, of course, the 1981 Ashes – sacking himself as captain before getting sacked, then shining as the glorious heart of the most legendary summer in English cricket history.

Every new twist felt like a chapter in some mythic parable. BOTHAM'S A MIRACLE, ran the *Daily Express* headline in the wake of his match-saving 149 not out at Headingley. And it certainly seemed that way. Botham did not really make sense as a human being, beset with flaws, troubles and insecurities. He was more like a supernova of power – a bolt of unstoppable energy sent from the gods.

But Bellany's image is hardly a cheerful one. A celebration of Botham it may be – but if so, it is a celebration full of shadows. Bellany was an interesting choice for the commission – a troubled figure, whose life was laced with tragedy. Prone to depression, he battled alcoholism for many years – he was hospitalised for it in 1984 and required a liver transplant a few years later. In 1985 – the same year he painted Botham – his second wife, Juliet Gray, committed suicide. The human forms he fashioned were often disturbing figures with deformed faces. After his transplant, he made several self-portraits – sinister images of himself on the hospital bed, skin a livid yellow, drip stuck in his nose, bare belly ravaged by scars. His friend, the poet Alan Bold, described him as 'a painter whose temperament broods on dark and mysterious forces'.

The Botham–Bellany pairing was unexpected, although the artist developed a good bond with Botham over the sitting process. A surprising connection even emerged between their two fields of expertise. 'I never talk when I begin painting,' Bellany said, 'but later, when the sitter's getting tired, I encourage it. Botham said the way I painted reminded him of bowling. He would study a batsman with the same intensity, looking for their strengths and weaknesses and then lull them into a state of false security before delivering a killer ball.'

Bellany tackled the project in good faith – with a genuine aim to honour a sporting legend. And it was the heroism of his subject, most of all, that he sought to show: 'I wanted to capture Ian's presence, both physical and spiritual, the aura he commands when he steps on to the cricket field and the crowd trembles.'

Opinions on the final product, to say the least, were mixed. When the painting was unveiled at the National Portrait Gallery, the public reaction was largely hostile. Cricket fans branded it 'rubbish'. The papers ran withering headlines such as HOWZAT, BOTHAM and ART LOVERS HIT FOR SIX. The oversized body was seen as excessive, even ludicrous. In the *Daily Telegraph*, Michael Wharton – under his pseudonym Peter Simple – did not hold himself back from satire: 'Mr Bellamy [sic] is not the only artist who was sought to capture the titanic cricketer's physical and spiritual presence. John Gasby, the neo-explosionist sculptor, has produced, after months of dedicated work, a statue of Botham, several times life size, which he hopes will be erected outside Lord's, involving the diversion of several roads.'

John McEwen, Bellany's biographer, called the portrait 'one of the most contentious contemporary acquisitions by a public gallery in post-1945 Britain'.

Such dismissals, though, miss the clash of moods that makes Bellany's painting so intriguing. The painter's effort to lionise Botham – someone he saw as 'a magnificent specimen, a physical giant of a man' – is clear not only in the huge, hulk-like body. The background is a flame-like mix of orange and yellow, as if Botham stands in front of some vast bonfire. The board beside him promotes 'IAN BOTHAM' in big capital letters – and underneath it, 'ENGLAND'. On the surface at least, this is very much Botham the patriot, the hero of English sport.

But there is a darkness to that face. It is not enough to say it is intense; it has a strained, even haunted quality. The forehead is clouded by a faint frown. The cheeks are etched with lines. Under the droop of the moustache, the mouth is tense and sour. The warped proportions give the feel of a disorientating bad dream. There is a disquieting aspect to Bellany's portrait – it is a long way from being a straightforwardly reverential depiction. Perhaps it hints at a murkier truth behind the conventional glorification of Botham; his life was, after all, far more complicated than the sanitised hero narrative allows. In those blazing blue eyes maybe there is a sign not just of all the wickets, runs and catches, but also the bruising tabloid scandals, the alleged affairs, the mood swings, the pub fights, the drug charges. It is a painting of a hero – but a hero with a dark side.

In general, though, a simpler characterisation of Botham remains dominant in the English imagination. He is fêted as a folk hero to stand alongside King Arthur and Robin Hood – a British bulldog, an archetype of John Bull patriotism. The nickname, 'Beefy', may in truth have stemmed from his bulky size; but there is something apt about the way it echoes age-old *rosbif* caricatures of the English temperament. It is as if he is not simply English, but is made out of Englishness itself. French journalist Philippe Auclair saw him as 'essentially an eighteenth-century Englishman' – a revival of a lost England, a ghost returned from Broadhalfpenny Down. In a homage to Botham on his sixtieth birthday, Michael Henderson hailed him as 'a very English hero', a player who 'spoke for England. Whenever he picked up his bat, or had a ball in his hand, he left spectators in no doubt.' In Henderson's view, he represented 'all those people who understand instinctively what England means, not in a narrow way, but through something that is in the blood'.

Botham has certainly always worn his patriotism on his sleeve. 'I'm a massive royalist,' he explained on the eve of collecting his knighthood. 'The monarchy stands for everything that makes me proud to be English . . . I listen to all these republicans and if it was down to me I'd hang 'em! I honestly would. It's a traitor's game for me.' It came as little surprise, with Brexit looming, to find him firmly in the Vote Leave camp. 'Anyone who is proud of their country and cares about its future should take their share of personal responsibility for what happens to it,' ran his article in *The Times* in the run-up to the 2016 referendum. The accompanying photo showed Botham sporting a Union Jack bow tie. 'As a patriot,' ran the title, 'I'm going in to bat for my beliefs.'

After retiring from first-class cricket, Botham transitioned into the commentary box. It was, in some ways, not a natural move; as he confessed himself, 'To say the least, I wasn't an over-analytical cricketer.' But working largely for Sky Sports, he became one of TV cricket's stalwart pundits. It is this post-retirement Botham – a smarter, more refined media dignitary – that we find in Nick Botting's 2001 portrait, now hanging at Lord's:

The sky-blue shirt – plus Rohan Kanhai International XI Tour tie – lend an appropriately professional air. In the background is the stand of the Qaddafi stadium in Lahore. Botting had been commissioned to record England's 2000 tour of Pakistan and the Botham portrait is one of a range of resultant pieces (other subjects included the Barmy Army, the crowd at Faisalabad, and Alec Stewart and Michael Atherton practising in the nets).

Botting's paintings are placid and charming – devoid of the unrest to be found in Bellany's work. He was 'a bit of a hermit, living in an isolated little bubble looking out at the world', he once explained. This quiet detachment is reflected in his peaceful depiction of Botham, who sits in relaxed fashion – gazing not confrontationally at the viewer, but out into the middle distance. The facial expression is thoughtful – perhaps even philosophical – but calm. On this occasion, the blue eyes are cool and composed. At the same time, though, reminders of his rebellious spirit are easy enough to find. The tie is a little loose round that neck; Botham, ever the maverick, appears not to have done up his top button. More obviously, the right hand clutches a fat cigar – a marker of Botham as *bon viveur*, a vibrant sampler of life's pleasures.

To some, it is a sign of something rather less palatable about the man – a kind of boorishness, a tendency towards macho posturing. But Botham was never the sort to care what other people thought. As a working-class kid from rural Somerset, in English cricket's class-infected world, he was inured from the start to the threat of social snobbery. 'I'm just a country boy from Yeovil,' he once said, 'who knew what he wanted from life and went for it.'

II
ORIGINS

28 July 1978. The Oval.

It had been a cool summer – unseasonably so, even by English standards, with daily temperatures well below average and most days overcast. 'The biggest test for any cricketer in England is the weather,' claimed the great Indian all-rounder Kapil Dev, and this was the kind of summer – grey, dull, cut with wintry chill – that seemed to prove his point.

But this particular day – the second day of the first test against New Zealand – was a scorcher. Sunlight burned like white fire on the players, the sort of hot, parched light that evoked the unforgettable summer heatwave of two years earlier. England had lost two quick wickets and so, in theory, there was pressure on new batsman David Gower, just twenty-one years old and in the middle of his first season of international cricket.

But Gower – lithe and willowy as a dancer in his baggy shirt, hair a cherubic sea of blond curls – seemed to know nothing about pressure. Already, he was a player of such unreal grace and ease that strange things happened as he batted. The ball seemed slower, somehow, when bowled to him; time seemed half asleep. It was as if, via some gift for prophecy, he already knew where each ball would be going, readying himself with lazy expectation. Each shot looked like it had been pre-prepared – too beautiful to be spontaneous, carefully rehearsed into aesthetic perfection.

The New Zealand bowlers were powerless as Gower sauntered towards his maiden test century. And after getting there with a sweep off spinner Stephen Boock, he hardly raised his bat at all in celebration – introducing England fans to a nonchalance that bordered on apathy. It was a trait they would come to love and resent, in equal measure, over the years to come. There was something ethereal about this angelic young prodigy – as if he had been lifted straight from a religious painting or an illustration to a Medieval English dream-poem . . .

3

'PLAYING AT CREAG': VISIONS
OF MEDIEVAL CRICKET

No one knows when cricket began. Every account of cricket's origins must start with an admission of failure. The records we have only go back a certain way. Beyond them, there is a blank space where the answer lies. Cricket began inside a silence forever out of our reach.

The reason we cannot supply cricket with a date of birth is that there really is no such thing – no single galvanic moment when games of stick and ball suddenly ripened into the game we recognise. And no literature or visual art is going to reveal a full picture; there is a hidden history outside the history we know. One of the few things we can safely say is that it evolved gradually – over not just decades, but centuries. Some form of cricket will have existed for a certain amount of time – perhaps for a very long time – before anyone chose to record it.

But while we do not have the full story of cricket's roots, there is plenty to suggest that these roots – the deep roots of the game – are ancient ones.

The most popular source for the word 'cricket' is that it stems from the Anglo-Saxon *cricc* – sometimes *cricce* or *cryc* – meaning a stick or staff. And stick and ball games have been around for pretty much as long as humans have. A Greek relief sculpture from the sixth century BC shows two players battling for a ball with curved, hockey-like sticks. There was a game, *seker-hemat*, played by the ancient Egyptian pharaohs, involving a batter hitting a ball as fielders ran to catch it.

Some have suggested that cricket's origins may even go back to primeval man. 'The instinct to throw and to hit,' wrote cricket historian H. S. Altham, 'is the basis of man's primitive armoury.' Writers Ralph Dellor and Stephen Lamb imagined that a bat was first brandished to rehearse 'the hunting techniques of their elders by clubbing, not one another, but, say, a stone or lump of wood thrown in their direction'. Poet and folklorist Andrew Lang felt cricket was discernible in old Irish epics of 600–700 BC or earlier – in one of which, warrior and demigod Cuchulainn plays a game that 'consisted in the batsman defending with a bat or thick club, a hole in the ground, into which his opponent tried to pitch a ball'.

If crude ancestors of cricket extend into the prehistoric past, where are we supposed to start? What actually is the earliest evidence of the game? Ancient images of players hitting balls with sticks, bats and clubs have often been claimed as prototypes for tennis, baseball and golf; cricket cannot claim them for its own. And – of course – a game involving a bat and a ball does not automatically mean a game of cricket. There is a complicated family tree stretching from antiquity through the centuries, their threads of influence spreading into modern sport in intricate, enigmatic ways.

In the end, part of the answer must come from the imagination. What inescapably grabs us is a sense of identification, a gut feeling that something recognisable is present. And it is that feeling – of something more than just a bat and a ball, but a distinctively *cricketing* spectacle – that makes an illustration from the twelfth century so compelling.

Nearly two hundred years before the first written reference to anything that might be cricket, a picture was made that looks remarkably like the game. It is a lightning bolt from the depths of medieval England – a beacon from cricket's unwritten prehistory. It just might be the earliest recorded representation of a group of cricketers, in the acts of batting, bowling and fielding.

The right shoulder is thrust forward, and the bat lifted dramatically high behind the head. There is even a hint of a smile on his face, as he stands waiting for the delivery. This is a player with dash and flair. The bat is curved – a little like a hockey stick, perhaps, but much more like a shepherd's crook, which it almost certainly was. Overall, the impression this figure gives is princely, arrogant, swaggering: a young man, one might say, with plenty of faith in his ability to score big runs.

Here – perhaps – is the very first batsman in history. He was drawn in the twelfth century, between 1120 and 1130, and appears in a manuscript of Bede's *Life of St Cuthbert*.

He may not have any predecessors, but he is obviously no rookie. He stands with the assured air of someone who has played the game plenty of times before. The feet are splayed wide apart, creating an aura of imposing confidence.

The bowler, meanwhile, has a look of focused concentration. He is a very different character, for sure. He appears a little nervous. The facial features are contracted into an uptight look. Perhaps his adversary has a reputation. Perhaps he has already amassed a significant innings. In any event, the bowler grips the ball carefully in both hands with preternaturally long fingers, fingers perfect for the application of spin, which is what he seems to be doing as he prepares to deliver the ball underarm.

There are five other figures in the image – wearing differently coloured tunics, clearly suggesting a team game, the reds versus the greens. There is no particular aim at mid-match realism, as a second ball is also included; one figure is spectacularly diving towards it, bent backwards, in the process of taking an acrobatic catch. A third squats between batsman and bowler, posed with one hand jutting upwards from his chin – an unorthodox fielding position, perhaps, or a coded feature of some umpiring role. Much more likely, though, it is a signal up to the heavens: this, in the picture's very middle, is probably the young Saint Cuthbert himself, hand pointing up to God as he sits watching the revels. In Christian iconography, an open palm symbolised honesty, salvation and freedom from evil.

The final three figures are not watching the main action. Perhaps they got bored. They may be playing their own game, in fact, separate from the others; one of them appears to be tickling another on the neck. The third seems lost in his own thoughts – a finger pointed towards his own face in contemplation or self-blame. The overall effect is somewhat chaotic – not a carefully orchestrated contest, but a disorganised scene of youthful play.

This illustration sequence has been heralded as a supreme example of medieval English art. 'It is the return,' wrote historian T. S. R. Boase, 'of the native graphic genius . . . Here we have the hand of a master.' And it is difficult to look at the batsman without being struck by a very particular resemblance, a visual bond shining across eight centuries. With his flowing locks and nonchalant air, this Adam of batting looks rather like David Gower . . .

Sometime in the twelfth century, an unknown monk sat down to draw an archetype of imperious left-handed batsmanship that would take human shape over eight hundred years later. Two strutting lyricists; ghosts of each other.

Another intriguing detail is that Bede's original text does not actually say anything about a bat or a ball. Cuthbert, we are told, excelled at 'wrestling, jumping, running'. Here is Bede's description of the scene:

> One day a great crowd of lads were at their usual games in a field, Cuthbert among them, twisting themselves about in all kinds of contortions in the excitement of the game.

The illustrator has chosen to introduce the batting and bowling elements. There is some artistic licence at work. We must assume that the image shows a game known to the artist, being played in England around 1120 when the illustration was made. It is a twelfth-century scene applied to an eighth-century text. Not only that, it hints that such a game was recognisable enough to justify the inclusion.

Perhaps this mysterious medieval version of cricket was more popular than we will ever be able to know.

The truth of what was being played on the fields of England, in the first hundred years or so after the Norman invasion, might elude us, but there are certain things we do know about cricket's birth. The curved crooks of early bats show us that the game developed among shepherd boys. And we can deduce that this happened in the south-east, across the Downs and the Weald, as journalist and commentator John Arlott explained:

> There the sheep-cropped grass was short enough to allow the earliest bowling to be – as it was – simply trundled all along the ground. If the entrance gate to the hurdle sheepfold was the

bowler's target, that would account for the term 'wicket' for it consisted of two forked uprights with a crossbar – called a 'bail' – laid across them; and the whole was called a wicket.

The ball may have been 'trundled', but this does not mean batting will have been easy. The Bede manuscript – with its intense, neurotic bowler – hints that, even then, complex and subtle spins may have been imparted in an effort to trick the batsman.

Almost two hundred years later, the first mention of cricket appeared in writing. Or, at least, perhaps it did. The legitimacy of the reference has been hotly disputed. In the spring of 1300, according to the wardrobe accounts of Edward I, the king's son, Prince Edward, was recorded as 'playing at creag and other sports'. No explanation exists of what, precisely, 'creag' might have been. The phonic similarity – the closeness to *cricc* – is tantalising. Some historians have accepted it, while others have been more sceptical. Arlott concluded that the claim 'awaits confirmation'. Former prime minister John Major dismissively said it requires 'a mighty leap of faith to claim that it was cricket; the kindest judgement that can be made upon this romantic assumption is "not proven"'. Writer Jim Pipe suggested it might not even describe a specific game at all, but 'could simply mean fun' – a variant, he suggests, of the Irish *craic* (or *crak* in Middle English).

In the end, it is another enigma. Untold stories lie behind it, but we cannot know its secrets.

What can be established is that, with the arrival of the four-teenth century, more art started to appear across England bearing an intriguingly cricketing air. At some point in the early part of the century, a copy of the Decretals of Pope Gregory IX made its way to London. Local artists were then commissioned to deco-rate the blank areas of each page with borders, designs, and pictures. One such picture is this:

It appears to be a scene of instruction – a coaching session of some sort. The figure on the right, older and bearded, has a teacherly aspect. His frowning look suggests he is in the process of explaining some points of batting technique. He certainly looks like someone who takes his job seriously. And once again, he adopts a southpaw stance. A satisfying surprise emerges: the earliest two surviving images of batsmen in England both depict left-handers.

The technique is competent, even to a contemporary eye – side on, feet apart, weight evenly distributed, eyes level and looking over the front shoulder. But there is something awkward about it too. This is not the dashing figure of the Bede manuscript. He looks hunched, constipated. The limbs are stiff, giving him a geriatric air. The backlift is low and watchful. Everything about him exudes nuggety caution. This is a long way from David Gower and much more like the squat belligerence of Mike Gatting. Or, if it is an echo of any left-hander, it is Allan Border – a hard-as-nails specialist in gritty batsmanship, disdainful of flair and all about effectiveness. 'You can overcomplicate batting,' Border once wrote. 'I counsel young people to keep it as simple as possible: "See the ball, hit the ball".'

The bat is oddly shaped. Straight rather than curved, it does not resemble a shepherd's crook. Slender all the way along, it has a spike at the end, as if it is supposed to be stuck in the ground and has been unearthed for the purposes of instruction. In short, the man appears to be demonstrating with a cricket stump.

On the other side stands what looks like his pupil, perhaps even his son. This figure is more casual. In one hand he holds a melon-sized ball, which he might be about to lob towards his companion. In the other he holds a narrow, stump-like bat. He wears a melancholy expression and looks faintly bored. He gives the impression that he does not appreciate whatever advice he is in the process of receiving.

Between them, at the image's centre, is a strange and beautiful tree. The long, slender trunk and neat sphere of leaves perhaps suggest a scots pine or a birch. Or maybe, with its leaves of spikes, it is a holly tree, symbol of protection and good luck in Celtic mythology. The bright blue leaves, though, give it an unearthly air. It appears not just to be any old tree, but something transcendent and magical.

The roots of trees run deep in the folklore of England, stretching back to the forest worship of the druids and beyond. Their significance is reflected in much Old and Middle English literature. In the eighth-century poem *The Dream of the Rood*, the narrator dreams of a 'most wondrous tree' – the tree from which Christ's crucifix was carved. The tree begins to speak and tells its story. In William Langland's fourteenth-century *Vision of Piers Plowman*, the trees of England are destroyed in a vision of the apocalypse: 'Pyries and plum-trees/Were puffed to the erthe . . . Beches and brode okes/Were blowen to the grounde.'

The presence of this particular tree, blazing with sapphire light between these two early cricketers, gives an ethereal quality to what might have been an everyday scene. Their play is being watched over by an ancient motif of the English imagination.

And with its green grass and wreathes of curling flowers, the image seems peaceful on the surface. But there is also something tense about it. A tetchy atmosphere. The two figures look grumpy with each other. It might even be said to capture a part of the game destined to become one of its defining features across the ages – the antagonistic nature of the bowler–batter dynamic.

Another manuscript, dated 1344 and now in the Bodleian library, shows a group of monks and nuns playing with bat and ball. It may be that the figures are being mocked for their frivolous ways – or it may be a sign that such games were popular inside the cloisters. There is nothing in the text – a French translation of the *Alexander Romance* – that helps to shed any light.

A nun is preparing to bowl – holding the ball carefully, as if worried she might drop it. There is some overlap, here, with the bowler from the Bede manuscript two centuries earlier. Again, we find ourselves looking at an anxious figure – suggesting that bowling was perhaps a struggle, a tense or difficult affair. 'Cricket is a batsman's game,' wrote Harold Larwood in his autobiography, 'When somebody says, "It's a perfect wicket," they mean perfect for the batsman, not the bowler.' Maybe, in medieval England, this was already the way of things.

The monk batsman is a more relaxed-looking character. He holds the bat one-handed, in his left hand, like a club or a sword. It is an alien, rounders-style stance – so different to the techniques of the modern game that some might query if this could really be cricket. But the bat itself is not dissimilar to modern bats; it is straight rather than curved and the narrow handle and wider blade are of familiar proportions.

The manuscript is lushly decorated; the players stand upon a golden platform laced with branches, tendrils, leaves and flowers. A quartet of monks and nuns are shown with hands raised. There is some uncertainty about what they are doing. Are they praying – perhaps to absolve the sins of their merrymaking friends? Or are they fielders, waiting for a catch? To a contemporary eye, the latter feels more fitting. And this is how observers have tended to read the scene. 'The lady must have bowled a mean outswinger to justify a slip cordon of four,' quipped Ashley Mote, 'although the manner in which the monk is holding his bat suggests that he was not a good player of fast bowling.'

The glimpses of cricket's dawn in the art of medieval England are a tantalising string of cryptic fragments. It was an era fraught with conflict; sports and games were popular across the land, but they were also treated with mistrust. A series of laws aimed to ban most games altogether. In 1363, Edward III passed a proclamation designed to outlaw everything except archery – choice of the noble classes – which he wanted to make compulsory.

But the medieval images of figures with bats, sticks and balls reveal the spread of other English games – ones that were played by peasants and shepherds on the country's pastures or by monks and nuns on cloistered lawns, games outside the networks of the nobility. The banned sports in Edward III's proclamation – originally in Latin – included *'pilam manualem'* (ball games played with the hands), but also games played with the foot (*'pedinam'*), with a club (*'bacculoream'*), and with a curved stick (*'cambucam'*). The ban did not just indicate hostility towards these games – it also showed their popularity. Clearly, enough people were playing them for the king to be concerned.

It was, inevitably, the poet Geoffrey Chaucer who best captured the centrality of sport to medieval England. His works are crammed with games and play. In his epic poem *Troilus and Criseyde*, he references 'raket', or racquets, an early ancestor of tennis. Elsewhere he evokes chess, checkers, dice and 'tables', a variant word for backgammon. Even the storytelling competition in the *Canterbury Tales* is framed as a game: 'Trewely,' announces the Host, 'the game is wel bigonne.' The Host berates the Monk for telling a joyless tale he believes to be against the game's spirit:

> Sir monk, na-more of this, so god yow blesse!
> Your tale anoyeth al this companye;
> Swich talking is nat worth a boterflye;
> For therinne is ther no desport ne game.

'Nay,' is the Monk's grumpy reply. 'I have no lust to pleye; Now let another telle, as I have told.'

And it is in Chaucer's England, an England steeped in sports and games, that cricket took its first steps. As historian Kevin Stroud has said, 'The king may have preferred for his subjects to practise archery, but Chaucer shows us that the people actually enjoyed playing other games and that's probably why the king's restrictions never had much of an impact on the games that people played in their spare time.' Somewhere on medieval English fields, shepherds had begun to reimagine their crooks and were wielding them with a new purpose. Their companions began to fling back at them matted balls of sheep's wool. A game was being forged – a game that was, almost certainly, not yet called cricket. But in the fabric of the English imagination, the opening overs were already being bowled.

4

'Creckett and other plaies': Cricket in the English Renaissance

Clean distinctions between the old games of England cannot be drawn; the histories of hockey, golf, baseball, tennis and cricket cannot be insulated from each other. But by the sixteenth century, we can say with certainty that a game called 'cricket' was being played in England. This is evident from a famous document, generally recognised as the first clear written reference to the game.

In a 1598 court paper, John Derrick was recorded to have played in his youth on some land of disputed ownership. 'Being a scholler in the Ffree schoole of Guldeford,' it runs, 'hee and diverse of his fellows did runne and play there at creckett and other plaies.' As Derrick was in his late fifties at the time, this schoolboy cricketing activity can be placed in the middle of the century.

Despite this, Elizabethan England is a shadowy era with regard to cricket. Few images exist that can be linked to the game in any reliable way. And the literature of the period is quiet on the cricketing front. The plays of Shakespeare are stuffed with sports and games – containing mentions, for instance, of billiards, rugby, bowling, football, backgammon, tennis, croquet, bear-baiting, archery, chess, wrestling, dice, cards, board games, jousting, hunting, and falconry. About cricket, though, the bard apparently had little to say.

Historians have pondered the likely reasons for this. In an 1870 essay, Charles Box argued that the lack of cricket in Shakespeare came down to two things. One of them was Shakespeare's preoccupation with the past more than the present. 'The England of his own day interested him no farther than that it recalled the England of days long gone by,' Box wrote. 'His allusions are therefore generally to things that had long ago since died out, or which were shortly to disappear.'

The other was that cricket – while it did *exist* in England – remained 'comparatively unknown'. In short, Shakespeare did not write about it because he had not heard of it. Box criticised the urge to seek out Shakespearean cricketing references that were not actually there. 'To force any of his allusions in this particular in the direction of cricket,' he complained, 'is as dishonest as it is preposterous.'

The small number of alleged cricketing glimpses in Shakespeare are either thin pickings or full-on red herrings. It might be fun to see Costard, in *Love's Labour's Lost*, remark that 'He is a marvellous good neighbour, faith, and a very good bowler,' but it is only a reference to the game of bowls. In the long poem 'A Lover's Complaint', a young woman abandoned by her lover weeps by the side of a river. An old man comes to sit with her:

> So slides he down upon his grained bat,
> And comely-distant sits he by her side;
> When he again desires her, being sat,
> Her grievance with his hearing to divide

The 'grained bat' here is the man's shepherd's crook, which he uses to ease himself down next to the girl. It is a word choice that gestures, just maybe, towards its secondary use for sport – but there is no evidence to suggest that Shakespeare intended this meaning. And the 'bats and clubs' held by rioting citizens, in the opening scene of *Coriolanus*, are certainly not being swung with any cricketing purpose in mind.

There are, though, some games that resembled cricket so closely it is tempting to read them as variations of the same essential spirit. One game in particular, stoolball, had been widely played in England since at least the fourteenth century. In his 1801 work, *The Sports and Pastimes of the People of England*, antiquarian Joseph Strutt offered the following description:

> I have been informed, that a pastime called stool-ball is practised to this day in the northern parts of England, which consists in simply setting a stool upon the ground, and one of the players takes his place before it, while his antagonist, standing at a distance, tosses a ball with the intention of striking the stool; and this it is the business of the former to prevent by beating it away with the hand, reckoning one to the game for every stroke of the ball.

'Stool-ball,' he adds, 'seems to have been a game more properly appropriated to the women than to the men.'

The defence of a wooden target, with bowler as adversary, has a familiar ring. The most obvious difference is the use of hands rather than bats. But other accounts suggest that a bat was used from early on in stoolball's history and even that the very earliest form of stoolball bat might have been a milking bowl. Altham stressed that cricket and stoolball were closely intertwined, with a shared ancestry: 'In a dictionary of "Sussex Dialect" the word "Stool" is defined as the stump of a tree and it is at least possible that the earliest variety of forest cricket may also have been known as stool-ball, though the latter game of course later developed an independent and different technique.' Historian David Underdown has suggested that 'until the eighteenth century there may not in fact have been much difference between the two sports.'

Stoolball survives to this day and remains popular in Sussex. It is now played with bats made of willow; it involves two wickets, suspended at shoulder height, and two teams compete to score the most runs. One of its most common nicknames is 'cricket in the air'.

Originally, it was strongly associated with Easter courtship rites between young lads and lasses. And the connection with love is reflected in sixteenth- and seventeenth-century literature. In Mary Sidney Herbert's 1596 poem 'A Dialogue Between Two Shepherds', one figure consoles his lovesick friend as follows: 'A tyme there is for all, my mother often sayes,/When she, with skirts tuckt very hy, with girles at stoolball playes.' Once again, it is a game played by women. Whether the mother's high skirts imply athletic focus, or something much flirtier, is open to interpretation.

There was certainly a sense of stoolball as bawdy, risqué, perhaps even ungodly. In 1592, religious scholar John Rainolds warned as follows: 'Time of recreation is necessary, I graunt, and think as necessary for schollers . . . as it is for any. Yet in my opinion it were not fit for them to play at Stoole-ball among wenches, nor at Mumchance or Maw with idle loose companions.'

And Shakespeare may not have mentioned cricket – but he did make one of the clearest references to stoolball as a seduction ritual. In *The Two Noble Kinsmen*, a 1613 collaboration between Shakespeare and John Fletcher, the game is playfully used as a metaphor for such exploits. Two young lovers converse:

Daughter: Will you goe with me?
Wooer: What shall we doe there, wench?
Daughter: Why, play at stoole ball:
What is there else to doe?

It is a 'nudge-nudge, wink-wink' moment, with the playing of 'stoole ball' transparent code for something else entirely.

The sexual suggestiveness reflects how both stoolball and its cousin cricket came to be portrayed as the seventeenth century advanced. They were games for lovers, gamblers, drinkers, shirkers. Shakespeare himself had placed plenty of emphasis on the intemperance of the English people – mocked by Macbeth as 'English epicures' and who, according to Iago, could comfortably outdrink folks of all other countries. It is this England – lewd, seedy, indulgent – that became the primary dwelling place of cricket in the 1600s.

In 1658, Edward Phillips – nephew of John Milton – published the snappily titled *Mysteries of Love & Eloquence, Or, the Arts of Wooing and Complementing; As they are Manag'd in the Spring Garden, Hide Park, the New Exchange, and Other Eminent Places*. It is generally acknowledged as a rebellion against his Puritan upbringing – a kind of cross between serious philosophical tract and a lighthearted pick-up manual.

In a chapter called 'At the Inn', two lovers, Richard and Kate, engage in conversation:

Nay 'tis true *Kate*, and I'le lay our pie-bald Mare against any Horse in the Town, that thou hast as pretty a smelling brow as any Lass in the Countrey.

Ay, but *Richard* will you think so hereafter? Will you not when you have me throw stools at my head; and cry, Would my eyes had been beat out of my head with a cricket-ball, the day before I saw thee.

Kate, My Infections are greater toward thee yn so. But if I should chance to call louder then ordinary, why, 'tis but saying hold your tongue *Dick*, here's piece of bag-budding for you: I and my mouth is stopt presently.

Richard, thou dost well to tell me some of thy humors; But art thou not terrible mad when th'art drunk, and quarrelsome withall?

No *Kate*, as quiet as any Lambkin: All that I shall do is onely this, that when I come home, I may snore an hour or two perhaps with my head in thy lap; then I start up and cry, Hoh *Kate*, what's a clock? and so go to bed.

The squalid ambiance is hard to miss. Kate's description of being blinded by a cricket ball is both comical and violent. The dialogue oozes with drink, fighting and lecherous intent. This ale-house scene is not, exactly, the most salubrious locale for the first reference to a cricket ball in the history of English literature.

Much later, at the height of Victorian patriotism, cricket would be marketed as an archetype of civilised English values. But in the civil war era it was keeping very different company. The Puritans attempted to enforce strict social codes. In 1642, theatres were closed. It was a move that ironically turned people to other recreations that the Puritans also loathed.

Sport became a subversive act. On Sundays it was not allowed, but it happened anyway. In 1652, a group of men were charged with playing 'a certain unlawful game called cricket' in Cranbrook, Kent. The group comprised of one 'gentleman', John Rabson, esq. – plus an earthier bunch of two clothiers, a barber, a husbandman and a labourer. In this kind of social atmosphere, cricket had an edge. It was not only a mechanism for revelry – it was a gesture of rebellion against authority.

And the game could be dangerous. In 1622, a group of young men were charged with playing cricket on a Sunday. They were accused of smashing church windows and putting a child in danger of having 'her brains beaten out with a cricket bat'. In 1624, a man was killed at Horsted Keynes after being hit on the head with a bat. In 1647, another died in the same fashion, in a game near Bosgrove. In 1693, a group of people accused of assault claimed that they 'had only been spectators at a game of cricket' – a defence, according to Underdown, that suggests 'violence at matches was common enough to be excusable'.

Cricket had always been primarily a game for peasants, yeomen and working men, and it remained this way as the seventeenth century progressed. Members of the nobility were occasionally drawn in, but largely as spectators rather than players. And the game remained tangled up with vice, indulgence, bad habits.

Booze started to be sold at matches. Betting was becoming commonplace. The first recorded instance was in 1646, when a man wagered six candles on the result of a match at Coxheath. By the century's final decade, the aristocracy were in on the action – in 1694, a member of the Pelham family had a wager 'about a cricket match' at Lewes. A year later, two Sussex teams played for the princely wager of 'fifty guineas apiece'.

Even as the century drew to a close, a sense still lingered that cricket was a game for rogues and wayward types – played on fields, but belonging to the streets. In 1699, Edward 'Ned' Ward published *The World Bewitch'd: A Dialogue Between Two Astrologers and the Author*. In it, he took aim at George Parker and John Parridge – two rival quack doctors in late seventeenth-century London – by having them farcically quarrel in the book's first part. 'I should either lay my strap cross your Schoulders, fling a Last at your Head, or stick my Aul in your Arse,' Parridge at one point threatens.

An author's interjection follows – titled 'Infallible Predictions for the year 1699'. This involves a series of satirical prophecies, one of which runs:

> Persons of Quality will now be going to their Contrey Houses, and Shop-keepers will put on as Melancholly Aspects as if their Books and their Bags had scarce ever a Cross in 'em. Quoits, Cricket, Nine-Pins, and Trap-Ball, will be very much in Fashion, and more Tradesmen may be seen Playing in the Fields, than Working in their Shops. It will be Fine Weather both for those who have Money, and such who want it: He that has it to spare, may spend it with much Pleasure, and he that hath none, may Sleep under a Hedge, without the Danger of having his Pocket Pick'd.

Cricket, here, is a distraction – one of a number of unruly games taking tradesmen away from their work. In a disintegrating society, laziness prevails, and pleasure crushes industry. This is a dark London scene – one of poverty and inequality, in which penniless people sleep on the streets while the wealthy retire to their 'Contrey Houses'. In Ward's scathing vision, cricket is associated with corruption and societal failure. Its popularity was a bad sign.

In the story of cricket and the English imagination, the sixteenth and seventeenth centuries give quiet hints of the wonders that lay ahead. References to the game often came in brief glimpses. But this was also a stretch of time in which it grew into one of the established games of England. Altham wrote that 'the last half of the seventeenth century was really the critical stage in the game's evolution, the era in which it developed from the pastime of boys, or, at best, of the yeomen of the exclusive Weald into a game with a national appeal'. Cricket's popularity and impact were expanding fast. The ground was prepared for everything to blossom.

5

'VERE NOVO': EIGHTEENTH-CENTURY IMAGININGS, PART I

At first, the arrival of a new century suggested little more than the same old story. Cricket had been pinned as a roguish pursuit, and so it would remain. The game's betting culture continued to thrive. In March 1700, a series of games were to be played 'on Clapham Common near Foxhall on Easter Monday next, for £10 a head each game and £20 the odd one'. In every recorded match from this era, a wager of some sort was involved. As John Major noted, the sponsors of such games were 'often innkeepers, keen to attract a thirsty crowd'.

This disreputable shadow is reflected in the literature of the time. In 1701, *A Rod for Tunbridge Beaus, Bundl'd up at the Request of the Tunbridge Ladies, &c.* was published anonymously in London. Billed as 'a burlesque poem', it is a satire on social pretension – packed with shady characters, drunkenness and fighting. And cricket does not escape its web of ridicule.

The narrator – seeking 'some distant Rural pleasure' beyond the confines of the city – makes his way out to Tunbridge Wells. There, he encounters the phenomenon of 'upstart Beaus' – a class of person conspicuously short of redeeming qualities, labelled as 'self-admiring Fops that hate, All that is Generous, Good or Great'. They are avatars of vanity, interested only in arrogant posing and their own advancement.

The first to be described is a sporting specialist:

At Nine-pins lies his Excellence;
. . . It's true he can at Cricket play,
With any living at this day:
And fling a Coit, or toss a Bar,
With any Driver of a Car:
But Little Nine-pins and Trap-ball,
The Knight delights in most of all,
Conceiving like a prudent Man,
The other might his Honour stain,
So scorns to let the Publick see,
He should degrade his Quality.

This upstart beau is – in equal measure – idiotic, pompous and
excellent at sport. And his expertise has a socially coded quality.
He openly allows himself to enjoy nine-pins and trap-ball.
Cricket, though, is one of several about which he needs to be
more discreet – otherwise, he might 'degrade his Quality'.
Clearly, at the beginning of the eighteenth century, it was not the
kind of sport that suited the goals of a cynical social climber.

A few years later, though, cricket would be given a very different spin. In 1706, William Goldwin published *Musae Juveniles*,
a collection of verse in Latin. One of the poems – '*In Certamen
Pilae*' – has the distinction of being the first piece of literature to
be exclusively focused on the game. As such, it plays a crucial
role in cricket's relationship to the English imagination. And it
has been an unjustly neglected work – not translated for over two
centuries, rarely republished and little studied.

As literature's opening cricketing opus, the poem demands
more recognition. Goldwin's decision to write in Latin lends
the poem a grandeur – and a tie with tradition – that reflects
his aim. He was keen to elevate cricket into something illustrious and heroic, placing it alongside the grand epics of the classical world.

The start of the poem is worth quoting in its full glory:

Vere novo, cum temperies liquidissima coeli
arridet, suadetque virentis gratia terrae
veloces agitare pedes super aequora campi;
lecta cohors juvenum, baculis armata repandis
quos habiles ludo manus ingeniosa polivit,
in campum descendit ovans . . .
(Springtime comes, with mild and limpid air
Smiling, with kindness coaxes earth to bear
And active feet to sport where fields spread wide;
A team of youths with crooked bats supplied,
By cunning hand trimm'd fitly for their game,
Thither troop gaily down . . .)*

The very first word – '*vere*', 'spring' – summons an atmosphere of new beginnings. And in addition to the springtime promise, it can also be seen to hint at another beginning – the new spring of English cricket literature, bursting into life at this very moment.

Goldwin bathes his poem in literary echoes: the first line alludes to Virgil's *Georgics*, while also recalling the general prologue to Chaucer's *Canterbury Tales* and its celebration of new life among the sweet showers of April. In Chaucer's poem, the coming of spring inspires people to go on pilgrimages – but in Goldwin's, they are inspired towards cricket. The echo not only provides a link to England's literary heritage – it also lends cricket a form of religious significance. These young men are on their own pilgrimage – a pilgrimage, in this case, to a cricket pitch.

The match is described in detail. Goldwin is at pains to describe the ferocity of the contest – using plenty of military

---

* This is the translation by Percy Francis Thomas, first published under the pen name of 'H. P.-T.' in *Early Cricket: A Description of the First Known Match; And Some Comments on Creag, Cricket, Cricce and Shakespeare's Clue* (Nottingham: C. H. Richards, 1923).

language and drawing heavily from the war stories of Latin and Greek epics. There is nothing gentle or peaceful about the game of cricket as he presents it. This is cricket through the lens of the battles of ancient legend – a pursuit requiring the strength and bravery of the classical hero. It is not for the faint hearted; 'In Certamen Pilae' offers an allusion-soaked feast of avid, brawny combat. A minor masterpiece of sporting literature, it is a piece of Latin verse that is also, at the same time, a jewel in England's literary heritage. It deserves to keep its place in the cultural memory.

These early eighteenth-century years were, in many ways, a boom time for cricket. Money was swimming into the game from a growing range of aristocratic patrons, some with a dubious reputation. There was the profligate landowner Edward Stead, who combined his support of cricket with a brutal gambling addiction until he dropped dead in his early thirties. There were the Sackville brothers – Charles, Earl of Middlesex, an arty opera lover, accused by Horace Walpole as 'seldom sober' on a two-year tour of Italy and Lord John Sackville, womaniser and gamester, who was consigned to an asylum before being exiled to Switzerland.

It all led to a strange brew of respectability and vice. Impish members of the nobility played alongside farmers, tradesmen, labourers. Betting was constant; at times, vast sums were wagered. All classes partook in the revels, as Cesar de Saussure noted in his account of life in England in the 1720s: 'Everyone plays it, the common people and also men of rank.' It was a world in which the light and the dark had become bedfellows. At the same time as being a thriving, prosperous game, it was also, in many places, seen as a sign of wayward habits.

And it could still be a violent business. A match on Chelsea Common in 1731 descended into a fistfight after gambling disputes. In the same year, a match involving the Duke of Richmond ended in cricket's first recorded draw; a mob invaded the field and tore the shirts off some of the players. Six years later, a woman had her leg broken at a match on Kensington Common. Similar incidents continued as the years rolled on. The brute force, if not the propriety, of William Goldwin's vision was alive and well.

In 1734, J. Wilford published *Priestcraft: or, the Way to Promotion* – another sharp-edged spoof from the golden age of satire. In it, the poet urges clerics to leave the church behind in search of political success. In one passage, a new educational vision is mockingly rolled out:

No more with Birch, let Eton's pupils bleed;
No more with Learned Lumber stuff their Head.
Her Rival see! Like Nursery of Fools,
Who practise Cricket, more than Busby's Rules.
Learn'd, or unlearn'd, to College when you please,
Nor fear Admission if you pay the Fees:
There in sweet Slumber, doze the sev'n long Year,
No harsh-tongu'd Greek shall hurt your nicer Ears.
To Musick, French, and Dancing, bend your Eye,
Instead of Ethicks, or Philosophy:
For who would e'er perplex his Head with these?
When without Learning he may take Degrees.

The boys of Eton need not bother themselves with learning. They can just play cricket instead. 'Busby's Rules' refers to Richard Busby – headmaster of Westminster, whose Latin and Greek grammar books were widely used at the time. Etonians would not require such tomes – busy as they were with the frivolities of leather on willow. Cricket is presented as the enemy of intellectualism: it is a dunces' game.

And speaking of dunces, another hurt to cricket's name was visited by the foremost literary figure of the age. Alexander Pope had originally published his *Dunciad* in the 1720s. The poem was an assault on the narrow-mindedness of his contemporaries, in which he fired shots at a wide range of targets including Whig politicians, Protestant agitators and the new king, George II.

In 1742, he published a rewritten and expanded version. In one of the new passages, the goddess of 'Dulness' addresses her own children:

Go, Children of my care!
To Practice now from Theory repair.
All my commands are easy, short, and full:
My Sons! be proud, be selfish, and be dull.
Guard my Prerogative, assert my Throne:
This Nod confirms each Privilege your own.
The Cap and Switch be sacred to his Grace;
With Staff and Pumps the Marquis lead the race;
From Stage to Stage the licens'd Earl may run,
Pair'd with his Fellow Charioteer the sun;
The learned Baron Butterflies design,
Or draw to silk Arachne's subtile line;
The Judge to dance his brother Sergeant call;
The Senator at Cricket urge the Ball . . .

Cricket is part of a tasteless, foolish world. It is – like dancing – the sort of activity Pope associates with vapid types. It is not clear who, exactly, the 'Senator' is intended to be, idly fixed on his cricket game; Altham reckoned it was Lord John Sackville. Whoever it might be, they are one of society's dunces – proud, selfish and dull. Pope, it seems, was not a cricket fan. But the game was clearly influential enough to warrant the sharp blade of his satirical knife.

Cricket's hold on the English imagination was tightening. Its relationship with social respectability may have been complicated, but it had developed into one of the country's most

popular recreational pursuits. Organised matches were prolifer-
ating. Representative county teams were beginning to form.

And as the middle of the century approached, art and literature were also shifting – away from satirical digs at cricket and
towards gestures of homage. Francis Hayman was one of the foremost painters of the time. He built a reputation for historical
subjects and scenes taken from literature – illustrating an edition
of Shakespeare's plays, as well as works by John Milton, Samuel
Richardson and Tobias Smollett. Artist Edward Edwards lauded
him as 'unquestionably the best historical painter in the kingdom
before the arrival of Cipriani'.

In 1743, he painted *The Cricket Match*, an image of a game
played at the Artillery Ground in London:

There is a great deal happening in this intricately composed
scene. It is an action shot, capturing a moment just after the
bowler has released the ball. The batsman – front leg forward,
face fixed in a determined look – prepares to play a drive. The
shin-high two-stump wicket is clearly visible (it would be several
decades before a middle stump was brought in). The curved bat

has a thin, flimsy-looking handle that widens into a fat head – suitable for playing low, skimming underarm deliveries, such as the one depicted here.

The players are wearing a wide mixture of clothing, suggesting that they represent a range of different social backgrounds. Most wear simple white linen shirts and breeches – no-nonsense, practical attire. The batsman sports the sort of cloth working-men's cap worn by ale-swigging revellers in William Hogarth's *Beer Street* (1751). Others, though, are much more formally dressed – wearing long coats and gold-trimmed tricorn hats that radiate a more fashionable, wealthy air. The sartorial diversity of the painting seems to reflect the socially blended culture of cricket in the era.

Among the players, levels of attention vary. Some – not just bowler and batsman – are keenly focused. The wicketkeeper is attentively, if awkwardly crouched: this is thought to be a portrayal of Hogarth, of whom Hayman was a pupil – and the bald-headed figure does bear a striking resemblance to Hogarth's self-portrait of 1757. Two fielders in the outfield hover, legs spread and knees bent, ready for action. An umpire watches on, arms folded.

But the two on the left appear to be more interested in their own conversation – leaning in towards each other, as if confidentially gossiping. One, leaning on his bat, is the non-striking batsman; the other, holding a stick, must be the second umpire. Their sidetracked demeanour sits oddly with the energy of the main action. Out in the deep, another pair seem to be doing the same. And the fielder standing behind the first umpire seems distracted by something, his gaze aimed over at the trees. These detached figures imbue the painting with a strange, ruptured quality; intense competition and idle relaxation appear side by side, in a dreamlike fusion.

The image feels like a rural scene – an expansive green, bordered by trees, under a typically English sky of piebald grey and blue. But this was the Artillery Ground, in Finsbury. In the distance, a group of indistinct stone buildings can be seen – a reminder that, for all the pastoral ambiance, this was a city location, less than a mile from St Paul's cathedral. Cricket was not just a game for the shires: more and more, it thrived in London too.

Hayman's painting is an example of the way cricket was increasingly presented as a key feature of English culture. A year earlier, Thomas Gray composed 'Ode on a Distant Prospect of Eton College' – a series of reflections on the days of his youth. The school's ancient surroundings lead Gray to ponder the contrast between his carefree childhood, and the more challenging realities of adult life:

Ah, happy hills, ah, pleasing shade,
    Ah, fields belov'd in vain,
Where once my careless childhood stray'd,
    A stranger yet to pain!
I feel the gales, that from ye blow,
A momentary bliss bestow,
    As waving fresh their gladsome wing,
My weary soul they seem to soothe,
And, redolent of joy and youth,
    To breathe a second spring.

Say, Father Thames, for thou hast seen
    Full many a sprightly race
Disporting on thy margent green
    The paths of pleasure trace,
Who foremost now delight to cleave
With pliant arm thy glassy wave?
    The captive linnet which enthrall?
What idle progeny succeed
To chase the rolling circle's speed,
    Or urge the flying ball?

As a boy, he was still a stranger to pain . . . the decline into his present condition is acute. The children become something more than schoolboys – they are symbols, of a blissful lightness of being. Young people playing cricket, urging the 'flying ball', have nothing to worry about. Cricket is part of a tapestry of childhood innocence in which the weight of the world ceases to exist.

In its own quiet way, this is a revolutionary outlook. The reasons why some had previously scorned the game have become the precise reasons why the game was valuable. Wilford's disdainful vision – of schoolboys idly playing cricket instead of studying – has been reimagined, as cricket becomes an activity whose very lack of depth makes it precious. The sports of childhood are a paradise of naïve happiness. 'Where ignorance is bliss,/'Tis folly to be wise,' Gray writes, in the poem's closing lines. Cricket does not *mean* anything – but for that very reason, it means everything.

It was a sea change in eighteenth-century portrayals of cricket. A rationalist concern with activities in relation to their social util-ity was being traded for something new – a proto-Romantic focus on individual feeling and sentiment. Gray's poem makes only brief reference to the game. But in the story of cricket's relation-ship to the English imagination, it is a significant fork in the road.

6

'Glorious, manly, British game': Eighteenth-Century Imaginings, Part II

Certain years hold a special, almost religious significance in particular fields: 1922, for instance, has been hailed as a miraculous year for Modernist literature – supplying James Joyce's *Ulysses*, T. S. Eliot's 'The Waste Land' and Virginia Woolf's *Jacob's Room*. Rock fans will wax lyrical about 1969, the year of the Beatles' *Abbey Road*, the Rolling Stones' *Let It Bleed*, the first two Led Zeppelin albums and the iconic bedlam of Woodstock.

For cricket, a year that will always hold such power is 1744.

This, for starters, is the year in which the first ever Laws of Cricket were drafted. These were touted as being 'settled by ye cricket club at ye Star and Garter in Pall Mall'; envoys from several clubs were involved. The laws differ, in a number of obvious ways, from the game as it would evolve; just four balls in an over, no boundaries, no fixed number of players in a team, no mention of an l.b.w. rule. But here was the basis for a new level of stability. Now, wherever it was played, a clear code could be upheld. The fact they were 'Laws' implied something grand, even menacing: these were more than guidelines, they were precepts pointing to a deep authority. Transgress them at your peril.

The same year also saw the appearance of a milestone in the history of cricket literature.

There had been a match between Kent and an all-England team at the Artillery Ground; it was arranged by a certain Lord John Sackville, captain of the Kent side. The game, which went right down to the wire, immediately became famous. 'Yesterday was play'd in the Artillery Ground the greatest Cricket-Match ever known,' claimed the *London Evening Post*. The presence of various grandees, including members of the royal family, helped to boost the import of the occasion. 'There were present their Royal Highnesses the Prince of Wales and Duke of Cumberland, the Duke of Richmond, Admiral Vernon and many other Persons of Distinction.'

The match was destined to be immortalised in *Cricket: An Heroic Poem* by James Love, the pen name of James Dance, an actor as well as a writer (performing was clearly in his blood). Publication was nothing short of momentous. Here, at last, across three books and 316 lines, was the dawn of cricket literature in English. Almost three centuries later, it remains one of the most celebrated pieces of writing on the sport.

At one level, the poem is a patriotic hymn to the game of cricket. Its tone, though, is complicated at every turn by the presence of sardonic humour. What could easily have slipped into empty jingoism is counteracted by something usually ignored in discussions of the poem – a wit, and an irony, inherited from Pope and Jonathan Swift.

James Love was a child of the age of satire. As a writer of plays, his specialisms were pantomimes, comedies and burlesques. He is credited with a comic adaptation of Samuel Richardson's *Pamela*, performed at the Goodman's Theatre in London in 1742. The play's epilogue mockingly proclaims the author's patriotic intentions: 'He knew his Judges, and he wish'd to find/A Theme might justly please a British Mind:/A Tale, which Albion's Sons might deign to hear,/And without Shame, let fall the pitying Tear.'

Love, in other words, wrote with a cocked eyebrow and a wry smile. Much like William Blake's lyric 'Jerusalem', his ode to cricket has often been misread as a tubthumping British anthem – a kind of poetic equivalent of a mid-match pub singalong. But it is a much cleverer, more interesting work.

The poem is accompanied with notes by 'Scriblerus Maximus' – the *nom de plume* of the Scriblerus Club, a group of satirical authors that included Swift and Pope in its ranks. These notes – probably not written by Love himself, but in collaboration with him – give the poem a sense of mischief that does not exactly *undermine* the patriotic sentiment, but sits alongside it, creating a more elusive text. A note on the author's functional title for the first Book, 'Cricket: Book I', shows the influence of Pope and his *Dunciad*:

> There is no Doubt, but that . . . this Title might have been dulcified; and by the ingenious Help of an AD tag'd to it, render'd extremely polite and unintelligible. But I think it is a high Compliment to CRICKET itself, that our Poet thinks proper to set before its Work, in its own plain unadulterated Signification.

The droll suggestion here – that Love should have called his poem the *Cricket-iad* – shows plainly enough the tradition in which he stood.

In the poem's most famous lines, the poet celebrates the game's wonders:

> Hail CRICKET! glorious, manly, British game!
> First of all Sports! be first alike in Fame!
> To my fir'd Soul thy busy Transports bring,
> That I may feel thy Raptures, while I sing!

Not only is cricket a glorious game, it is also *manly* – a game for strong and courageous types – and a peculiarly British game, too. How are we to read these claims, which are at once passionate and also faintly ludicrous? In some ways, it marks the beginning of a proudly patriotic sentiment that would linger in the culture of cricket from this point onwards – a belief, or a contention, that the game somehow expresses the best of British values.

Historian Anthony Bateman felt that Love casts cricket as a 'symbol of British national identity', legitimising it 'as a suitably manly pursuit that is therefore worthy of its status as a national pastime'.

But this does not capture the tonal ambiguity here. After all, these lines appear in a poem that adopts the voice and the form of Alexander Pope and is studded with humorous, mock-scholarly notes. 'Hail CRICKET! Glorious, manly, British game!' . . . Are we really to take the avowal at face value, or is Love – actor, satirist, pantomime writer and associate of the Scriblerus Club – to some extent having us on? The oft-quoted words are, in the end, both authentic and deliberately overblown – suffused with layers of irony that cannot be fully resolved.

As the poem progresses, the mixture of brashness and satire is deliciously enriched. Love contrasts cricket with a range of inferior pursuits. The notes, though, lend everything an arch quality. Tennis, for example – confined to a 'small space' – must 'yield/To nobler Cricket, the disputed Field'. But the accompanying note reads:

> It must be confess'd, that Tennis is very nearly ally'd to CRICKET, both as to the Activity, Strength and Skill that are necessary to be exerted on each important Occasion. But as the latter happens to be the present Subject, our Author with great Propriety and admirable Taste, makes all other Games knock under. When he gratifies the World with a Poem upon Tennis, no doubt, he will do the same, in favour of that also.

The integrity of the poem's claims – that cricket is 'first of all sports' – is undercut by the suggestion that, at some point, Love will get round to writing a tennis poem that says the same thing. Cricket's superiority is not *objectively* true – it is part of a rhetorical performance, in a work of art such as this. It is Love's job in writing this poem to make 'all other Games knock under'. But is it just an act, a stage turn from a professional actor-poet?

Love affects a xenophobic stance, in order to argue for cricket's pre-eminence. Billiards is 'Frenchifi'd' – a suspiciously continental product that is no match for a noble British game. He slams the hedonistic pursuits of Europe:

O Parent Britain! Minion of Renown!
Whose far-extended Fame all Nations own;
Of Sloth-promoting Sports, forewarn'd beware!
Nor think thy Pleasures are thy meanest Care;
Shun with Disdain the squeaking Masquerade,
Where fainting Vice calls Folly to her Aid.
Leave the dissolving Song, the baby Dance,
To sooth the Slaves of Italy and France:
While the firm Limb, and strong brac'd Nerve are thine,
Scorn Eunuch Sports; to manlier Games incline;
Feed on the Joys that Health and Vigour give;
Where Freedom reigns, 'tis worth the while to live.

On the surface, the anti-European sentiment is clear. It certainly contrasts with the claims of Wilford and Pope that cricket is a trivial affair, to be bracketed with singing and dancing. Here, masquerades, singing, and dancing are the 'eunuch sports' – idle pursuits for emasculated foreigners. Cricket is submitted as a kind of antidote: a 'manlier' game that could not be any more different to the wimpy claptrap found on the continent.

But the simple-minded nature of the rhetoric – the bombastic flag-waving, the bicep-flexing machismo – is exaggerated enough to raise questions about how seriously it should all be taken. There is an edge of humour to the haughty dismissal of 'sloth-promoting', 'eunuch' sports. 'There is great Reason . . . to think that [cricket] is a European invention,' runs another of the notes, before admitting that the game may indeed be British – since 'the Chinese, who claim Printing, Gunpowder, &c. so long before we had any Notion of them, to our great Satisfaction, lay not the least claim to it.' Love's poem presents an attitude of patriotic fervour that it also, at the same time, satirises.

The enigmatic sophistication of 'Cricket: An Heroic Poem' put the game firmly on the literary map. It also reflected its rising popularity and profile, as the middle of the century approached. The prevalence of cricket – in both countryside and city – was underscored by Samuel Johnson, in an August 1751 edition of the *Rambler*. In a piece called 'An account of an author travelling in quest of his own character. The uncertainty of fame,' he tells the story of a writer who is desperate to hear some praise for his new work – and so heads off into London, 'to learn the various opinions of his readers'.

But he hears no mention of his book. As he moves from place to place, he finds only the everyday chatter of urban society:

> The same expectation hurries him to another place, from which the same disappointment drives him soon away. His impatience then grows violent and tumultuous; he ranges over the town with restless curiosity, and hears in one quarter of a cricket-match, in another of a pick-pocket; is told by some of an unexpected bankruptcy; by others of a turtle feast; is sometimes provoked by importunate inquiries after the white bear, and sometimes with praises of the dancing dog.

Cricket is offered as an example of gossip around town. It has become the kind of topic you would inescapably encounter, as you rambled around the city streets – whether you wanted to or not.

Meanwhile, out in a small Hampshire village called Hambledon, a parish cricket team had formed and were beginning to play local matches. Hambledon would develop into the finest team in England, a side so formidable that they would become a match for any all-England outfit. And the characters and culture of the club would ultimately enter into fable, becoming an enduring fairy tale of rural English life. In many ways, the whole second half of the eighteenth century is a kind of cricketing folk dream – so steeped in legend that it can be difficult to separate history from a swirling cauldron of mythology.

At the same time, London was becoming a more powerful nerve centre for cricket – abounding with teams, one of which was based at the White Conduit Club in Islington. They were a well-heeled bunch, stuffed with gentry and aristocracy. But the location of their ground lacked privacy: it was not ideal. Two members – the Earl of Winchelsea and Charles Lennox, later to become Duke of Richmond – commissioned one of the club's players, a young and ambitious Yorkshireman, to help. In 1787, he established the first of three grounds in north-west London, near Marylebone. His name was Thomas Lord.

The blustering violence of much eighteenth-century writing on cricket casts it with a macho air. One might have expected it to be a hostile environment for women.

The truth, though, was very different. From the 1740s onwards, women's cricket matches were common. Not only that, but they could be big occasions, involving hefty wagers and watched by large crowds. In 1745, a match played on Gosden Common, near Guildford, was described in the *Reading Mercury* as, 'The greatest cricket match that was played in this part of England . . . the girls bowled, batted, ran and catched as well as most men could do in that game.' Women's matches ranged from games between village sides to more eccentric affairs, such as contests between married women and spinsters. As Underdown noted, 'Eighteenth-century Englishwomen clearly had more opportunities for physical exercise than their Victorian successors.'

And within the aristocracy, it was not just the men who partook. A 1779 drawing depicts a match played two years earlier, involving 'The Countess of Derby and other ladies', at the Oaks estate in Surrey:

The picture shows a woman in a blue dress bowling the ball watchfully, with obvious concentration. She adopts a lower position than most eighteenth-century depictions of bowlers – almost fully down on one knee, keen to deliver the ball as low and as fast as possible, trying to sneak it under the bat. This is not a novice, or a reluctant cricketer: she is a proficient and focused presence.

The batswoman, waiting with a smile, looks more laid-back. In fact, the whole scene – rather like Hayman's 1743 Artillery Ground portrait – offers a dislocated combination of concentration and distraction. The wicketkeeper points at the stumps, perhaps to urge the bowler on. A fielder stands watching the action, but with arms casually spread – more of a gesture of surprise than readiness. And the others are scattered round the outfield in groups, interested in their own conversation rather than the game in question. All are dressed fashionably – in long dresses and bonnets. The implication is that this match is not just a sporting event: it is a social occasion.

And history tells us that romance was indeed in the air. At this very game, the Duke of Hamilton fell in love with the top scorer, Elizabeth Burrell. In the 22 January 1778 edition of the *Morning Post*, it was reported that Burrell 'took bat in hand' and 'her Diana-like air created an irresistible impression'. They were married in April of that year.

The Countess of Derby herself – organiser of the match – was conducting an affair with none other than John Sackville, the Duke of Dorset (son of Lord John Sackville, the great early cricketing patron). Dorset was present at the game and later penned an extraordinary letter published in *Sporting Magazine* 'to a Circle of Ladies, his intimate Friends, describing a Cricket Match played at the Oaks, in Surry, by some of the first Female Characters in the Island'. In it he offered a progressive message of support for his mistress' sporting goals: 'What is human life but a game of cricket? and, if so, why should not the ladies play at it as well as we? . . . Mind not, my dear ladies, the impertinent interrogatories of silly coxcombs, or the dreadful apprehensions of demi-men. Let your sex go on, and assert their right to every pursuit that does not debase the mind. Go on, and attach yourselves to the athletic.'

Not everyone, though, was quite so supportive of women in sport. Other artworks from the period present a very different view.

MISS WICKET and MISS TRIGGER.
Miss Trigger you see is an excellent Shot, And forty five Notches Miss Wicket's just got.

Miss Wicket and Miss Trigger, by satirical artist John Collet, takes a swipe at women who ignored their expected social role. One figure proudly holds up a clutch of game birds she has just shot; in her other hand, she grips a rifle. Her transgressive comrade coquettishly smiles while leaning on a cricket bat. The caption runs: 'Miss Trigger you see is an excellent Shot, And forty five Notches Miss Wicket's just got' ('notches', here, being runs – the latter term would not appear for several decades). On the ground, there is a letter marked 'Effeminacy': Miss Trigger tramples on it with a black leather boot. The message is not a subtle one. Women's involvement in such things is simply not natural.

Matches between representative county teams became more and more frequent as the century wore on, with the strongest outfits being Hampshire, Kent, Middlesex, Surrey and Sussex. The rivalry between Kent and Surrey was captured in two 1773 poems about a match at Bourne Paddock, seat of Sir Horatio Mann. The game had initially been called off after biblical rain. But after some quarrelling and a string of rejected proposals, it was restarted later in the week in a slightly different, less flooded spot. The needle between the two sides might be one reason the match gathered infamy.

The first of the poems – 'Surry Triumphant' by John Duncombe – tells the story of Surrey's victory after amassing what was, in those days, a gargantuan second innings score of 217. Duncombe gleefully portrays the beaten Kent cricketers' miserable return home:

Their husbands woful case that night
Did many wives bewail,
Their labour, time, and money lost,
But all would not prevail.

Their sun-burnt cheeks, though bath'd in sweat,
They kiss'd and wash'd them clean,
And to that fatal paddock begg'd
They ne'er would go again.

The 'money lost' was certainly not trivial; it had been a high-stakes game, with a pot of two thousand pounds. The poem ends by noting that, not long after this humiliating defeat, Kent got their revenge in a rematch 'on Sevenoaks vine'.

John Burnby's riposte, 'The Kentish Cricketers', is an al-together more intense affair. It begins with an angry attack on the vices of the aristocracy:

In Times like these, when VICE can rear
Her pois'nous Crest – make VIRTUE fear;
When Dukes and Lords, are daily known,
To swarm like Locusts o'er the Town,
Eager to grasp the golden Prize,
As FOLLY blinds the gamester's eyes.

The lines set a dark tone: Burnby is denouncing the corruption of a broken society. 'Vile effeminacy reigns,' he writes, 'With timid Blood in ENGLISH veins' . . . the words resemble those of James Love, but there is little of Love's arch humour in Burnby's indignant rhetoric.

And what possible redemption might there be, in such a weak and crooked world? The answer, of course, is cricket. When Burnby turns to the match, he presents the players as archetypes of English honour. They become ideals of rural life – merging with the surrounding landscape, so that they form a part of nature's beauty:

The matchless CRICKETERS were seen
In milk-white Vestments tread the Green;

Where the smooth Grass was laid compleat
Before Sir HORACE MANN's retreat;
Where the sweet Lawn, with shady Trees
Encompass'd round – Sensation's please!
The rural Prospect of the Grove,
Nature so kindly made for Love –
The tow-ring Hill, and neighb'ring Vale,
The gliding Stream of the Canal:
But view the Scene! Description's faint;
My Pen cannot its Beauties paint.

The cricketers in their 'milk-white' vestments are part of an Edenic pastoral paradise. And all around them are the 'smooth Grass', the 'sweet Lawn', the 'shady Trees', the 'tow-ring Hill', the 'neighb'ring Vale', the 'gliding Stream' . . . Burnby puts emphasis not only on the cricket, but on the charm of the natural environment in which the match is played.

It is an inkling of what was to come: a gateway into Romanticism. Burnby is not just praising the beauty of nature; by the end of his description, the scene is no longer expressible. 'My Pen,' he explains, 'cannot its Beauties paint.' And in suggesting nature is beyond language's reach, the line anticipates a reflection made some years later, in the very first year of a new century:

For the Reader cannot be too often reminded that Poetry is passion: it is the history or science of feelings: now every man must know that an attempt is rarely made to communicate impassioned feelings without something of an accompanying consciousness of the inadequateness of our own powers, or the deficiencies of language.

Poetry aims, paradoxically, to describe a world that is too beautiful to be captured in words. The author of the note was William Wordsworth.

III
ROMANTICS

'The Eton v. Harrow match will no longer be played as a regular annual fixture at Lord's after 2022.'

So ran a statement from the MCC, in February of that year. It went on to explain that 'this move aims to further MCC's goal to broaden the scope of the fixture list, extending playing opportunities at Lord's to a wider range of players.'

To some, it was a no-brainer. Conventions like Eton versus Harrow were no more than an elitist disgrace – a hangover from English cricket's class-blighted history, best consigned to the past. In his role as MCC president, Stephen Fry promoted a more democratic future. 'If you really love cricket,' he argued, 'don't you want more kids to play? Don't you want it to lose that image that it sometimes still has – a turgid image of snobbery and elitism?'

Others, though, were not so happy. One member threatening to hand back his egg-and-bacon blazer was legendary cricket commentator (and Old Etonian) Henry Blofeld. 'To play cricket implies honesty and loyalty,' he protested, 'and the committee should be the epitome of everything cricket stands for. I do feel for the first time that the club is not coming clean and is going behind my back . . . There is a nasty taste to this.'

Bedlam ensued at the home of cricket. A group of 180 members revolted against the decision; a vote was forced. And in September 2022, the decision was spectacularly reversed – initially Lord's was confirmed for one more year and the following spring it was revealed that the fixture would stay there for another five years at least.

'Without tradition,' said Winston Churchill, 'art is a flock of sheep without a shepherd. Without innovation, it is a corpse.' For the moment, Eton versus Harrow was safe; this time round, tradition had triumphed over change. Views were split on whether this was a grim defence of something toxic or the triumphant survival of something precious. It was, after all, a fixture with a long history; not only that, but a literary history too. In its very first year – all the way back in 1805 – the Harrow eleven even included a spirited all-rounder by the name of Byron . . .

7

'OUR SPORTS HAVE AN END': CRICKET AND ROMANTICISM

Although the aggressive tenor of eighteenth-century cricket may not seem the natural place for children, the game had been long established in the public schools of England. Many portraits from the latter part of the century presented young boys as cricketers. It was a sign that the game was popular amongst the young – but also that it was in some way a badge of social esteem. Here is a portrait of a young Charles Collyer by Francis Cotes, painted in 1766:

The boy's pose is confident, even faintly arrogant. The fine attire, with gold trim on the hat and waistcoat, confers social status. But another status symbol is the cricket bat he holds – insouciantly gripped between two fingers, despite its heavy appearance. It suggests an elevated level of cricket's prestige by this point in the eighteenth century. If you wanted to look dignified and important, it was a good move to pose as a cricketer.

Another striking image from this era was once attributed to Thomas Gainsborough, but is actually the work of portraitist Thomas Alleyne:

Alleyne made his living visiting the country houses of England, painting aristocratic subjects. This boy is finely dressed, indicating a degree of social standing. Even the stance, with legs crossed, is telling – an established signal of noble birth. He is surrounded by a green idyll, with trees on either side and a distant backdrop of typically English fields and rolling hills – much of which, maybe even all – will have been owned by the boy's family.

The set of stumps, in the foreground, is also noteworthy for the reason that there are not two stumps, but three. Alleyne's portrait is one of the earliest depictions of this innovation. For many years, the wicket had been composed of two stumps with a single bail on the top. But in 1775, a controversial incident took place. Edward 'Lumpy' Stevens had gathered a reputation as the finest bowler in England. He bowled at a brisk pace, and with matchless precision; cricketer and author John Nyren would later note that he could bowl 'the greatest number of length balls in succession'. He is often cited as cricket's earliest example of a true master bowler – able to vary flight, pace and length with infallible control, bringing forth unplayable deliveries seemingly at will. And he was an honest, salt-of-the-earth chap to boot. 'He had no trick about him,' wrote Nyren, 'but was as plain as a pike-staff in all his dealings.' In the fable-rich tapestry of eighteenth-century English cricket, he is one of the most enduring figures of all.

In 1775, Lumpy was playing for Surrey in a match against Hambledon. It was a big game: one of England's leading counties up against the legendary, all-conquering parish club. He was bowling to John Small, the most eminent of all Hambledon's batsmen ('A star,' according to Nyren, 'of the first magnitude'). And at some point in the match – three times in a row – Lumpy bowled the ball right through the middle of John Small's stumps. A flaw in the game was instantly exposed. How could it be right, to defeat a batsman in such a manner, and not receive any reward? Not long after, the middle stump was introduced.

The images of bat-wielding youths associate cricket with a more innocent world – a world not of fighting, boozing and wagering, but one of childhood play. The second half of the eighteenth century was a time of revolutionary ideas surrounding childhood. A key Romantic concept was beginning to germinate – that childhood held unique properties worth cherishing and the ideas of the adult world should not be despotically enforced. 'Childhood has its own way of seeing, thinking and feeling,' wrote

Jean-Jacques Rousseau in 1762. 'Nothing is more foolish than to try and substitute our ways.' There was, perhaps, a new era on the horizon.

William Blake was a Londoner, born and bred in the city. The extent of his involvement in cricket is not known. As we have seen, though, the game was flourishing in London by the time of his birth in 1757. He will have been familiar with it from a young age. Within close range of his childhood home in Soho, there were cricket grounds at Lamb's Conduit Fields, Gray's Inn, Chelsea Common, Kennington Common and White Conduit Fields, as well as the famous Artillery Ground in Finsbury.

An Island in the Moon, one of Blake's earliest works, is a satirical piece in which a series of acquaintances – with names such as Suction, Inflammable Gass and Obtuse Angle – sit around conversing, philosophising and singing poems. The tone is puerile and vulgar. 'The trumpeter shit in his hat,' sings Suction at one point. And towards the end of the manuscript, a character named Tilly Lally recites the following lyric:

O I say, you Joe,
Throw us the ball.
I've a good mind to go,
And leave you all.

I never saw such a bowler,
To bowl the ball in a tansey,
And to clean it with my handkercher
Without saying a word.

That Bill's a foolish fellow
He has given me a black eye.
He does not know how to handle a bat
Any more than a dog or a cat.

He has knock'd down the wicket
And broke the stumps,
And runs without shoes to save his pumps.

There is a distinctly comic quality here. The ball is bowled
wrapped in a 'tansey' – a kind of pudding. The tone is lowered
further if we note that Blake's original choice for the word was
'turd'. And there are implications of violence in the lines, too –
ones that echo Edward Phillips' *Mysteries of Love & Eloquence*
from over a hundred years before. Blake had initially written 'That
Bill's a foolish fellow/To hit me with a bat', but crossed out the
latter line. The vision of cricket offered in this poem is dark and
ribald, gesturing back to the tawdry aspects of the game's history.

It could not be more different to what he created a few years
later in 'The Ecchoing Green' from his *Songs of Innocence*, first
published in 1789:

Two cricketers appear in the main image – a happy rural scene, featuring children and adults gathered around a tree. A pair of boys face each other, playing. One of them holds his hands aloft – in celebration, excitement or maybe in anticipation of a catch. The ball hovers in front of the other boy, who wields a bat boldly in one hand, like a club, preparing to knock the ball back to his friend. Any cricket fan will recognise it instantly, the setup, the arrangement – an informal fielding practice session.

The third cricketer appears in the left margin, by the opening lines – leaning on his bat, gazing into the distance. And the fourth, another young boy, appears at the poem's end, face turned away from the viewer:

He is looking up at a man – whose white hair and wisp of white beard suggest old age, though there is something youthful about the face, too, a cheerful, ever-young air. The man appears to be instructing the boy, guiding him home, perhaps, after his day of games. Twilight approaches: the man's finger points into a purple-black swirl of gathering night. And as the boy turns to listen, he grips the curved crook of a cricket bat. It is a tool that appears to be too big for him, the handle reaching up to his chest, highlighting his juvenile years.

Here is cricket, shown as play on the pastures of England. The baser connotations of the game are dramatically discarded, in favour of a beautified, idealised vision. And – crucially – it was now children playing it. Blake was not only honouring the game as a ritual of the rural space; he was merging it with the bliss of youth. Cricket had been reshaped, as a game played by children at their happiest – a signifier of joy. The young cricketers he engraves – playing, thinking, inquiring – represent qualities of childhood wonder central to his model of innocence.

How, then, might we best appreciate 'The Ecchoing Green' from an angle that has usually been ignored – a cricketing angle? The poem starts with a beautiful sunlit scene:

> The sun does arise,
> And make happy the skies.
> The merry bells ring
> To welcome the Spring.
> The sky-lark and thrush,
> The birds of the bush,
> Sing louder around,
> To the bells' cheerful sound,
> While our sports shall be seen
> On the Ecchoing Green.

All elements of the natural world work together to form a harmonious tapestry. The sun's rise provides the sky with happiness; sounds of bells and birdsong blur into each other. It is an opening within a clear tradition – one that can be traced back through James Love and William Goldwin – that places cricket in a springtime landscape of optimism and possibility.

The speaker of the poem is one of the playing children, but the second stanza introduces an adult presence:

> Old John, with white hair
> Does laugh away care,
> Sitting under the oak,
> Among the old folk,
> They laugh at our play,
> And soon they all say.
> 'Such, such were the joys.
> When we all girls & boys,
> In our youth-time were seen,
> On the Ecchoing Green.'

Cricket's healing effect on 'Old John' is clear. Watching the game being played brings him joy and peace; the 'care' of the adult world is washed away, leaving laughter instead. It also brings nostalgia – for memories of similar such games in the adults' own youth, there on the very same echoing green. Alongside the sounds of laughter and play, Blake's green echoes with the memories of old folks, reminiscing in a manner that mingles elements of merriment and sadness.

In the final lines, the sun goes down and the games come to an end. The journey home is both peaceful and faintly ominous, hinting that the playfulness of these children – the liberated childhood they inhabit – will have its own expiry date:

> Till the little ones weary
> No more can be merry
> The sun does descend,
> And our sports have an end:
> Round the laps of their mothers,

Many sisters and brothers,
Like birds in their nest,
Are ready for rest;
And sport no more seen,
On the darkening Green.

Together with the cosy withdrawal into snug homes, there is the poignant and even vaguely threatening presence of the 'darkening Green' . . . night has come. Perhaps summer has ended. Perhaps childhood has ended, too. The cricket is no more. The poem highlights the transience of life's pleasures, the sense that sport is precious because it only lasts for so long. For everyone, a day will come when they will play no longer – when the kit is packed away for the last time and it has become the next generation's turn to bat, and bowl, and field on the echoing green. Cricket is not a game for the adult world. It belongs to the young.

Blake's vision of cricket, in 'The Ecchoing Green', reflects a distinctively Romantic reverence for childhood's spiritual purity. 'Heaven lies about us in our infancy!' wrote Wordsworth some years later, in his ode 'Intimations of Immortality'. 'Shades of the prison-house begin to close/Upon the growing boy'. The idea that adult systems cause damage to the welfare of children can be found in other Blake poems, such as 'The School Boy' ('to go to school in a summer morn,' he wrote, 'O it drives all joy away!'). For Blake, play was far from a trivial matter. All round him, every day – in the grime and toil of London – he witnessed the crushing effects of childhood poverty, chronicling it in famous lyrics such as 'London', 'Holy Thursday' and 'The Chimney Sweeper' from *Songs of Experience*. As an emblem of escape from the pain of a cruel world, play could not have been any more important.

Another artistic giant of the era, who turned to cricket more than once, was J. M. W. Turner. A game features in his magnificent early watercolour of Wells Cathedral:

The grandeur of the cathedral's west front dominates the scene. But Turner has selected the perspective in order to draw attention to the surrounding life of the city. The smaller buildings in the distance include the music schools of Wells Cathedral School – a reminder that, alongside the majesty of the twelfth-century cathedral, the education of the young continues.

And human life appears, too, in the scattering of people in the foreground. They are playing two different games – one group plays hoop, while the other plays cricket. The figures are small, dwarfed by the ancient stone, as if to underline the insignificance of individual lives in the light of grand historical designs. Turner offsets the monument of the cathedral and the game of cricket against each other, in a counterbalancing of the enduring and the everyday.

As the eighteenth century drew to a close, William Wordsworth and Samuel Taylor Coleridge brought greater awareness to the character of English rural life with the publication of *Lyrical*

Ballads. The focus of the poems was on 'humble and rustic life', as Wordsworth explained – 'because, in that condition, the essential passions of the heart find a better soil in which they can attain their maturity, are less under restraint, and speak a plainer and more emphatic language.' And even though London had become cricket's power centre, it is as a simple, rustic pursuit – a game for crude country types – that two late-century plays lightheartedly cast the game.

In George Colman's *The Heir at Law*, first performed in 1797, a Gosport shopkeeper improbably inherits a lordship title together with an income of fifteen thousand pounds. The play follows the new lord's efforts to transform his family from coarse bumpkins into respectable members of society. In an early scene, his son Dick – a young roisterer – recounts his skills as a cricketer:

> Dick: I can shoot a wild-duck with any lawyer's clerk in the
>   country, I can fling a bar – play at cricket –
> Zekiel: That you can: I used to notch for you, you know.
> Dick: I can make a bowl of punch –
> Zekiel: That you can: I used to drink it wi' you, you do know.

Colman uses cricket here as a sign of rural simplicity. Dick has just arrived in the maelstrom of London as an affable, thoroughly unrefined youth from the country. Cricket, the play implies, is the sort of game for chaps like this – unworldly yokels, who enjoy a drink and a bit of fun, but who exist in comic contrast to a world of social sophistication. The game is a rural pursuit – but in a manner that could not be much more different from the idealised innocence of Blake's 'The Ecchoing Green'. It is, instead, a game for ale-slurping revellers.

And the game has a similar function in *Speed the Plough* by Thomas Morton, first performed the following year. Here, Bob Handy, the son of a local nobleman, Sir Abel Handy, patronisingly queries a farmer named Ashfield about his way of life:

Handy Jnr: I say, Farmer, you are a set of jolly fellows here, an't you?

Ashfield: Ees, Zur, deadly jolly – excepting when we be otherwise, and then we beant.

Handy Jnr: Play at cricket, don't you?

Ashfield: Ees, Zur; we Hampshire lads conceat we can bowl a bit or thereabouts.

Handy Jnr: And cudgel too, I suppose?

Sir Abel: At him, Bob.

Ashfield: Ees, zur, we sometimes break oon another's heads by way of being agreeable, and the like o'that.

Handy Jnr: Understand all the guards? [*Putting himself in an attitude of cudgelling.*]

Ashfield: Can't zay I do, Zur.

Handy Jnr: What! Hit in this way, eh? [*Makes a hit at Ashfield, which he parries and hits young Handy violently.*]

Ashfield: Noa, zur, we do hit thic way.

Handy Jnr: Zounds and fury!

Sir Abel: Why, Bob, he has broke your head.

All elements of the scene – Ashfield's countrified dialect, the superior tone of Handy junior, the sudden onset of violence – reinforce the idea of cricket as a game for rugged country folks. The farmer's Hampshire roots gesture towards the strength of that county's cricketing pedigree, as well as the legend of the Hambledon Club, which by this point was firmly established.

These plays poke fun at cricket while also affirming it to be a motif of rural English life. As Anthony Bateman has observed, 'Cricket was being written into existence as a legacy of a near-extinct folk culture, as uncontaminated by modernity, and hence as authentically English.' In the tumult of the Industrial Revolution, the increasingly urbanised reality of cricket – with London the new sovereign – was countered by a sentimental fantasy of cricket as synonymous with the countryside.

And as a new century dawned, the game would repeatedly surface in the lives and work of the great Romantic poets. In late 1791, Wordsworth travelled to France. Political principles stirred by the revolution were only one reason for the trip; he was also keen to escape, or at least delay, a family expectation that he would head into law or the church. While there, he fell in love with a young Frenchwoman, Annette Vallon, who bore his child. And his commitment to anti-monarchist, revolutionary politics deepened into a passionate conviction. 'Bliss was it in that dawn to be alive,' he would famously write of his youthful idealism, 'But to be young was very heaven!'

As time passed, though, the brutality of Robespierre's reign of terror swept away his political ideals. He became disillusioned. In 1802 – after returning from Calais, where he had visited Annette and his daughter – he wrote 'Composed in the Valley Near Dover, on the Day of Landing':

Dear Fellow-traveller! here we are once more.
The Cock that crows, the Smoke that curls, that sound
Of Bells – those Boys that in yon meadow-ground
In white-sleev'd shirts are playing – and the roar
Of the waves breaking on the chalky shore –
All, all are English. Oft have I looked round
With joy in Kent's green vales; but never found
Myself so satisfied in heart before.
Europe is yet in Bonds; but let that pass,
Thought for another moment. Thou art free,
My Country! and 'tis joy enough and pride
For one hour's perfect bliss, to tread the grass
Of England once again, and hear and see,
With such a dear Companion at my side.

The lines fondly describe the landscape and character of England. It is as if he is returning not just to a place, but to a kind of loyalty to the nature of Englishness itself. The boys playing cricket 'in white sleev'd shirts' form part of a view that is meaningful because it is distinctively, archetypally English.

And, in contrast to the 'bonds' of Europe, the English landscape before Wordsworth's eyes is one of freedom. It is a patriotic, sanitised scene. The cricketers are really no more than an agreeable component of the tableau, along with chimney smoke, church bells and the sound of the sea against Dover's white cliffs.* Wordsworth is not so interested in the game's human reality, but more in its aesthetic qualities, at the core of a beautiful rural setting.

John Keats made several references to cricket in his letters. In October 1818, he wrote to his brother George, who had emigrated to America earlier that year:

> I intend to write you such Volumes that it will be impossible for me to keep any order or method in what I write: that will come first which is uppermost in my Mind, not that which is uppermost in my heart – besides I should wish to give you a picture of our Lives here whenever by a touch I can do it; even as you must see by the last sentence our walk past Whitehall all in good health and spirits – this I am certain of, because I felt so much pleasure from the simple idea of your playing a game at Cricket.

Like Wordsworth, Keats pictured cricket as a symbol of England. His letters reveal a close relationship with his brother ('I hope you will have a Son,' he wrote elsewhere, 'and it is one of my first wishes to have him in my Arms'). In the wake of a painful transatlantic separation, he takes comfort in the thought of his

---

* The 'dear companion' mentioned in the poem is Wordsworth's sister, Dorothy. She had accompanied him on the trip and would later describe the 'crowds of people at a cricket-match, the numerous combatants dressed in "white-sleeved shirts"' in her notebook.

far-away brother playing a game of cricket, in a tender dream of his return.

And the game also offered Keats other consolations. It was not until the spring of 1820 that he was diagnosed with tuberculosis, but he had been troubled with illness all his life. His keen interest in physical endeavour – he enjoyed both boxing and street-fighting – was mixed with understandable fears about ill health; his mother died from tuberculosis when he was fourteen and his brother Tom died at nineteen from the same disease.

For Keats, sport and activity were medicinal prospects – affirmations of physicality, and celebrations of aliveness. Even injuries were to be hailed as badges of vitality. 'Yesterday I got a black eye,' he wrote to George in 1819, 'the first time I took a Cricket bat . . . I am glad it was not a clout. This is the second black eye I have had since leaving school – during all my school days I never had one at all – we must eat a peck before we die.' The vigour of his own imagination was something he once framed in cricketing terms. 'My Mind is heap'd to the full; stuff'd like a cricket ball,' he wrote to his lover Fanny Brawne. 'If I strive to fill it more it would burst.' It is a peculiar image – one that forges a surprising associative bond between cricket and creative fertility.

By far the most celebrated cricketer amongst the great Romantic poets, though, was Lord Byron. In the English imagination, he is the Romantic archetype of cricket-playing youth made flesh – playing for Harrow against Eton in 1805 and recording the experience in some of his earliest verse. It was not his only sporting interest. His appetite for swimming was immortalised in his crossing of the Hellespont in 1810 – the first person officially to make it across the three-mile stretch. He was also a keen fencer, rower, boxer, rider and shooter. It was all, it seems, a way of keeping dark thoughts at bay. 'The more violent the fatigue,' he noted in 1814, 'the better my spirits for the rest of the day.'

His addiction to exercise was also a display of determination in the face of a badly deformed right foot. In the Eton v. Harrow cricket match, he was able to play but needed to bat with the aid of a runner. Afterwards, he was keen to stress the strength of his own performance. He *claimed* that he had scored eleven runs in the first innings and seven in the second – 'which was more than any of our side, except Brockman and Ipswich, could contrive to hit'. It was, though, a tall tale; the records show he scored seven in the first innings and two in the second. In terms of runs, this was only the seventh-best effort in the team. The Harrow captain, J. A. Lloyd, wrote afterwards that 'Byron played very badly . . . he should never have been in the XI had my counsel been taken.'

The 1805 match was the first of what became a historic annual fixture. It took place at Lord's Old Ground – the earliest of the three grounds that Thomas Lord set up in the area. Evidence suggests that the game was not officially organised by the schools' authorities but the boys themselves. The original challenge was despatched from the Harrow side: 'The gentlemen of Harrow School request the honour of trying their skill at cricket with the gentlemen of Eton, on Wednesday 31 July at Lord's Cricket Ground. A speedy answer, declaring whether the time and place be convenient, will oblige.'

The match itself, eventually played on 2 August, turned out to be a one-sided affair. Harrow only managed fifty-five in their first innings. Eton responded with a sturdier 122. As Byron rightly noted, Lord Ipswich was one of Harrow's top performers – the only player to make it into double figures in the first innings and top scoring with twenty-one in the second. But it was all to no avail. Harrow were bundled out again, this time for sixty-five.

Byron did get a bowl – contributing with one wicket, clean bowling Kaye for seven. His side, though, had been hammered by an innings and two runs. 'We played the Eton and were most confoundly beat,' he admitted.

More drama happened in the hours after the match, in the form of swaggering schoolboy mischief. It appears that booze was consumed. Byron found himself embroiled in a fight at the

Haymarket theatre with members of the Eton team. After the brawl ended – rather improbably – peace was made and members of both sides squeezed into a box to watch the play. According to biographer Benita Eisler, though, they had to make a 'speedy exit', as their 'noisemaking made it impossible for other theatre-goers to hear the performance'. Byron would look back on the day with a mixture of embarrassment and satisfaction. 'How I got home after the play, God knows,' he wrote to his friend, 'as my brain was so confused by the heat, the row and the wine I drank, that I could not remember in the morning how the deuce I found my way to bed.'

In the days that followed, a teasing piece of doggerel from Eton emerged:

Adventurous boys of Harrow School,
Of cricket you've no knowledge,
You play not cricket but the fool,
With men of Eton College.

It was hardly the most sophisticated piece of English verse. But it was enough to instigate a riposte from Harrow, which has often been thought to be by Byron himself:

Ye Eton wits, to play the fool
Is not the boast of Harrow school;
No wonder, then, at our defeat
Folly like yours could ne'er be beat.

If this is indeed by Byron, it is one of his earliest surviving pieces of work. The budding young poet was not just a player in the Harrow XI; he was also the team's literary spokesman.

Byron's cricketing feats were sources of pride for the rest of his life. He would continue to refer to them many years later. 'I played in the Harrow match against the Etonians in 1805, gaining more notches (as one of our chosen eleven) than any except Ld. Ipswich & Brockman on our side,' he wrote to John Murray in 1820, repeating his fib of fifteen years before. And the cricketing memories were not just an opportunity to boast. They had a personal significance for him, too. In 1821, he wrote in his journal, 'I was besides a very fair Cricketer – one of the Harrow eleven when we played against Eton in 1805.' He may not have been quite as fine a cricketer as he wished to claim, even to himself. But there can be little doubt that the game was close to Byron's heart.

8

'There was high feasting held': Dreams of Merrie England

On 3 October 1811, a cricket match took place at Balls Pond, Newington, between the women of Hampshire and the women of Surrey. It was the first official women's county game and a high-stakes affair, with a thousand guineas in the pot (around fifty thousand pounds in today's money). Thomas Rowlandson produced a caricature of the occasion:

'The Performers in the Contest were of all Ages and Sizes,' the caption explains. According to historian John Ashton, players ranged from fourteen to 'upwards of forty'.

And despite what must have been a distinct chill, coming so late in the season, the scene Rowlandson depicts is bright and colourful. He appears keen to mark the drama of the occasion as well as gently mocking it. Comedy and competitiveness are both present. The game is poised at a key moment, with a fielder in a pink dress stretching to take a catch – although her off-balance posture suggests she might be destined to drop it. Meanwhile, the batswomen sprint between the wickets with obvious intent. The rest of the fielding side watch on in attitudes of suspense – hands on hips, or heads, or knees or in the air. Some members of the crowd are waving their hats, overcome by the tension. It is a spirited scene, suggestive of high drama.

Other elements, though, are more mischievous. One fielder trips over a dog as she desperately runs at the ball. Another has already toppled over, performing a graceless belly flop. On close inspection, several of the couples at the field's far perimeter are more interested in romance than in the match, locked as they are in amorous embraces (over his career, Rowlandson would carve out a handy sideline in explicit erotic pictures for wealthy clients). The marquee on the far side – its flag sporting the ineptly spelled slogan, 'Jolly Criketers' – appears to be overflowing with bibulous patrons. Overall, the picture sits somewhere between a celebration and a send-up.

But this is not quite the full story. There are aspects of the image that give it a strange, even surreal quality. The green fields, stretching out to the horizon, create the feel of an open rural space; even the title of the image is *Rural Sports, or a Cricket Match Extraordinary*. But the truth was rather different. London was rapidly expanding: in the opening years of the nineteenth century, its population increased by almost fifty per cent to over 1.4 million. Urban sprawl had not *quite* reached the location of this match in Newington – but with Islington High Street less than a mile away, it was getting very close. Rowlandson paints a pastoral picture of an event that was, in fact, happening right on the cusp of the metropolis. He offers just one hint of the city's proximity – an industrial chimney in the far corner, bellowing its smoke into the pale blue sky.

The stumps are another curiosity. Rowlandson depicts a pair of two-stump wickets – but these had long been obsolete. Why did the artist choose to include such an outmoded detail? The wickets create a dated, retro feel. It is an early nineteenth-century picture of an eighteenth-century game. It is not only misleadingly rural in character – it is also nearly half a century out of date.

And as we shall see, Rowlandson was far from the only artist at this time who was keen to summon the past – presenting visions of cricket that were not so much historically accurate as construc-tions of the imagination, nostalgic dreams of an unreal yesteryear.

The opening decades of the nineteenth century were a time of dynamic change. In 1800, Alessandro Volta developed the 'voltaic pile' – the world's first electric battery. Inspired by Volta, Humphry Davy used the voltaic pile to discover several new elements, before inventing the electric arc lamp and the miner's lamp. The invention of high-pressure steam engines led to George Stephenson's first passenger-carrying locomotive in 1814. Over these years, gas lighting was installed across London. In 1818, James Blundell performed the first successful blood trans-fusion. The Industrial Revolution was in full swing – and tech-nology was advancing with dizzying pace.

The game of cricket was also changing fast. The moneyed, aristocratic body of the MCC was now well established as the game's most powerful force and county teams were regularly hosted at Lord's – the third and final incarnation of the ground, at St John's Wood, which opened for business in 1814. Very large stakes were often at play. Betting remained omnipresent. Skulduggery was widespread. Altham describes a single-wicket match at Lord's, in which both bowler *and* batsman had been bought, leading to a ludicrous double-cross stalemate: 'There was the bowler refusing to bowl within the batsman's reach ... and the batsman vigorously refusing to make any stroke at the ball for fear he might happen to score a run and so lose his money.' As the years went on, cricket's authorities would become stricter, and gambling laws more rigorous, but the spectre of corruption would not fully disappear.

After the end of the Napoleonic wars in 1815, there was a rapid growth in activity across many English counties. The game was becoming increasingly popular in the north. The international reach of cricket was widening, too, with clubs springing up in Australia, Argentina, Barbados, India and South Africa. And cricket was about to see a dramatic revolution in technique – something both controversial and transformational. The old, tried and trusted method of underarm bowling was about to come under threat.

Precisely how round-arm originated is a matter of uncertainty. The first evidence comes from the 1790s. Tom Walker, of Hambledon, was generally more of a batsman; but on the occasions he did bowl, he had a taste for experimental approaches. One novelty was the trialling of super-slow, high lobs – deliveries that scarcely reached the batsman and that were later scorned by his teammate, Billy Beldham, as 'baby bowling'. But another experiment involved a provocative departure from the accepted underarm manner of releasing the ball. Instead, Walker tried delivering it with the arm swung out away from his body, at right angles to his chest. The effects were dramatic. But it did not go down well. As Ashley Mote noted, 'It was decided this method of delivery was "foul play", due to the tremendous pace that such bowling generated.'

Built into the mythology of round-arm is the beguiling suggestion that women, in fact, were instrumental to the innovation. John Willes of Kent was a key pioneer and one account runs that it was his sister Christiana, bowling to him in the garden, who employed the technique to avoid the hindrance of her hooped skirts. Another early round-arm bowler, George Knight, was the focus of a similar tale, told years later by an ex-cricketer named R. H. W.: 'One Knight, a south country bowler, used to practise with his sister to keep his hand in, and his sister bowled to him in turn. As she put no steam on, he asked her to shy the ball, which she did in the way women usually do shy that is without using the wrist. He observed that the pace improved ... He laid the matter before the Lord's committee and the style was at once legalised and adopted.'

Only one of these tales can plausibly be true and it is possible that neither of them are. But the presence of such accounts adds richness to the imaginative origins of the round-arm rebellion.

The plot thickens upon the discovery that George Knight had distinguished relatives; more precisely, he was the nephew of a writer by the name of Jane Austen. John Major has mused that – if it is true that Knight's sister bowled to him – 'might not his famous aunt, Jane Austen, have done so as well?' The notion that *Jane Austen herself* may have had a shadowy background role in the development of round-arm bowling is, if nothing else, an enticing thought – especially given the fact that cricket does make an appearance in her novels.

In *Northanger Abbey*, a young Catherine Morland is more interested in cricket than in girls' usual pursuits: 'She was fond of all boy's plays, and greatly preferred cricket not merely to dolls, but to the more heroic enjoyments of infancy, nursing a dormouse, feeding a canary-bird, or watering a rose-bush.' The idea of a young woman, disdaining girlish interests in favour of sporting endeavours – pertinent to the status of Austen as an early feminist icon – has inspired later accounts of Austen's own life, despite the absence of direct evidence to suggest she was a cricketer. In the 2007 biopic *Becoming Jane*, Austen (played by Anne Hathaway) marches onto the field during a local cricket match to belt the winning runs. 'You've played this game before,' sighs opposition bowler and would-be love interest, Tom Lefroy, as she turns away with the bat rested on her shoulder.

*　　*　　*

Despite the primacy of innovation in the playing of the game, the art and literature of cricket often seemed fixed on the past. Peter Bailey has written that cricket 'carried with it long-standing associations of a bucolic, pre-industrial society; it was, in fact, a perfect vehicle for the myths of Merrie England'. In these opening decades of the nineteenth century, there is a strong sense of cricket evoking something dreamlike and folkloric that was both precious and in danger of dying out.

In 'Merry England', first published in 1819, essayist William Hazlitt aims to explain the essence of the English character. It, was, he felt, a contradictory brew, in which pessimism and merriment were obscurely interlinked. There is a dourness within the English disposition that shapes – and even heightens – the presence of jollity when it appears. 'The jest,' he wrote, 'is not the less welcome, nor the laugh less hearty, because they happen to be a relief from care or leaden-eyed melancholy . . . we are glad when any occasion draws us out of our natural gloom.'

The English appetite for sport, Hazlitt argues, stems from the embracing of cheer as a welcome escape from a default state of sullenness. It is precisely *because* of the dour English temperament that 'no people are fonder of field-sports, Christmas gambols, or practical jests'.

He moves into a description of cricket that oozes with nostalgia:

There is no place where trap-ball, fives, prison-base, football, quoits, bowls are better understood or more successfully practised; and the very names of a cricket bat and ball make English fingers tingle. What happy days must 'Long Robinson' have passed in getting ready his wickets and mending his bats, who, when two of the fingers of his right hand were struck off by the violence of a ball, had a screw fastened to it to hold the bat, and with the other hand still sent the ball thundering against the boards that bounded Old Lord's cricket-ground! What delightful hours must have been his in looking forward to the matches that were to come, in recounting the feats he had performed in those that were past! I have myself whiled away whole mornings in seeing him strike the ball (like a countryman mowing with a scythe) to the farthest extremity of the smooth, level, sun-burnt ground; and with long, awkward strides count the notches that made victory sure!

'Long Robinson' here is Robert Robinson, renowned batsman of Hambledon and Surrey. An unconventional character, he was the first player to experiment with both cricket pads and spiked shoes. Known variously as 'Long Bob' and 'Three-Fingered Jack', his deformed hand – injured not by a ball, as Hazlitt suggests, but in a childhood fire – forced him to craft a modified bat together with a highly unorthodox, left-handed technique.

The passage unmasks Hazlitt as an avid cricket fan, revelling in Robinson's displays of power and skill. But it is also, importantly, a scene dragged up from the past. By the time this essay was published, Robinson was well into his fifties – and although he did play to a late age, his heyday was decades earlier, in the closing years of the eighteenth century. The image of Robinson as a 'countryman mowing with a scythe' turns him into an expression of rustic labour. Hazlitt's reference to Old Lord's, too, shows that the scene in his mind is not one of the present day. It is a reminiscence, a wistful dream of days gone by.

John Nyren, born in 1764, had played alongside Long Bob in Hambledon's twilight years. He was the son of Richard Nyren, landlord of The Bat & Ball inn, who had been captain of both Hambledon and Hampshire. In the early 1830s, John Nyren began collaborating with Charles Cowden Clarke on a work that aimed to tell the tale of Hambledon's glory days. The product – *The Cricketers of My Time* – would become one of the most celebrated books in the history of cricket.

By the time of its publication, John Nyren was in his seventies and the precise nature of his collaboration with Clarke has been much debated. What cannot be debated, though, is the powerfully nostalgic nature of the recollections in the book. The halcyon era of Hambledon is transported to the realm of mythology; in weaving a tale of folk customs and revelry, Nyren goes way beyond the documentation of cricketing skill.

Instead, he paints a richer picture in which the artistry of the players is critical. The great batsman John Small, for instance, is praised for his musicianship: 'He was a good fiddler, and taught himself the double bass.' Small's musical ability forms the core of an anecdote suggesting a mystical oneness with the world of nature: 'Upon one occasion he turned his Orphean accomplishment to good account. Having to cross two or three fields on his way to a musical party, a vicious bull made at him; when our hero, with the characteristic coolness and presence of mind of a good cricketer, began playing upon his bass, to the admiration and perfect satisfaction of the mischievous beast.'

Elsewhere, wicketkeeper Tom Sueter is revered for the beauty of his singing voice: 'With what rapture have I hung upon his notes when he has given us a hunting song in the club-room after the day's practice was over.' It is noteworthy that the focus is not on the field of play, but on the club-room revelry come evening time. The Hambledon Club evokes something much more than just cricket. It is a repository for the rituals of rural life. The members are not just cricketers, but symbols, with much broader, deeper resonances; they are participants in a lost ideal, a dream of Merrie England.

Nyren combines sentimentality with an open, heart-on-sleeve patriotism. 'The game of cricket is essentially English,' he reminds us. The book's most famous passage details a scene of hedonistic merriment so legendary and magnificent that it must be quoted in its entirety:

There was high feasting held on Broad-Halfpenny during the solemnity of one of our grand matches. Oh! it was a heart-stirring sight to witness the multitude forming a complete and dense circle round that noble green. Half the county would be present, and all their hearts with us. Little Hambledon pitted against All England was a proud thought for the Hampshire men. Defeat was glory in such a struggle – Victory, indeed, made us only 'a little lower than angels'. How those fine brawn-faced fellows of farmers would drink to our success! And then, what stuff they had to drink! – Punch! – not your new *Ponche à la Romaine*, or *Ponche à la Groseille*, or your modern cat-lap milk punch – punch be-deviled; but good, unsophisticated John Bull stuff – stark! – that would stand on end – punch that would make a cat speak! Sixpence a bottle! We had not sixty millions of interest to pay in those days. The ale too! – not the modern horror under the same name, that drives as many men melancholy-mad as the hypocrites do; – not the beastliness of these days, that will make a fellow's inside like a shaking bog – and as rotten; but barleycorn, such as would put the souls of three butchers into one weaver. Ale that would flare like turpentine – genuine Boniface! – This immortal viand (for it was more than liquor) was vended at twopence per pint. The immeasurable villany of our vintners would, with their march of intellect (if ever they could get such a brewing), drive a pint of it out into a gallon. Then the quantity the fellows would eat! Two or three of them would strike dismay into a round of beef. They could no more have pecked in that style than they could have flown, had the infernal black stream (that type of Acheron!) which soddens the carcass of a Londoner, been the fertiliser of their clay. There would this company, consisting most likely of some thousands, remain patiently and anxiously watching every turn of fate in the game, as if the event had been the meeting of two armies to decide their liberty. And whenever a Hambledon man made a good hit, worth four or five runs, you would hear the deep mouths of the whole multitude baying away in pure Hampshire – 'Go hard! go hard! – Tich and turn! – tich and turn!' To the honour of my countrymen, let me bear testimony upon this occasion also, as I have already done upon others.

Although their provinciality in general, and personal partialities individually, were naturally interested in behalf of the Hambledon men, I cannot call to recollection an instance of their wilfully stopping a ball that had been hit out among them by one of our opponents. Like true Englishmen, they would give an enemy fair play. How strongly are all those scenes, of fifty years by-gone, painted in my memory! – and the smell of that ale comes upon me as freshly as the new May flowers.

There are few more vibrant descriptions of drinking and feasting in the whole of English literature. Nyren's book would be immortal on the strength of this passage alone. It is a celebration of a specifically English sensibility, requiring specifically English materials – 'good, unsophisticated John Bull' punch, rounds of beef, old-fashioned barleycorn ale. Proper hairs-on-the-chest stuff. His hostility to foreign imports, and diluted modern variants, could not be clearer. And the scene he presents is not a mess of mindless indulgence; moral principles survive along with the pleasure. Nyren highlights an ethics of honesty that he perceives to be distinctively English: 'Like true Englishmen, they would give an enemy fair play.'

The Cricketers of My Time assembles the unashamedly nostalgic recollections of an old man looking back at his golden years; and it is soaked with all the rose-tinted idealism that such an enterprise inevitably involves. The book's vividness and beauty are intertwined with an inclination to romanticise. Published in the 1830s, it tells the story not of an England on the cusp of the Victorian era, but one that existed half a century before – if, indeed, it can be said to have ever existed at all. *How strongly are all those scenes, of fifty years by-gone, painted in my memory . . .*

Elsewhere, Nyren quotes a poem by the Reverend John Cotton that praises cricket at the same time as it celebrates the club's lavish epicurean rites:

Assist, all ye Muses, and join to rehearse
An old English sport, never praised yet in verse;
'Tis cricket I sing, of illustrious fame,
No nation e'er boasted so noble a game.
. . . Then fill up your glass, he's the best that drinks most.
Here's the Hambledon Club! – who refuses the toast?
Let's join in the praise of the bat and the wicket,
And sing in full chorus the patrons of cricket.

This, he notes, is an 'old-fashioned song', one 'which was very popular fifty years ago'. In *The Cricketers of My Time*, the story that Nyren tells is an old story, of an old English sport – a delicious fable of honour, companionship, and festivity.

Alongside Nyren's account, a tantalising sketch exists showing cricketers – including three legends of Hambledon – in a range of poses. It was made by George Shepheard in the early 1790s:

John Arlott described it as 'perhaps the most historically important, and unique, of all cricket pictures'. Little is known of Shepheard, who played briefly for Surrey, but appears not to have been a cricketer of the first rank. He would have been a young man of around twenty when he drew these figures – little anticipating their iconic destiny as a priceless artefact of cricketing folklore.

Near the middle of the page, there is 'Silver' Billy Beldham – one of the greatest of all Hambledon batsmen, but fixed here in a rather curious, French cricket-like pose, the bat directly in front of his awkwardly bowed legs. He looks ill-positioned to play any actual shot; it seems more like he is taking guard. Next to him is Tom Walker, the famed round-arm innovator, inspecting the blade of his own bat in wonder or confusion. In the top-right corner, there is David Harris – perhaps the finest underarm bowler of the eighteenth century – his right arm grandly aloft, preparing to bowl.

The Hambledonians are surrounded by a range of late-eighteenth-century cricketing notables. Just a few years before the sketch was made, Thomas Lord would have purchased the first of his grounds in north-west London; and Shepheard depicts him twice. First, he is shown taking a catch in the slips – carefully, if not gracefully – his cupped hands drawn close to the face. Then he is shown batting, knees bent towards the ground, whole body thrust forwards – a crooked stance, but certainly an aggressive one. Elsewhere, Colonel Charles Lennox and Edward Bligh are shown deep in mid-pitch conversation and Henry Tufton, elegantly attired as if attending the opera, is having a quiet word with Lord Frederick Beauclerk. The names of the other three figures are very faded; one of them can just about be deciphered as Captain Charles Cumberland, but the final two remain a mystery. Hailed by Gideon Haigh as 'the oldest surviving image of cricketers involved in an actual match', Shepheard's sketch is a compelling window into the look and feel of the eighteenth-century game.

In 1828, Mary Russell Mitford published *Our Village: Sketches of Rural Character and Scenery*. This, she explained, was 'an attempt to delineate country scenery and country manners, as they exist in a small village in the south of England'. The village in question was Three Mile Cross in Berkshire. Once again, though – despite Mitford's claim to render things 'as they exist' – the impulse towards historical faithfulness is mixed with a desire to offer up idealised visions of the countryside.

Chapter fourteen is charmingly titled 'A Country Cricket-Match', and the charm of the occasion is precisely what Mitford wants to emphasise. Here is the opening passage:

I doubt if there be any scene in the world more animating or delightful than a cricket-match: I do not mean a set match at Lord's Ground for hard money, between a certain number of gentlemen and players, as they are called – people who make a trade of that noble sport, and degrade it into an affair of bettings, and hedgings, and cheatings, it may be, like boxing or horse-racing; nor do I mean a pretty fête in a gentleman's park, where one club of cricketing dandies encounter another such club, and where they show off in graceful costume to a gay marquee of admiring belles, who condescend so to purchase admiration, and while away a long summer morning in partaking cold collations, conversing occasionally, and seeming to understand the game; the whole being conducted according to ball-room etiquette, so as to be exceedingly elegant and exceedingly dull. No! the cricket that I mean is a real solid old-fashioned match between neighbouring parishes, where each attacks the other for honour and a supper, glory and half-a-crown a man. If there be any gentlemen amongst them, it is well — if not, it is so much the better.

There is an effort here to distinguish village cricket from the urban, moneyed cricket of London and the gentry. Whether it be a big match at Lord's or a fashionable game in a gentleman's park, such occasions are just vulgar opportunities for corruption and vanity. But rural cricket – village cricket – is an altogether more noble thing. The focus on good, honest moral principles and the praising of the old – 'a real solid old-fashioned match' – is similar in mood to Nyren's chronicle.

Mitford's account brims with affection for the game of cricket as an expression of all that is best about a close-knit, rural community. The team members each have their role in the village social fabric – not as a divisive hierarchy, but as a compassionate, democratic unit in which fun is allowed to flourish without snobbery or judgement. 'A village match is the thing,' she writes, 'where our highest officer, our conductor (to borrow a musical term), is but a little farmer's second son; where a day-labourer is our bowler, and a blacksmith our long-stop; where the spectators consist of the retired cricketers, the veterans of the green, the careful mothers, the girls, and all the boys of two parishes, together with a few amateurs, little above them in rank, and not at all in pretension: where laughing and shouting, and the very ecstacy of merriment and good humour, prevail.'

The match had been set up after the boastful challenge of a rival village team. And with infectious glee, Mitford details how the Three Mile Cross XI took them down a peg or three:

These challengers – the famous eleven – how many did they get? Think! imagine! guess! – You cannot? – Well ! – they got twenty-two, or rather they got twenty; for two of theirs were short notches, and would never have been allowed, only that, seeing what they were made of, we and our umpires were not particular. – They should have had twenty more, if they had chosen to claim them. Oh, how well we fielded! and how well we bowled! . . . Well, we went in. And what were our innings?

Guess again! – guess! A hundred and sixty-nine! in spite of soaking showers, and wretched ground, where the ball would not run a yard, we headed them by a hundred and forty-seven; and then they gave in, as well they might.

It is a lively scene, steeped in cheerfulness and joy. Mitford's 'Country Cricket-Match' is a kind of paradise, a fairy tale in which everything is tuneful, happy and sweet – a summertime version of a Christmas picture postcard. But whether it is a fully authentic presentation is a different story. The narrative often feels contrived, and deliberately idealised. Mitford often draws attention to the artifice of her own descriptions. We see this sort of thing towards the end of the chapter:

William Grey made a hit which actually lost the cricket-ball. We think she lodged in a hedge, a quarter of a mile off, but nobody could find her. And George Simmons had nearly lost his shoe, which he tossed away in a passion, for having been caught out, owing to the ball glancing against it. These, together with a very complete somerset of Ben Appleton, our long-stop, who floundered about in the mud, making faces and attitudes as laughable as Grimaldi, none could tell whether by accident or design, were the chief incidents of the scene of action.

The action here is framed as a 'scene' – as if it is all a performance on a stage. The long-stop, too, is compared to Grimaldi, one of the great actors and clowns of the age. Mitford is hinting that the cricketing spectacle is a show, a fabrication – a product less of reality than of the imagination. In *Our Village*, Mitford turns cricket into a picture-perfect, sentimental dream. Perhaps not quite cricket how it really happens; but cricket as it is meant to be.

*　　*　　*

The value, in this era, of English cricket as a dreamscape – an antidote to industrial uproar – is encapsulated in another picture by Turner. At some point between 1828 and 1830, he produced a sketch of *Cricket on Goodwin Sands*:

Goodwin Sands in Deal, Kent, is a corner of England that has a rich cricketing history. The earliest recorded match was in 1813 – and it proved a controversial affair, condemned by some as an affront to all the sailors who had perished in the vicinity. These sands were notorious as a dangerous spot for ships, involving erratic tidal variations of up to five metres. Over a thousand lost their lives there in the Great Storm of 1703. In 1740, the Dutch merchant ship, the *Rooswijk*, was wrecked a few miles from shore and no crew members survived. In 1748, the same fate befell a British schooner, the *Lady Lovibond*; legend tells that it reappears as a ghost ship every fifty years, out on the lonely waters.

But you would not know any of this from Turner's picture. A series of blurry figures play a game of cricket on the beach, in a tranquil, delicate tableau. The indistinct shapes and forms anticipate aspects of his late maritime masterpieces, such as *Snowstorm, Steam-Boat Off a Harbour's Mouth* (1842), but without any of the unrest. Here, a calm flat blue sea forms the backdrop to the contemplative stillness of the game. The players are little more than shafts of light, almost part of the sand itself. The sun is only a smudge of white in a peaceful bath of grey. Here is cricket, preserved in the safety of a dream-world, far away from the harsh reality of things.

9

'ALL-MUGGLETON HAD THE FIRST INNINGS': CRICKET IN DICKENS

In the final years of her life, Mary 'Mamie' Dickens wrote a memoir about her famous father, published in the months after she died in 1896. It is a fond account, one that steers clear of the darker aspects of his personal life and promotes the great novelist as an equally great human being, brimming with warmth and cheer. His love of Christmas, his generosity to guests and strangers, his affection for children and his delight in the comforts of home are all given prominence. 'My love for my father has never been touched or approached by any other love,' she declares. 'I hold him in my heart of hearts as a man apart from all other men, as one apart from all other beings.'

In the midst of this tender chronicle, she recalls the wide-ranging love Dickens had for sports and games. Cricket, she notes, was a source of particular joy:

> Outdoor games of the simpler kinds delighted him. Battledore and shuttlecock was played constantly in the garden at Devonshire Terrace, though I do not remember my father ever playing it elsewhere. The American game of bowls pleased him, and rounders found him more than expert. Croquet he disliked, but cricket he enjoyed intensely as a spectator, always keeping one of the scores during the matches at 'Gad's Hill'.

The location – Dickens' final home at Gad's Hill – was a hive of cricketing activity. It became the site of regular charity matches, organised by Dickens himself, and played in the field directly behind his house; Dickens would personally contribute a guinea if the first ball in a match was hit to the boundary. And as Mamie suggests, he was an enthusiastic scorer. His friend Percy Fitzgerald recalled: 'I myself have seen him sit the whole day in a marquee, during a match got up by himself at Gad's Hill, marking (or "notching") in the most admirable manner.'

There is some evidence that he played too. His first biographer, John Forster, may have dismissively written that 'he was a very little and a very sickly boy' and 'was never a good little cricket-player'; but in adulthood, Dickens grew phenomenally active. Specimens of his cricketing accomplishments might be scarce – but in a letter to his friend, the journalist W. H. Wills in 1861, he allowed himself a brief boast about some recent heroic feats: 'Cricket came off, and the "Governor" your present correspondent got a hit high over the apple tree, for which he scored three, and which covered him with glory.'

Dickens, in short, adored the game of cricket. George Dolby, manager of his reading tours, verified that 'Mr Dickens was a great lover of cricket, and in the summer of 1866, he would often hurry back to Gad's Hill after a visit to town, in order to be present at a cricket match in the field at the back of his house.'

Inside the Dickens home, a swathe of cricketing pictures hung on the walls. And in one of them, a familiar figure is depicted preparing to bowl. It is a painting of a Gad's Hill match, happening just yards away from the very wall where the painting stood.

The bowler here is Mr Charles Dickens himself. The fact that he is dressed in formal black wear – more like an umpire than the white-clad players – suggests this is a ceremonial rather than a competitive moment. Dickens is getting things started, by bowling the first delivery. The match, which took place in September 1868, will have been one that he personally organised. As a mark of respect, the fielders all clutch handkerchiefs that they are waving above their heads, in an affectionate salute to the great man.

Dickens' son Henry wrote about the picture: 'I cannot recall the "Charity Match" which it represents; but it may have taken place when I was away at school or college. My father used to take the part of "scorer" at the games we played there, and was sustained in that arduous job by the "cooling drinks" provided for the guests who were staying in the house at the time or for the neighbours who came to see the games. Having regard to his interest in cricket itself and his keen interest in promoting the cause of charity, I can, I think, safely say that the incident did happen.'

And on several occasions, Dickens' passion for cricket made itself present in his writing. Its most famous appearance in his fiction – arguably the most famous scene of cricket in any fiction – is from *The Pickwick Papers*. It is a much-referenced, much-mythologised passage; but as a cricketing account, it has also often been unfairly maligned, a victim of major misunderstandings regarding the author's intent.

The backdrop to the match in the novel is as follows. Mr Wardle, the benevolent country squire, is playing host to a quartet of travelling Pickwickians – Mr Winkle, Mr Tupman, Mr Snodgrass and Mr Pickwick himself. When Mr Winkle suffers a nasty injury in an unfortunate shooting accident, the presence of a local cricket match surfaces in conversation:

'Are you a cricketer?' inquired Mr Wardle of the marksman.

At any other time, Mr Winkle would have replied in the affirmative. He felt the delicacy of his situation, and modestly replied, 'No.'

'Are you, sir?' inquired Mr Snodgrass.

'I was once upon a time,' replied the host; 'but I have given it up now. I subscribe to the club here, but I don't play.'

'The grand match is played to-day, I believe,' said Mr Pickwick.

'It is,' replied the host. 'Of course you would like to see it.'

The big game in question is Dingley Dell Cricket Club v. All-Muggleton. The Pickwickians promptly head out to watch.

They enter into a kind of utopian paradise of fun and farce. Dickens evokes the spirit of Merrie England in a manner plainly influenced by John Nyren and Mary Russell Mitford. Even the characters' journey to the cricket ground is past 'delightful scenery', 'through shady lanes and sequestered footpaths' – a pilgrimage into the heart of rural bliss.

And when they arrive at the ground, it is a location for drinking and dining as much as for sporting spectacle: 'The wickets were pitched, and so were a couple of marquees for the rest and refreshment of the contending parties.' The eccentric rascal, Mr Jingle, provides a vivid summary of the festivities in his characteristic staccato style: 'This way – this way – capital fun – lots of beer – hogsheads; rounds of beef – bullocks; mustard – cart-loads; glorious day – down with you – make yourself at home – glad to see you – very.' The spirit of Nyren's high feasting on Broadhalfpenny is keenly apparent. A game of cricket is where revelry happens, a gateway into indulgence and pleasure.

The match itself is given a light-hearted, comic spin:

All-Muggleton had the first innings; and the interest became intense when Mr Dumkins and Mr Podder, two of the most renowned members of that most distinguished club, walked, bat in hand, to their respective wickets. Mr Luffey, the highest ornament of Dingley Dell, was pitched to bowl against the redoubtable Dumkins, and Mr Struggles was selected to do the same kind office for the hitherto unconquered Podder. Several players were stationed, to 'look out', in different parts of the field, and each fixed himself into the proper attitude by placing one hand on each knee, and stooping very much as if he were 'making a back' for some beginner at leap-frog. All the regular players do this sort of thing; – indeed it is generally supposed that it is quite impossible to look out properly in any other position.

The umpires were stationed behind the wickets; the scorers were prepared to notch the runs; a breathless silence ensued. Mr Luffey retired a few paces behind the wicket of the passive Podder, and applied the ball to his right eye for several seconds. Dumkins confidently awaited its coming with his eyes fixed on the motions of Luffey.

'Play!' suddenly cried the bowler. The ball flew from his hand straight and swift towards the centre stump of the wicket. The wary Dumkins was on the alert: it fell upon the tip of the bat, and bounded far away over the heads of the scouts, who had just stooped low enough to let it fly over them.

Dumkins and Podder, the All-Muggleton batsmen, lead their team to a total of fifty-four. It turns out to be more than enough: 'in an early period of the winning game Dingley Dell gave in, and allowed the superior prowess of All-Muggleton'.

Dickens' warm-hearted portrayal, though, has not always been well received. In excluding the chapter from an anthology of sporting literature, golfer and Dickens scholar Bernard Darwin explained, 'John Nyren might have turned in his grave if the writings of one so ignorant of his beloved game had been found next door to his own.' Cricket writer R. C. Robertson-Glasgow said, 'I don't know if Dickens ever watched cricket at Lord's. Judging solely from his description of the cricket match in the Pickwick Papers, I should doubt it.' Poet and novelist E. V. Lucas was even more forthright: 'The odd things that happened when All-Muggleton met Dingley Dell convince me that the Inimitable, much as he knew of everything else, was not even a theoretical cricketer.'

Not even a *theoretical* cricketer . . . brutal dismissals like these sit oddly with the abundant evidence that Dickens keenly followed the game and knew it well. His habit of operating as scorer reveals not just a passive enjoyment in spectating: it is a task that requires active engagement, concentration and a sharp understanding of the rules. Moreover, we have Percy Fitzgerald's testament that he was not just a keen scorer – he was a good one.

But at a technical level, it has to be said that the cricketing action described in *Pickwick* hardly stands up to scrutiny. The language used is naïve and clumsy. Both of the umpires are 'stationed behind the wickets'. Later in the game, there is a bizarre implication that both sides should be able to score runs at the same time: 'When Dumkins was caught out, and Podder stumped out, All-Muggleton had notched some fifty-four, while the score of the Dingley Dellers was as blank as their faces.'

How could such a cricketing enthusiast as Dickens produce an account so riddled with errors?

Part of the answer lies in the author's comic purpose. Back in 1970, the centenary of Dickens' death, cricket writer Irving Rosenwater wrote a perceptive essay on Charles Dickens and cricket. He noted that this early chapter from *Pickwick* 'was conceived almost entirely in a spirit of farce . . . Of course the technical descriptions are ridiculous – but so ridiculous as to be deliberately so, and all the time possessing the sort of basic "truth" that Lear's nonsense displays.' It is, he contended, precisely

Dickens' strong knowledge of cricket that allowed him to produce a scene so absurd and stubbornly unserious – 'just as, for example, a violinist is able to fool about successfully on his violin only if he is an expert performer, so Dickens was able to indulge in farce to such effect because he *did* understand the game.'

And it is away from the sharp edges of reality that Dickens travels, in all aspects of his representation. Like the recollections of Hazlitt, Nyren and Mitford, the cricket of Dickens' *Pickwick Papers* is a nostalgic dream – set in an otherworldly, rural English paradise and surrounded on all sides by bursts of festivity.

After the match is over, the day culminates with a raucous banquet at the Blue Lion Inn. Mr Jingle explains that it promises to be a 'Devilish good dinner – cold, but capital – peeped into the room this morning – fowls and pies, and all that sort of thing – pleasant fellows these – well behaved, too – very'. The evening plays itself out in a deluge of hedonism. Following the meal, a range of toasts are delivered. Copious amounts of wine are consumed. And the chapter ends with a picture of tipsy sing-song merriment that – whether or not it consciously echoes the rites of the Hambledon Club – could not more perfectly evoke their spirit:

> . . . within some few minutes before twelve o'clock that night, the convocation of worthies of Dingley Dell and Muggleton were heard to sing, with great feeling and emphasis, the beautiful and pathetic national air of
> *We won't go home till morning*
> *We won't go home till morning*
> *We won't go home till morning*
> *'Till daylight doth appear.*

When *The Pickwick Papers* was first published as a complete edition in 1837, artist R. W. Buss was commissioned to provide some additional illustrations alongside the originals by Robert Seymour, who had committed suicide the previous year. Buss would later become most famous for *Dickens' Dream*, an unfinished watercolour in which scenes from the great novelist's work float round him as he sleeps. The process of etching required for book illustrations, though, was out of his comfort zone. Here is one of the two plates he produced for *Pickwick*:

A portly batsman – wielding his bat rather like a high-striker mallet – hits the ball at a bald and bespectacled close fielder, whose top hat is knocked off by the blow. The fielder's mouth hangs open in shock. Umpire and non-striking batsman anxiously watch on.

According to Rosenwater, Buss's *Pickwick* sketches were 'disastrous failures and were suppressed after some seven hundred impressions of each had been printed'. Buss himself was not satisfied with what he delivered, feeling that the need to hand his original pencil drawings to an engraver, for etching, erased his own, distinctive style. 'The free touch of an original work was entirely wanting,' he later complained. 'My name appeared to designs, not one touch of mine being on the plates. I felt greatly annoyed at this, and had I been allowed time, would have cancelled those two plates and etched designs with my own hand.' It is just possible, in any case, that his contribution has been unfairly disregarded. The print may be clunky and contrived, but it does manage to capture the capering spirit of the match; it is not exactly realistic, but Dickens' description is far from realistic either.

Throughout the rest of Dickens' work, cricket is repeatedly associated with the joys of the countryside. In *Oliver Twist*, it is a motif of escape from the crime of the city. A wounded Oliver, shot in the arm in a bungled burglary, is nursed back to health by the intended victims – the kindly trio of Mrs Maylie, Rose Maylie and Mr Losberne. When summer comes round, they take Oliver out to a cottage in the country. Dickens casts the spot as a healing tonic to London's toil: 'Who can describe the pleasure and delight, the peace of mind and soft tranquillity, the sickly boy felt in the balmy air, and among the green hills and rich woods, of an inland village! Who can tell how scenes of peace and quietude sink into the minds of pain-worn dwellers in close and noisy places, and carry their own freshness, deep into their jaded hearts!'

Oliver regains strength in this rural wonderland like some figure out of Blake or Wordsworth, an innocent youth sweetly communing with nature. And a key component of the environment is cricket:

When the birds were made all spruce and smart for the day, there was usually some little commission of charity to execute in the village; or, failing that, there was rare cricket-playing, sometimes, on the green; or, failing that, there was always something to do in the garden, or about the plants, to which Oliver . . . applied himself with hearty good-will.

Cricket, along with other nourishing pursuits such as gardening and charity work, is offered up as a feature of blissful rural life. It sits in vivid contrast to the traumatic nightmare Oliver suffered at the hands of Fagin and Bill Sikes in London.

This example is characteristic of Dickensian cricket. References to the game in his novels tend to be brief outside *The Pickwick Papers*, but there are plenty of them and they tend very much to resemble one another. In *The Old Curiosity Shop*, 'The men and boys were playing at cricket on the green.' In *Martin Chuzzlewit*, a coach passes at twilight 'beside the village green, where cricket-players linger yet, and every little indentation made in the fresh grass by bat or wicket, ball or player's foot, sheds out its perfume on the night'. In *Barnaby Rudge*, the protagonist ponders the carefree days of his childhood: 'Barnaby had been thinking within himself that the smell of the trodden grass brought back his old days at cricket, when he was a young boy and played on Chigwell Green.' Cricket in Dickens is consistently portrayed in this sort of way, as a signal of a happy existence in rural England – free from the suffering and misery that he details elsewhere.

And on some occasions, Dickens went as far as to associate cricket not just with happiness, but with moral integrity. For instance, David Copperfield points out his skill at cricket in an effort to emphasise the decency of Steerforth's character:

'Yes! That's just his character,' said I. 'He's as brave as a lion, and you can't think how frank he is, Mr Peggotty.'

'And I do suppose, now,' said Mr Peggotty, looking at me through the smoke of his pipe, 'that in the way of book-larning he'd take the wind out of a'most anything.'

'Yes,' said I, delighted; 'he knows everything. He is astonishingly clever.'

'There's a friend!' murmured Mr. Peggotty, with a grave toss of his head.

'Nothing seems to cost him any trouble,' said I. 'He knows a task if he only looks at it. He is the best cricketer you ever saw. He will give you almost as many men as you like at draughts, and beat you easily.'

Something similar can be seen in Dickens' final, unfinished novel, *The Mystery of Edwin Drood*, where the virtuous qualities of the Reverend Septimus Crisparkle are underlined in a cricketing image:

Good fellow! manly fellow! And he was so modest, too. There was no more self-assertion in the Minor Canon than in the schoolboy who had stood in the breezy playing-fields keeping a wicket. He was simply and staunchly true to his duty alike in the large case and in the small. So all true souls ever are. So every true soul ever was, ever is, and ever will be. There is nothing little to the really great in spirit.

In cases such as these, cricket becomes something more than a sport; it appears as a sign of virtue, a standard-bearer for morality itself.

Over a century and a half since his death, Charles Dickens remains one of English literature's most cherished and eminent cricket fans. And his love for the game endured until the very end of his life. The conservatory at Gad's Hill, at the house's rear, looked out across the lawn; it would have offered a fine view of the cricket matches played in the adjoining field. It was Dickens' pride and joy – the last room that he managed to complete before his death in June 1870. And it was the site of the very final cheques he signed – including what was, according to William R. Hughes, 'the last cheque which he drew' in his entire life. The cheque was a subscription; and it was made out to the Higham Cricket Club.

IV
VICTORIANS

The drama of the 2023 Ashes lasted all the way through to the final test at the Oval. By that point, the urn itself had gone; but England, if they won, could still square the series, and protect an unbeaten Ashes home record stretching all the way back to 2001. So there was much to play for.

On the very last day, tensions were high. Australia were chasing what had looked like an implausible target of 384. But they had made a good start and at the crease was Steve Smith, whose form had been modest, by his standards, but his jittery genius always inspired fear. Batting alongside Travis Head, he had taken the score past 200, with seven wickets still left. England were feeling the pressure.

Just before the lunch break, Smith played forward to a full delivery from Moeen Ali that found a bit of turn and bounce – flicking Smith's glove and ballooning to Ben Stokes at leg slip. As he took what was a pretty straightforward catch, the nearby fielders began leaping in delight – before stopping their celebrations a moment later, as if they had all simultaneously run out of battery. Stokes stood shaking his head and smiling in disbelief. The ball lay beside him on the grass. He had dropped it.

After some discussion with his teammates, though, the England captain asked the umpires for a review. Replays showed that he had, initially, taken the catch cleanly above his head – but as he swung his arm round to toss the ball up, already bellowing in triumph, his hand had clipped his thigh and the ball had fallen loose.

Had Stokes really thought that it might be out? It was difficult to believe, looking at the replays. To many, it looked less like genuine uncertainty, and more like crafty opportunism.

The Australians did not hesitate to highlight a whiff of hypocrisy. 'The spirit of the game's out now the shoe's on the other foot,' suggested Aussie batsman Marnus Labuschagne. Ronny Lerner, sports reporter for the Sydney Morning Herald, could not resist a jibe at Piers Morgan – who, since the saga of the Bairstow stumping, had been in the business of claiming England were winning the 'moral Ashes'. 'Never looked like he controlled it in real time,' wrote Lerner on Twitter. 'He would've known it, and yet he still reviewed. The captain of the country no less, Piers Morgan!! Why I never!! What a scandal! Spirit of cricket has officially died old boy.'

A spotlight shone on English claims of honour – and it seemed to expose an uncomfortable truth. For generations, the English had been in the business of claiming moral ascendancy – and in the summer of 2023, the envoys of Perfidious Albion were no less duplicitous than they had been at the very zenith of high-minded Victorian moralising. 'Victorian values . . . those were the values when our country became great,' former prime minister Margaret Thatcher had once claimed – and there is also a story, perhaps apocryphal, that she favoured the revival of all Victorian values except hypocrisy . . .

10

'FOR MEMBERS ONLY': VICTORIAN CRICKETING VISUALS

On 10 and 11 July 1837, a match was played at Lord's to mark the fiftieth anniversary of the Marylebone Cricket Club. It was a transitional moment in the history of English culture; just a few weeks earlier, an eighteen-year-old Victoria had taken the throne. The match brought together representative teams from the south and the north of England. A picture was produced to mark the occasion, printed on commemorative handkerchiefs that were given to every member of the ground staff:

It was billed as a big occasion, featuring some serious cricketing talent (the drapery hanging from the top of the picture tells the story of the match; in a low-scoring affair, the south won by five wickets).

According to John Arlott, 'Two outstandingly strong teams were composed of the leading professionals and a single amateur, William Ward.' The involvement of Ward is notable. A fine batsman, he was the record holder for the highest score in first-class cricket – a mighty 278, for the MCC against Norfolk in 1820. And as a patron of the game, his relationship with Lord's could not have been much more significant; back in 1825, he had put up the five thousand pounds required to stop the ground being sold for housing.

The image offers a fascinating insight into the early years of Lord's. Over in the right-hand distance is the Church of our Lady, on Lisson Grove, which had opened only a few years before. On the far left, the main gate into the ground is visible (roughly where the Heyhoe Flint Gate now stands). Next to it is the original tavern, with seating outside, at which a handful customers refresh themselves. The building to the right of the pitch is the ground's second pavilion – established by Ward himself, after the first was destroyed by fire.

It is a view of Lord's very different from the imposing grandeur of its contemporary character. The Lord's of 1837 has a much plainer, more rustic feel. The boundaries of the pitch appear indistinct; the ground looks more like an open field than a fully enclosed space. As John Major has explained, Lord's 'was still undeveloped and rural. It had a small wooden pavilion, but no seats for spectators. Beer was available from pot-boys and a pen held sheep which grazed the outfield.'

And despite the publicised importance of the game – hailed as a 'grand match' in Alfred D. Taylor's history of the MCC – the crowd is peculiarly scarce. A couple of dozen gentlemen sit stiffly on benches. Large parts of the perimeter lack spectators of any description. The scorers sit alone, isolated figures at an unimposing trestle table. The match actually attracted over five thousand people, but according to this portrayal, one feels it would have been quite possible to walk down St John's Wood Road without realising it was even happening.

It is almost as if the cricket is not, in truth, the main purpose of the image. The centrepiece is not really the match itself, but a gigantic White Ensign fluttering in the breeze – preposterously oversized, nearly fifty feet wide, and clearly the artist's invention. It bears the name of James Henry Dark, proprietor of the ground (Dark had taken over from Ward in 1835). This rather anodyne, formal-looking print gives greater prominence to the honouring of a patron than to the vibrant life of a cricket match. As the inaugural piece of Victorian cricketing art, it is a curiously fusty specimen – one that seems to pay more homage to Dark and the MCC than to the game of cricket itself. In its institutional focus, and its dutiful nod to power, it might be said to foreshadow aspects of the era that lay ahead.

By the middle of the nineteenth century, cricket had a more significant role in the expanding public-school system. The game was no longer just a recreation to be enjoyed – it could be taught. More than that, it *should* be taught. Increasingly, cricket was being thought of as a technical discipline, a science that could be studied and mastered. And this was accompanied by another conviction, that cricket should form part of the moral education of the young. It was, after all, not simply a game, but something much more profound – a morally edifying pursuit, expressing the best of English values. A child who learned the ways of cricket could, in doing so, become a better citizen – a wiser and more noble human being.

We see something of this in *Felix on the Bat*, published in 1845 – an erudite meditation on the game that doubles as a cricketing instruction manual. The author – Nicholas Wanostrocht – was born into education. His father had founded the Alfred House Academy, near Camberwell Green; and when he passed away, Nicholas inherited the running of the school at the tender age of nineteen. Worried, though, that parents of pupils might think his cricketing activities undignified, he developed a pseudonym – Nicholas Felix – by which, as a cricketer, he would invariably be known.

And as a cricketer, he was a fine batsman, playing for Kent for over two decades. His teammate, the great Fuller Pilch, rated him as the most attractive batsman in England: 'He knew the whole science of the game,' said Pilch, 'and had a hand and eye such as no one e'er best him at.' In the twilight of his career, Felix squared up against hulking all-rounder Alfred Mynn, the 'Lion of Kent', in perhaps the most famous single-wicket match in history.

His masterpiece, *Felix on the Bat*, is very much a schoolmaster-cricketer's work, armed with a clear pedagogical purpose. In the introduction, he offers a reading of cricket that stresses its philosophical substance:

> That it is not wholly unconnected with some of the high and honour-stirring principles of Moral Philosophy, is a suggestion which may hazard the contempt of the self-sufficient; nevertheless, we are prepared with good evidence in favour of our statement . . . we have only to consider how delightfully flows the game when it claims allegiance to the sovereignty of these temporising attributes, viz. laudable ambition, where the want of all angry feeling secures moral approbation; cheerfulness, which pervades the contest, giving spirit and activity to the body; courage, boldly to face, or prudently to yield to the extremities of Fortune – who takes a lively interest in the sport notwithstanding all our assumed proficiency; judgment, to apply experience upon which physical knowledge is founded; justice, in dealing fairly one by another; 'moderation in all things'; 'order, Heaven's first law'; and the true value and modest acknowledgment of praise and reputation.

There is a conviction here that cricket, at its best, should bring out the best attributes of people – cheerfulness, courage, judgement, justice and so on. The author hopes his readers might enjoy 'the gratification of associating with your fellow-mortals in the manly sport, teaching one another the grand moral lesson of bearing alike with becoming grace the victory or defeat'.

Any danger of pompous moralising, though, is kept firmly at bay by a taste for roguish japes. It is a character trait for which he was famed – Altham noted that 'Felix was never happy without his joke'. And his manual is a delightfully eccentric *tour de force*, mingling high-minded instruction with something much more mischievous.

Alongside his many other talents, Felix was a skilled watercolourist; and it is in the illustrations to *Felix on the Bat* that his humour most deliciously emerges. In order to explain the various technical deficiencies of young batsmen he has seen, he offers a series of diagrams that have been fashioned with a playful twinkle in the eye:

Felix critiques each of these ill-conceived stances as follows:

No. 1 will find it almost impossible to make the necessary spring preparatory to the driving hit; he can but imperfectly command the back block, back cut, and forward.

No. 2 must get up from this curious attitude, and, conse-
quently, has yet to prepare himself: thereby losing much time,
and disquieting the guard.

No. 3 is by no means the worst of the number; he is the best
prepared for a hard hit; but it is a dangerous position where the
bowling is very good. A shooter is almost certain destruction.
How is it possible to bring the bat down time enough to stop
this most cruel casualty?

No. 4, like Nos. 2, 5, 6, has to gather himself after getting
up, thereby disturbing the line of sight, which, be it well
remembered, should take in the eye, the bat, and the wicket:
that is to say, if a line were let fall from the eye of the batsman
to the ground, it should seem, to a person standing at the opposite wicket to pass down the centre of the bat, the bat being
held to cover the middle stump.

No. 6 is a very common one, and is selected by many young
players; but it has only to be seen to be rejected.

The seriousness of his aim – to explain the correct way of playing the game – is inseparable from a puckish, tongue-in-cheek
tone that runs across every page.

Even the book's frontispiece takes the form of an offbeat, visual
pun; it depicts a batsman, wielding his bat like an axe, riding on
the top of a giant flying bat. In a similar vein, the illustrations at
the end of every chapter – each titled 'What You Ought Not to
Do' – are a staunchly humorous affair. One presents a portly
cricketer stepping on another's foot as he stretches to catch a ball.
'If possible,' reads the caption, 'especially if you be a man of any
weight, you should avoid digging the spike of your heel into your
neighbour's instep. The consequences are likely to be loss of
blood, and ditto of temper.'

Felix on the Bat is certainly not your average instruction
manual, and it is all the better for it. As the inventor of the world's
first-ever bowling machine – the 'Catapulta' – and the first-ever

batting gloves, as well as being an author, artist, scholar, educator and distinguished cricketer, Nicholas Felix was one of the century's most remarkable cricketing polymaths.

Elsewhere in the visual landscape of Victorian cricket, a more self-important air was often apparent. Perhaps the most famous of all Victorian cricketing pictures is an 1849 print by W. H. Mason, depicting a contest between Sussex and Kent:

The location is the Royal Pleasure Gardens in Brighton; St Peter's church can be seen in the background. But once again – as with the 1837 Lord's jubilee print – the cricketing action is not the central focus. The picture, in fact, does not depict any specific game; instead, it is an assemblage of cricketers who played in the Sussex v. Kent fixture at some point or another in the 1840s.

A phalanx of eminent gents from the cricketing world line up in the foreground. Every one of them is facing away from the match, towards the viewer, posing. It is a star-studded cast of big names. James Henry Dark stands next to John Wisden, one of the country's finest all-rounders, who fifteen years later would publish the opening volume of his *Cricketers' Almanack*. In the middle of all the smartly dressed, waistcoated and top-hatted grandees, two white-clad players lean on their bats; the one on the left is Nicholas Felix and on the right is Alfred Mynn. At the picture's extreme right-hand edge, William Ward sits on a chair, a tiny dog looking up at him with a hopeful, raised paw. The provision of a chair for Ward is perhaps a mark of respect, but it may also hint at his frail physical condition; he passed away in June that year.

More than anything else, it is a picture that showcases status and reputation. The group of luminaries pay no attention whatsoever to the action taking place on the pitch, despite the prestige value of the players involved; behind their backs, the great round-arm pioneer William Lillywhite prepares to bowl to Fuller Pilch, at this point hailed as the best batsman in England.

Status, tradition, the institution: these were often, in various ways, at the foreground of Victorian cricketing art. The continuing ascendancy of Lord's formed one of the currents of conservatism that preserved the establishment. 'Conservative by education, habit, and principle,' ran an 1845 editorial of Samuel Carter Hall's *Art-Journal*, 'we shrink from the idea of aiding the adversaries of any established institution.' We see something of this ethos in Henry Barraud's 1874 painting of Lord's:

The ground's pavilion – replaced by the present version in 1889 – looms large in the background. Its grandeur is heightened by the presence of two flags at full mast: a Union Jack, and the distinctive stripes of the MCC. It is as if, one might say, these two flags go hand in hand, twin emblems of British spirit. As a further nod to the past, the union flag appears in its pre-1801 form, without the cross of Saint Patrick.

In the foreground, a crowd of distinguished members, players and wives mill about on the grass. In the middle of the picture, a tallish, dark-haired player can be seen mid-conversation, hands thoughtfully clasped together, his vast beard spreading like a blackberry bush down to his chest: the unmistakable figure of W. G. Grace, right at the heart of the parade of top hats, canes, smart suits and fashionable dresses. Lord's is presented as a social event of some significance. The venue's cricketing purpose is not emphasised at all; if it were not for the white attire of the players, it would be easy to miss the fact that this is a painting of a cricket ground. Lord's is valued, here, for its eminence and social clout.

Victorian England was the site of startling changes in the fabric of cricket, a time of dynamic growth, the blast furnace out of which the modern version of the game emerged. Cricket had by now spread all over the country; county matches were becoming more regular, with teams from Yorkshire, Lancashire and Gloucestershire joining the traditional south-east strongholds (the County Championship would be officially established in 1890). Since the 1860s, the appearance of representative All-England elevens was a step towards the emergence of international cricket.

But throughout it all, London remained the centre of power, in the hands of the dignitaries at the Marylebone Cricket Club. It was not without its times of trial – in the 1860s, for instance, a power struggle played itself out. At the time, the reputation of Lord's had dipped, partly as a result of shoddily kept grounds and the wicket's poor condition. The spread of cricket in the north had led to some calls for a 'cricket parliament', involving a more even spread of power across the country. In the end, though, Lord's prevailed and kept its grip at the helm. By 1870, the ground's facilities had been improved, and membership had risen to well over a thousand. 'The Club has at length passed through its most critical epoch,' affirmed historian Arthur Haygarth in his *Scores and Biographies*.

What, then, of village cricket in this era? There are some absorbing representations of the rural game from the latter part of the century. John Ritchie's best-known paintings were two London scenes – *A Summer Day in Hyde Park* and *A Winter Day in St James's Park*. But in 1855, he painted *Village Cricket*:

A group of locals from across the generations watch the game. The cricketing action has a competitive feel, with the batsman poised and the fielders attentively crouched; but the colours they wear, all green and russet and golden hay, blend them with the surrounding landscape as if they are natural forms or forest deities, spirits of the woods and fields. A stately, grey-haired scorer watches contemplatively at his table. Two other men lean in towards him, scrutinising the scorecard. A young boy sits by the scorer's table, gaze fixed on the game, a cricketer of the future. A little girl in a yellow frock selects goodies from a picnic hamper. For the most part, it is very much a peaceful, idyllic scene.

The one discordant note appears on the right-hand side. A woman is turned away from the cricket, looking out towards the viewer. There is an anxious expression on her face; another woman appears to be comforting her. Though it is possible she is the batsman's wife, simply too nervous to watch, it does not feel that way; she seems to have something on her mind more urgent than the cricket match. It is a detail that gives an air of unease to what is, otherwise, a cosy representation of village cricket and rural life.

An element of unease was, in truth, an understandable feature of Victorian village cricket – perhaps even an inevitable one. It was an era of decline for cricket in rural parts of England, as historian Gerald Howat has explained:

> The village cricketers of the nineteenth century played their games in a rural setting which remained substantially unchanged up to the outbreak of the First World War. Nonetheless, the game suffered in the second half of that century from the agricultural depression, when wages fell and unemployment was rife. There was a steady movement to the towns, village communities shrank and numbers declined. Furthermore, increased mobility led to some 'poaching' of players of ability to nearby town clubs. Those who stayed in the village often worked long hours in the fields and found it difficult to find the time for cricket. Some village sides collapsed through lack of support.

In a tough climate like this, the halcyon days of the Hambledon Club must have seemed a long way away.

Revealingly, John Ritchie's painting was initially thought to be a representation of Hambledon. There is no actual evidence to support the theory: the landscape and the church in the distance do not match any Hambledonian template. But the fact that people assumed Ritchie was channelling an almost century-old cricketing memory does indicate something – a sense that Victorian rural cricket yearned for a bygone era of happier, healthier climes.

Here is William Fisher's *A Match on Tunbridge Wells Common*, painted in 1877:

An improvised game is being played on patches of bare earth and rough grass, with a hat and jacket serving as a makeshift bowling mark. The scene could not be much more relaxed. One member of the party has rustled up the energy for some close fielding, but the others recline behind the stumps, more focused on their picnic. A dog frolics, chasing the flying ball.

But for a painting made in the 1870s, it is also very much a throwback. By this time, overarm bowling was firmly established in cricket – the Law had changed in 1864 – and round-arm had been around for nigh on fifty years. The bowler here, though, delivers the ball in old-school, underarm fashion. Even the bat wielded by the straw-boatered batsman is a curiosity. Its curved appearance – with the blade widening out, like a paddle, towards the bottom – is an anachronism that conjures up the glory days of Broadhalfpenny Down; it better resembles the blades in George Shepheard's 1790s sketchbook than anything a cricketer of the 1870s would have used. Fisher's scene, in other words, is a summoning of the distant past; a wishful fantasy of rural cricket at a time when it was struggling to survive.

Meanwhile, cricketing art continued to show interest in the affairs of high society. One of the most extraordinary of all late-Victorian cricket paintings is *The Imaginary Cricket Match*, by George Hamilton Barrable and Sir Robert Ponsonby Staples (1886):

The painting reflects the burgeoning international game. Touring All-England teams had been operating since the 1850s – initially playing in the United States and Canada before, a few years later, Australia. In 1878, an Australian XI visited England for the first time. It was in 1882 that the Australians' famous victory at the Oval led to the immortal declaration, in the *Sporting Times*, that since English cricket was dead, the body would be cremated and 'the ashes taken to Australia'. Test cricket was alive;

this supposedly most English of games was now a thoroughly international sport.

The scene depicted in the painting is 'imaginary' because the players involved did not all really play together in the same match; it is a dream team collection of stars from the early days of the Ashes. The facing batsman is W .G. Grace and the non-striker is William Walter Read, who made test cricket's first century at the Oval in 1884. The bowler is legendary Australia paceman, Fred 'The Demon' Spofforth. Fielding the ball on the boundary is Tom Garrett, who made his debut at eighteen, and who to this day remains the youngest Australian ever to play against England.

But once again – even in this all-star, cricketing fairy tale – there is much more to the picture than the cricket. Spectators dominate the foreground. Gentlemen and young ladies chat with each other – cricket, again, is a social event, a fashionable place to be seen. The *real* story here, though, is much spicier – nothing less, in fact, than a royal scandal. Walking around the perimeter of the pitch is the Prince (later King Edward VII) and Princess of Wales. All the female spectators are turned in the same direction – away from the strolling prince, as if they do not want to catch his eye. The provocative reason for this has been explained by John Arlott: 'Several ladies, whose names had been linked by gossip with the prince, are averting their heads from him.' In the foreground, to the immediate right of the pillar – gaze directed boldly out at the viewer – is Lillie Langtry, renowned actress, socialite, and former lover of the prince.

And this is not the only intrigue in the painting. Over to the left is a woman clutching a small square of paper; Gideon Haigh has proposed this is 'the hostess and enchantress Lady de Grey, receiving a note, perhaps from one of her lovers'. A close look reveals that the paper is actually a scorecard, emblazoned with the Lord's insignia. What kind of private message may or may not have been scrawled on the back of it, though, is anyone's guess. She is receiving some friendly attention from a cricketer whose focus is certainly not on the cricket. Leaning over her, dapperly dressed in an *I Zingari* blazer, is the distinctive moustachioed figure of Lord Harris, captain of England, who appears to be taking the opportunity, while his team bat, to indulge in a bit of amorous play.

The deep-set devotion to status in nineteenth-century cricket, and its entanglement with class division, is no more clearly apparent than in the distinction between amateur 'gentlemen' and professional 'players'. The consequences of this divide have been perceptively unpacked by cricket historian Keith Sandiford:

> When the Victorians accepted professionalism in cricket, they preserved the Georgian image of professionals as retainers and consistently treated their best cricketers as hired servants rather than as skilled artisans ... Class distinctions were so rigidly preserved by the Victorians that professionals and amateurs used different facilities, dressed in different pavilions, used different gates, travelled in different compartments on trains, and, generally speaking, maintained a discreet distance.

And it was not simply a matter of each keeping to their own. A widespread feeling persisted that the amateur cricketer was in pursuit of something more noble – playing not for money, but for a love of the game and its artistry. The professional, in contrast, was a more mercenary figure; not just lowlier in social status, but lowlier in moral intention. 'Cricket was essentially play, as opposed to work,' Sandiford explains. 'Professionalism tended to destroy the element of sportsmanship and to make the game too serious.'

One product of this was a curious mixture of dependence, collaboration and division. Cricket was hailed as a space in which people of all classes could play together in a single, unified team; at the same time, two distinct categories of cricketer existed, determined not by a player's skill or talent but by their birth and background.

This segregated culture was captured in another painting by Sir Robert Ponsonby Staples, *Gentlemen vs Players, at Lord's in the Pavilion Enclosure* (1891):

The 'gentlemen' are all gathered in front of the pavilion. They are huddled closely together – as if territorial in spirit or conspiring and wanting not to be overheard. On several of them, the striped blazer and cap of Lord's membership are visible. The signs by the gate make the point clearly enough: 'For Members Only'.

Not a single one of these gentlemen is deigning even to look at the 'players', who are gathering in the background of the picture, on their way out to the pitch. There is an eloquent geographical separation of the two groups; the pavilion's picket fence stretching between them becomes a symbol of the players' externality to the world of social privilege.

The background of our artist, Ponsonby Staples, could not have been much more aristocratic; he was the third son of Sir Nathaniel Staples, 10th Baronet of Lissan House in County Tyrone. But in this painting, the statement he makes about cricket's culture of class-based division is sharp-edged. The amateurs may be given prominence, in the foreground of the picture; but as they sit around idly chatting, every one of them is cast into shadow. It is the players – out on the field, filled with purpose, ready to play some cricket – who are bathed in a sea of sunlight.

11

'IT'S MORE THAN A GAME': VICTORIAN CRICKETING FICTIONS

'The national game of cricket,' wrote Lord William Lennox in 1840, 'has a peculiar claim to the people generally; and is one of those games open alike to all. It is free from selfishness, cruelty, or oppression; it encourages activity; it binds gentlemen to country life; it preserves the manly character of the Briton, and has been truly characterised as a healthful, manly recreation, giving strength to the body and cheerfulness to the mind, and is one of the few sports that has not been made the subject of some invidious anathema.'

As a sign of cricket's place in the Victorian imagination, Lennox's language is revealing. It is, first of all, a democratic game – 'open alike to all', as he puts it – a game in which lords and labourers can compete together in the same team. Cricket is 'manly', too, building the strength and the character of all those people – all those English people – fortunate enough to play it.

But most of all, cricket contains a kind of moral purity – it is 'free from selfishness, cruelty, or oppression'. In this distinctively Victorian vision, the game is no longer bound up with the vices or the corruption of society. On the contrary, it is an escape from such things – a haven of wholesomeness and noble instincts.

In Victorian England, cricket was no longer just a sport. It was philosophy; it was virtue; it was an imagined ideal of nationhood. The game had been remade as a fiction, a metaphor for all the things England wanted itself to be.

*   *   *

The rhetoric of Lennox – with its focus on the union of physical and psychological health – reflects aspects of Muscular Christianity, which by the middle of the century was rapidly gathering influence. Juvenal's line, '*Mens sana in corpore sano*', had gained new currency: a healthy mind was impossible without a healthy body to go with it. And it was a Church of England priest who produced the era's defining study of cricket.

In 1851, the Reverend James Pycroft published *The Cricket-Field* – a history of the game, and a philosophical reflection on its character. It is a work that perfectly encapsulates many of the Victorian attitudes towards cricket. 'There is something highly intellectual,' he proclaims, 'in our noble and national pastime.' A central message resounds – that the game's Englishness is inseparable from its integrity. At times, Pycroft drifts into a xenophobic bravado that has not exactly aged well: 'The game is essentially Anglo-Saxon. Foreigners have rarely, very rarely, imitated us. The English settlers and residents everywhere play; but of no single cricket club have we ever heard dieted either with frogs, sour crout [*sic*], or macaroni.'

For Pycroft, cricket offers a kind of moral code. To pursue the game is to follow a path towards a virtuous life. And as he is keen to remind us, such traits are, of course, uniquely English:

> The game of cricket, philosophically considered, is a standing panegyric on the English character: none but an orderly and sensible race of people would so amuse themselves. It calls into requisition all the cardinal virtues, some moralist would say. As with the Grecian games of old, the player must be sober and temperate. Patience, fortitude, and self-denial, the various bumps of order, obedience, and good-humour, with an unruffled temper, are indispensable. For intellectual virtues we want judgment, decision, and the organ of concentrativeness – every faculty in the free use of all its limbs – and every idea in constant air and exercise. Poor, rickety, and stunted wits will never serve:

the widest shoulders are of little use without a head upon them: the cricketer wants wits down to his fingers' ends.

Cricket is framed as a display of the English spirit. To play it well requires not just skill; it requires a proper dose of good old English decency. 'Of what avail is the head to plan and hand to execute,' he asks, 'if a sulky temper paralyses exertion, and throws a damp upon the field; or if impatience dethrones judgment, and the man hits across at good balls, because loose balls are long in coming; or, again, if a contentious and imperious disposition leaves the cricketer all "alone in his glory", voted the pest of every eleven?'

This purified, character-building view of cricket could only ever be an ideal; it was always much closer to fiction than fact. As writer and biographer Simon Rae has noted, 'In real life, high-minded proponents through selfless sporting endeavour were in a minority compared to those who simply saw cricket as one of life's pleasures.' Nevertheless, the image was to lodge itself in the patriotic storehouse of the Victorian English imagination; and it was memorably captured in one of the era's most popular novels.

Thomas Hughes had attended Rugby school as a boy; *Tom Brown's School Days*, first published in 1857, is a semi-autobiographical account inspired by his childhood memories. It delivers a portrait of public-school life that is unashamedly sentimental. Hughes' own headmaster at Rugby had been Thomas Arnold – famed for his compassionate leadership and influential reforms. In the novel, Tom Brown's headmaster is 'the Doctor', closely based on Arnold. He is presented as benign and wise – steering his ship with a firm commitment to the belief that school is about far more than academic learning. 'The object of all schools,' explains Hughes, 'is not to ram Latin and Greek into boys, but to make them good English boys, good future citizens; and by far the most important part of that work must be done, or not done, out of school hours.'

The story follows the fortunes of Tom Brown throughout his time at Rugby. He quickly befriends the boisterous Harry East; much of the novel's first part chronicles their adventures, as well as the violent bullying they suffer at the hands of the nefarious Flashman. But the novel also highlights Brown's changing character over the years, as he develops from a wayward youth into a mature young man. The second part focuses on his stewardship of George Arthur – a frail, scholarly, and pious boy, who ultimately helps to turn Brown away from his tomfoolery and towards a Christian path of good sense and rectitude.

Throughout the novel, cricket is a regular presence. We are given plenty of reminders of its importance as part of school culture. East has a cricket bat in the corner of his study. After a windfall on the horses, East and Brown go on a spending spree that includes 'two new bats and a cricket-ball'. To cure George Arthur's ill health, the doctor recommends 'some Rugby air, and cricket'. Brown strikes up a bond with Old Thomas, the school porter, who would 'come out in the afternoons into the close to Tom's wicket, and bowl slow twisters to him, and talk of the glories of bygone Surrey heroes, with whom he had played former generations'.

But it is at the end of the novel that cricket takes centre stage. The penultimate chapter, 'Tom Brown's Last Match', describes a game between the school and the MCC. By this point, Tom Brown is one of his school's leaders; a senior prefect and a model for those around him to follow. Not only that, he is also captain of the eleven.

While Rugby are batting, Brown watches the action along with Arthur and an unnamed young master. He admits that cricket has received rather more attention than his studies:

'There now,' struck in the master; 'you see that's just what I have been preaching this half-hour. The delicate play is the true thing. I don't understand cricket, so I don't enjoy those fine draws which you tell me are the best play, though when you or Raggles hit a ball hard away for six I am as delighted as any one. Don't you see the analogy?'

'Yes, sir,' answered Tom, looking up roguishly, 'I see; only the question remains whether I should have got most good by understanding Greek particles or cricket thoroughly. I'm such a thick, I never should have had time for both.'

'I see you are an incorrigible,' said the master, with a chuckle; 'but I refute you by an example. Arthur there has taken in Greek and cricket too.'

'Yes, but no thanks to him; Greek came natural to him. Why, when he first came I remember he used to read Herodotus for pleasure as I did Don Quixote, and couldn't have made a false concord if he'd tried ever so hard; and then I looked after his cricket.'

Arthur's bookish nature contrasts with the sporting feats of Brown, who embodies Hughes' line that the main purpose of school lies outside the schoolroom.

As the trio talk, they ponder the question of what makes cricket a special game:

'Come, none of your irony, Brown,' answers the master. 'I'm beginning to understand the game scientifically. What a noble game it is, too!'

'Isn't it? But it's more than a game. It's an institution,' said Tom.

'Yes,' said Arthur, 'the birthright of British boys old and young, as *habeas corpus* and trial by jury are of British men.'

'The discipline and reliance on one another which it teaches is so valuable, I think,' went on the master, 'it ought to be such an unselfish game. It merges the individual in the eleven; he doesn't play that he may win, but that his side may.'

'That's very true,' said Tom, 'and that's why football and cricket, now one comes to think of it, are such much better games than fives or hare-and-hounds, or any others where the object is to come in first or to win for oneself, and not that one's side may win.'

Cricket educates, at the same time as it provides pleasure; the principle of placing the team before the individual gives it edifying qualities. Pycroft's 'panegyric on the English character' is made flesh. Cricket, in the end, is more than a game. It is an instructor, a guru in sporting form, helping young men towards the pursuit of an honourable life.

One of the illustrations to the Macmillan & Co. edition depicts this pitch-side scene:

Brown here is a thoughtful figure, his bearing serious and philosophical. Arthur stares up at his mentor with obvious affection. The master, leaning back in his seat, watches Brown with interest, as if intent on what he has to say. The image sums up our hero's growth. He is no longer a boy; he has become a young man, both physically strong and wise. And in his hands, he grips a symbol of one of the things that has brought about this change – 'his favourite bat, with which he has already made thirty or forty runs to-day'. He holds it with reverential care, as if it is a sacred object, a grateful offering to the gods.

Tom Brown's School Days has become its own legend, a monument of its time that has by turns been admired, rebuked, mimicked and mocked. But not all Victorian depictions of cricket are quite so sanctimonious. In the very same year that Hughes' novel appeared, Wilkie Collins published *The Lazy Tour of Two Idle Apprentices*, written in collaboration with a certain Charles Dickens. In it, a young man named Thomas Idle – an avatar of Collins himself – suffers a calamitous cricketing ordeal:

Shortly after leaving school, he accompanied a party of friends to a cricket-field, in his natural and appropriate character of spectator only. On the ground it was discovered that the players fell short of the required number, and facile Thomas was persuaded to assist in making up the complement. At a certain appointed time, he was roused from peaceful slumber in a dry ditch, and placed before three wickets with a bat in his hand. Opposite to him, behind three more wickets, stood one of his bosom friends, filling the situation (as he was informed) of bowler. No words can describe Mr Idle's horror and amazement, when he saw this young man – on ordinary occasions, the meekest and mildest of human beings – suddenly contract his eye-brows, compress his lips, assume the aspect of an infuriated savage, run back a few steps, then run forward, and, without the slightest previous provocation, hurl a detestably hard ball with all his might straight at Thomas's legs. Stimulated to preternatural activity of body and sharpness of eye by the instinct of self-preservation, Mr Idle contrived, by jumping deftly aside at the right moment, and by using his bat (ridiculously narrow as it was for the purpose) as a shield, to preserve his life and limbs from the dastardly attack that had been made on both, to leave the full force of the deadly missile to strike his wicket instead of his leg; and to end the innings, so far as his side was concerned, by being immediately bowled out.

It is a glorious bit of comic writing, recalling nothing so much as the immortal farce of All-Muggleton versus Dingley Dell.

Elsewhere, though, Collins supplied cricket with a more serious meaning – as a defining icon of English culture. In his gothic masterpiece *The Woman in White*, the Italian language teacher Professor Pesca is determined to mould himself into an Englishman. And cricket, he believes, is essential to this project: 'The ruling idea of his life appeared to be, that he was bound to show his gratitude to the country which had afforded him an asylum and a means of subsistence by doing his utmost to turn himself into an Englishman . . . the little man, in the innocence of his heart, devoted himself impromptu to all our English sports and pastimes whenever he had the opportunity of joining them . . . I had seen him risk his limbs blindly at a fox-hunt and in a cricket-field; and soon afterwards I saw him risk his life, just as blindly, in the sea at Brighton.'

More often than not, in fact, Victorian fiction functions as a kind of mirror, with representations of cricket reflecting some of the era's chief preoccupations. Towards the end of George Meredith's 1871 novel, *The Adventures of Harry Richmond*, a coach driver extols the game's virtues. And his anecdotes have more than a touch of jingoistic spice:

> The driver was eloquent on cricket-matches. Now, cricket, he said, was fine manly sport; it might kill a man, but it never meant mischief: foreigners themselves had a bit of an idea that it was the best game in the world, though it was a nice joke to see a foreigner playing at it! None of them could stand to be bowled at. Hadn't stomachs for it; they'd have to train for soldiers first. On one occasion he had seen a Frenchman looking on at a match. 'Ball was hit a shooter twixt the slips: off starts Frenchman, catches it, heaves it up, like his head,

half-way to wicket, and all the field set to bawling at him, and sending him, we knew where. He tripped off: "You no comprong politeness in dis country." Ha! ha!'

To prove the aforesaid Frenchman wrong, we nodded to the driver's laughter at his exquisite imitation.

The anti-French jibes recall the punchiest parts of Pycroft's rhetoric. But the coach driver is not done. He goes on to hail the game's character-building qualities in a manner that sounds very much like something lifted from *Tom Brown*: 'Cricket in cricket season! It comprises – count: lots o' running; and that's good: just enough o' taking it easy; that's good: a appetite for your dinner, and your ale or your Port, as may be the case; good, number three. Add on a tired pipe after dark, and a sound sleep to follow, and you say good morning to the doctor and the parson; for you're in health body and soul, and ne'er a parson'll make a better Christian of ye, that I'll swear.'

Equally patriotic claims about cricket came from one of the Victorian era's finest novelists, Anthony Trollope. 'It is the English alone,' he wrote in the preface to *British Sports and Pastimes*, 'who take part in the game.' In Trollope's view, cricket was so quintessentially English that foreign players were unthinkable:

Into the causes of this peculiar institution not merely failing to flourish, but steadfastly declining to take the smallest root, in soils unshadowed by the British flag or its successors, it is needless to enter here. Few of those who understand the game at all, and have any knowledge of national character, will fail to recognise, if they cannot define, the inaptitude of aught but the Saxon element for such a sport.

Trollope also railed against the menace of professionalism in the game, which, he felt, had spawned a cheapening, mercenary spirit: 'Even Cricket has become such a business, that there arises a doubt in the minds of amateur players whether they can continue the sport, loaded as it is with the arrogance and extravagance of the professionals. All this comes from excess of enthusiasm on the matter; – from a desire to follow too well a pursuit which, to be pleasurable, should be a pleasure and not a business.'

Trollope's views on cricket appear to be archetypally Victorian. But his portrayal of the game in an 1882 novel, *The Fixed Period*, was – at least on the surface – much more eccentric. This satirical science-fiction tale was a stark departure from his usual terrain of realist fiction. It is set a hundred years in the future – in 'Britannula', a former British antipodean colony that has pioneered a programme of state-enforced euthanasia. This is the 'Fixed Period' of the title: citizens must be executed once they reached the age of sixty-eight years. The story is narrated by John Neverbend, mastermind of the Fixed Period system.

One chapter features a cricket match against a visiting English team laced with eminent figures (the tourists are playfully given names like Lord Marylebone, Sir Kennington Oval, and Sir Lords Longstop). The match features a number of surreal elements that reflect the futuristic setting. It is sixteen a side ('There used, I am told, to be eleven of these men,' wonders the narrator). Prophetically, the batsmen all wear 'machines' upon their heads to protect themselves. Bowling is performed mechanically, via a contraption known as a 'steam-bowler'. All in all, it is a bizarre episode – cricket on steroids, beefed up into bionic, sci-fi combat.

At times, though, a more serious political message is evident. Trollope seizes the opportunity to deliver a jibe at money-grabbing professionals:

Jack swore that the English would be 'nowhere' but for eight professional players whom they had brought out with them. It must be explained that our club had no professionals. We had not come to that yet – that a man should earn his bread by playing cricket. Lord Marylebone and his friend had brought with them eight professional 'slaves', as our young men came to call them – most ungraciously.

Jack is the narrator's son, one of Britannula's star cricketers. And he turns out to be the hero of the hour. The match seems in the hands of the English, when they amass over one-and-a-half-thousand runs; but in comes Jack, who steals the show. By the time he plays the winning stroke, his total stands at an eye-watering 1275 not out.

Trollope's critiques of professionalism are a reminder of the extent to which Victorian cricket was marked by webs of class division. And it is through the prism of class snobbery that another great novelist, Thomas Hardy, portrayed the game in his 1891 short story, 'The Son's Veto'.

Hardy's heroine is a parlour maid who marries a wealthy clergyman. After her husband dies, she is left to bring up her only son, Randolph – an arrogant public schoolboy, embarrassed by her uncultured ways. One day, she meets an old flame from her youth and they rekindle their romance – but when he proposes marriage, she explains she will need the approval of her son. She tries to seek it out at a familiar location:

She had not told him a word when the yearly cricket-match came on at Lord's between the public schools, though Sam had already gone back to Aldbrickham. Mrs Twycott felt stronger than usual: she went to the match with Randolph, and was able to leave her chair and walk about occasionally. The bright idea occurred to her that she could casually broach the subject while moving round among the spectators, when the boy's spirits were high with interest in the game, and he would weigh domestic matters as feathers in the scale beside the day's victory. They promenaded under the lurid July sun, this pair, so wide apart, yet so near, and Sophy saw the large proportion of boys like her own, in their broad white collars and dwarf hats, and all around the rows of great coaches under which was jumbled the debris of luxurious luncheons; bones, pie-crusts, champagne-bottles, glasses, plates, napkins, and the family silver; while on the coaches sat the proud fathers and mothers; but never a poor mother like her. If Randolph had not appertained to these, had not centred all his interests in them, had not cared exclusively for the class they belonged to, how happy would things have been! A great huzza at some small performance with the bat burst from the multitude of relatives, and Randolph jumped wildly into the air to see what had happened. Sophy fetched up the sentence that had been already shaped; but she could not get it out. The occasion was, perhaps, an inopportune one. The contrast between her story and the display of fashion to which Randolph had grown to regard himself as akin would be fatal. She awaited a better time.

The grandeur of Lord's, as a parade of status and money, is so daunting that Mrs Twycott cannot go through with her plan.

A better time, though, proves elusive. When she eventually tells her son, at home, his response could not be much more brutal: 'It was long before he would reply, and when he did it was to say sternly at her from within: "I am ashamed of you! It will ruin me! A miserable boor! a churl! a clown! It will degrade me in the eyes of all the gentlemen of England!"'

It is perhaps appropriate that Hardy's story was written in the same year that Ponsonby Staples produced his painting of the gentlemen and the players split by the Lord's pavilion fence. As the nineteenth century drew to a close, Victorian England was still the site of acute divisions; the cricket world, one might say, did no more than reflect the rifts in the fabric of England itself. There were different categories of cricketer, just as there were also different categories of Englishman.

It is a point made clearly enough by an anonymous author in an 1883 edition of the *Saturday Review* – who argued that, while professionals 'are for the most part a very well conducted and responsible body of men . . . it must be remembered that cricket brings them into association with men of the best manners, and above all of impeachable character, whose traditions of the game, brought from school and college, make unfairness or even sharp practice as impossible to them as cheating at cards. It is from these men that cricket takes its tone in this country.' The gentleman cricketer was not just wealthier, better educated, or more fortunate. He was a better class of human being: fairer, truer, more noble. Even, one might say, more English.

The schism between rhetoric and reality was stark. Byron's words, in a letter of 1821, seemed truer than ever. 'After all, what is the higher society of England?' he wrote to his friend Richard Hoppner. 'According to my own experience, and to all that I have seen and heard (and I have lived there in the very highest and what is called the *best*), no way of life can be more corrupt . . . In England, the only homage which they pay to virtue is hypocrisy.'

12

'They had their day and ceased to be': Suffragists at the Wicket

There are two of them, these 'Political Lady-Cricketers', and they stand together in attitudes of defiance. They wear the colours of the MCC, a club they would not be allowed to join for another hundred years. The badges on the shirts bear the logo of the Women's Liberal Federation. 'A team of our own?' runs the caption. 'I should think so! If we're good enough to scout for you, why shouldn't we take a turn at the bat?'

Both women are turning their heads, casting a disdainful half-glance back at an elderly, top-hatted and mutton-chopped batsman, who regards them with uncertainty while leaning on a bat marked 'SUFFRAGE'. It is none other than William Gladstone – whose wary demeanour might have something to do with a letter he had recently penned, challenging the extension of the vote to women.

Gladstone's letter – written in April 1892, a month before the *Punch* sketch appeared, and a few months before he became prime minister for the fourth time – expressed scepticism about the parliamentary franchise. It is full of typically Victorian views about gendered social roles. 'I think it impossible to deny,' he writes, 'that there have been and are women individually fit for any public office however masculine its character; just as there are persons under the age of twenty-one better fitted than many of those beyond it for the discharge of the duties of full citizenship. In neither case does the argument derived from exceptional instances seem to justify the abolition of the general rule.' It is not *entirely* clear what Gladstone means by the 'masculine' character of public office; but the sentiment is clear enough. While the occasional woman might be capable in such jobs, the vast majority are most certainly not.

He goes on to claim that protecting women from high-stress pursuits – such as voting – was very much for their own good:

> I have no fear lest the woman should encroach upon the power of the man. The fear I have is, lest we should invite her unwittingly to trespass upon the delicacy, the purity, the refinement, the elevation of her own nature, which are the present sources of its power . . . I admit that in the Universities, in the professions, in the secondary circles of public action, we have already gone so far as to give a shadow of plausibility to the present proposals to go farther; but it is a shadow only, for we have done nothing that plunges the woman as such into the turmoil of masculine life. My disposition is to do all for her which is free from that danger and reproach, but to

take no step in advance until I am convinced of its safety. The stake is enormous. The affirmation pleas are to my mind not clear, and, even if I thought them clearer, I should deny that they were pressing.

The turmoil of masculine life, says Gladstone, is no place for women. All of their most valuable qualities – 'delicacy', 'purity', 'refinement' – would be sullied by the strain of politics.

The *Punch* cartoon uses cricket as a sign of rebellion against male authority. With its strong female figures and hunched, shadowy Gladstone, it appears to express some sympathy for their cause. But as was the case with John Collet's sketch of a century earlier, a vein of ridicule is also present – mocking women for their commitment to such an absurd breach of the natural order.

This is evident in a tongue-in-cheek passage of dialogue that accompanies the sketch. Two 'Admiring Bystanders' are watching a master batsman practising in the nets. This is Gladstone himself, comically characterised as a mirror image of W. G. Grace. The bystanders give him a variety of Gracean nicknames, such as 't'other W. G.', 'The Champion' and 'The Old 'un', as they ponder his stance on women:

First A. B. Ah, by the way, what do you think of these here new-fangled Lady-Cricketers?

Second A. B. (*significantly*). Ask the Old 'Un what *he* thinks of 'em.

First A.B. Ah! Can't abide 'em, can he? And yet he likes the Ladies to look on and applaud, and even to field for him at times.

Second A.B. Yes; the Ladies have been good friends of his, and now he'd bar them from the legitimate game. I fancy it's put their backs up a bit, eh?

First A.B. You bet! And it *do* seem ray-ther ongrateful like, don't it now? Though as fur as that goes *I* don't believe Cricket's a game for the petticoats.

Second A.B. Nor me neither. But bless yer they gets their foot in in everything now; tennis, and golf, and rowing and cetrer. And if you let 'em in at all, for your own pleasure, I don't quite see how you're going to draw the line arbitrary like just where it suits *you*, as the Grand Old Slogger seems to fancy.

First A.B. No; and, if you ask me, I say they won't stand it, even from *him*. 'No,' says they, 'fair's fair,' they says. 'All very well to treat us like volunteer scouts at a country game, or at the nets, returning the balls whilst you slog and show off. But when we want to put on the gloves and pads, and take a hand at the bat in a businesslike way, you boggle, and hint that it's degrading, unsexing, and all that stuff.'

Second A.B. Ah, *that* won't wash. If it unsexes 'em to bat, it unsexes 'em to scout. And if the old cricketing gang didn't want the Ladies between wickets, why, they shouldn't have let em into the field, *I* say. Strikes me Lady Carlisle'll show 'em a thing or two. That 'operative mandatory resolution' of hers means mischief—*after* the next big match anyhow. 'Ladies wait, and wait a bit more, wait in truth till the day after to-morrow.' Yes; but they won't wait for ever.

First A.B. Not they. Why, look yonder! There's one of 'em in full fig. Lady-Cricketer from cap to shoes – short skirt, knickers, belt, blouse, gloves, and all the rest of it. D'ye think that sort means volunteer scouting only? Not a bit of it. Mean playing the game, Sir, and having regular teams of their own.

Cricket becomes a metaphor for women's transgression in the male space. Lady Carlisle is cited as a prominent champion of the suffragist cause. The skit pokes fun at Gladstone's uneven policies on women's rights and the problem of advancing rights in some places, but not others. At the same time, though – as made clear by the female player wearing 'short skirt, knickers, belt, blouse, gloves, and all the rest of it' – it also suggests that women's cricket is an unladylike, even demeaning spectacle.

The nineteenth century had seen a dramatic collapse in women's cricket, one that neatly coincided with the arrival of the Victorian age. As historian Dean Allen records, a 'pronounced and protracted slump occurred in female cricket from the 1830s until the 1880s'. It is difficult to avoid a conclusion that the strengthened associations between masculinity and cricket – the 'manly recreation' of Lord Lennox, the 'manly sport' of Felix on the bat – went hand in hand with an increasingly restricted view of women and their roles in society. The rigidly hierarchical culture of nineteenth-century England was a hostile space for budding female cricketers.

This is certainly how it appeared in a report of a women's village cricket match from the *Nottingham Review* in 1833. 'Last week, at Sileby feast, the women so far forgot themselves as to enter a game of cricket,' it dolefully begins, 'and by their deportment as well as frequent applications to the tankard, they rendered themselves objects such as no husband, father or lover could contemplate with any degree of satisfaction.' A brutal assessment indeed. Carousing in distinctly unladylike fashion, these cricketing women (something that should have been a contradiction in terms) disgraced not only themselves, but their entire families. They had no place upon England's cricketing greens.

By the 1880s, though, a distinct upturn in women's cricket was discernible. It came after fifty years in the doldrums. Significant links arose between cricket and the women's suffrage movements of the latter part of the century – links that, to this day, remain sorely under-appreciated. In 1882, the English Cricket and Athletic Association launched 'an initiative to show that cricket as a game was indeed a possibility for women'. It was advertised in *Lillywhite's Annual* as follows:

> With the object of proving the suitability of the national game as a pastime for the fair sex in preference to Lawn Tennis and other less scientific games, the English Cricket and Athletic Association Limited have organised Two Complete XIs of Female Players under the title of THE ORIGINAL ENGLISH LADY CRICKETERS. Trained by W. Matthews, S. B. Lohman and qualified assistants. Elegantly and appropriately attired.

The final sentence lends an inevitable touch of patriarchal condescension. But women's cricket was, at last, being given some help.

Later in her life, Dame Ethel Smyth would gain fame as the composer of 'The March of the Women', a feminist anthem to suffragette resistance. In her memoirs, Smyth recalled that the year 1889 had been charged with fervour for women's cricket:

> During the summer of 1889 the cricket mania possessed all the young women of my acquaintance, the fountain-head of inspiration being the celebrated White Heather Club, of which the Talbots, Lytteltons and Brasseys were the moving spirits. This club was the Zingaree of women's cricket and sported the prettiest colours I ever saw, a yellow, white, green and black ribbon with a faint line of pink in it.

White Heather was the first ever women's cricket club, formed in 1887. It had been founded in Yorkshire and consisted mostly of wealthy ladies from that county; Smyth compares the club to *I Zingari*, the legendary men's wandering team that had been established in 1845. She goes on to describe her friendship with Meriel Talbot – whose eminent work in government was preceded by success as a fine cricketer:

In the light of her subsequent career, and also apart from any such considerations, I am proud to say that my particular friend was Meriel Talbot, a cricketer compared to whom most of us were impostors. We all quite realised the fact, our feelings towards her being akin to those of schoolboys for W. G. Grace; and however that great man may have treated neophytes and other inferiors, I can only say that Meriel met our incompetence with the gracious indulgence of a true artist. In one respect only, rapidity of movement, were some of us her superiors, but as she made most of the runs for her side she had every right to make them at her own pace – a curiously majestic one. The Club spread its net wide; thus it came that my sister, myself, and Nelly Benson were members, and have played cricket under the very eyes of demigods such as Edward and Alfred Lyttelton and Jack Talbot.

Smyth's account unearths a women's cricket culture that was not only avid, but competitive. She lists some of her team's wins with distinct satisfaction: 'We thought the other XI were going to have a walkover, and in spite of their own efforts to disguise the fact, such was evidently their own expectation, but strange to say we beat them by three wickets.'

The Original English Lady Cricketers were the first ever paid women's cricket team. In 1891 they played exhibition matches around the country and were often well received. One match, in Liverpool, was watched by an estimated crowd of fifteen thousand people. A viewer commented that they 'did not burlesque the manly sport of cricket', but instead played 'in a thorough legitimate manner, having been properly coached by some of the best leading professionals of the day'. The patronising tone is palpable – cricket is still, here, a 'manly sport' – but it is, at least, combined with obvious admiration at the level of skill on display.

Not everyone, though, was quite so impressed. Voices of scepticism were not hard to find. As historian Jihang Park has noted, during this time, 'Women's cricket drew the greatest number of sneers; men wanted cricket to remain an exclusively men's game.' The cricketers all had to play under assumed names; women taking *money* to play would have been seen as a disgrace. At matches, they were hardly given proper freedoms; teams were always accompanied by a chaperone. Medical opinion inclined to the view that women playing sport was unnatural and dangerous; an 1890 edition of *The Lancet* warned that throwing could cause strained muscles and that blows to the chest could lead to breast cancer.

Women's cricket might have spiked in popularity; but it struggled to be taken seriously. In 1897, *Punch* offered some mocking Directions To Lady Cricketers: 'Get yourself bowled first ball so that you can spend the rest of the time at tea and flirtation with the five fielders who have been withdrawn from the field to give ladies a chance.' It was accompanied by an epigram:

CRICKET – LADIES V GENTLEMEN
The ladies came out as they had gone in, all 'Ducks'.
And what did the Gentlemen make? – Love.

The derisive message was clear enough. It was not a serious sporting spectacle; its only true value was as an opportunity for flirting. In such a scornful atmosphere, it is perhaps not a great surprise that the Original English Lady Cricketers disbanded after only one season.

And so the short-lived promise of late-Victorian women's cricket ended with something of a whimper. In an 1899 memoir, a cricketer of some renown recalled the episode as follows:

A new chapter – and a short one – was added to the annals of cricket by the appearance [in 1891] of two elevens of 'Lady Cricketers', who travelled about the country and played exhibition matches. They claimed that they did play, and not burlesque, the game, but interest in their doings did not survive long. Cricket is not a game for women, and although the fair sex occasionally join in a picnic game, they are not constitutionally adapted for sport. If the Lady Cricketers expected to popularise the game among women they failed dismally. At all events, they had their day and ceased to be.

They had their day and ceased to be . . . and that, it seems, was that. No more needed to be said, since the cricketing almighty had spoken. The author of these words was William Gilbert Grace.

13

'The field is full of shades':
Fin de Siècle Fantasies

There are three notable cricketing poems, from the nineteenth century's final years, that in their different ways convey the downbeat yearning of fin de siècle gloom. Henry Newbolt published his first collection of verse, *Admirals All*, in 1897. In it was '*Vitai Lampada*' ('The Lamp of Life'). Partly inspired by his own childhood memories at Clifton College, it begins with a schoolboy cricketing scene:

> There's a breathless hush in the Close to-night—
> Ten to make and the match to win—
> A bumping pitch and a blinding light,
> An hour to play and the last man in.
> And it's not for the sake of a ribboned coat,
> Or the selfish hope of a season's fame,
> But his captain's hand on his shoulder smote
> 'Play up! play up! and play the game!'

A tense atmosphere is evident. The match is building to a dramatic climax: one wicket left, with ten runs needed. But the focus here is not on whether the 'last man in' actually manages to get the runs. It is on the nature of their motivation – which lies not in the prospect of school colours, or short-lived fame, but in the principled power of the captain's words. 'Play up! Play up! And play the game!': the meaning of the occasion lies not in victory, but in moral decency, the spirit of the sport.

It is a familiar sanctification. James Pycroft's forty-year-old claim that cricket evokes 'all the cardinal virtues' of English character appears, in these lines, to be alive and well. But there is also a darker side to Newbolt's scene. The light is fading. Time is short; night looms. A sombre feeling emerges of things coming to an end. The next stanza shifts the action to the horrors of the battlefield:

> The sand of the desert is sodden red,—
> Red with the wreck of a square that broke;—
> The Gatling's jammed and the Colonel dead,
> And the regiment blind with dust and smoke.
> The river of death has brimmed his banks,
> And England's far, and Honour a name,
> But the voice of a schoolboy rallies the ranks:
> 'Play up! play up! and play the game!'

The lines allude to the Battle of Abu Klea in Sudan in January 1885; the dead colonel is Frederick Burnaby, who perished in the clash. Here is a much more disturbing context for the burning lamp of life. Newbolt's repeated refrain no longer applies just to sport, but to all of reality, including its most awful and tragic elements. 'This,' suggests author Michael Henderson, 'was poetry as metaphor, for life and the sense of duty essential for all officers of the Crown.'

Few literary works have become as synonymous with melancholy as A. E. Housman's *A Shropshire Lad*, published in 1896. Telling the cheerless story of a young man worn down by the cares of life, these sixty-three short lyrics recount miseries of lost love, suffering and the passage of time. The seventeenth poem in the collection begins – much like *'Vitai Lampada'* – with a sporting scene:

> Twice a week the winter thorough
> Here stood I to keep the goal:
> Football then was fighting sorrow
> For the young man's soul.

Stuck in the cold of winter, goalkeeping is not enough to keep the lad's spiritual malaise at bay. And when spring arrives, things do not particularly improve:

Now in May time to the wicket
Out I march with bat and pad:
See the son of grief at cricket
Trying to be glad.

Try I will; no harm in trying:
Wonder 'tis how little mirth
Keeps the bones of man from lying
On the bed of earth.

Cricket has replaced football in the hunt for happiness; but it still looks like a losing battle. The speaker's resigned air – 'no harm in trying' – suggests limited confidence in cricket as an antidote to sorrow.

Housman's lyric critiques a core Victorian claim – that an English public-school education provides a route to happiness through a healthy dose of fresh air and sport. The speaker of *A Shropshire Lad* discloses the failure of this philosophy. The doctor's belief, in *Tom Brown's Schooldays*, that George Arthur just needs 'some Rugby air, and cricket' is rewritten as no more than a delusion. Such things cannot redeem the melancholy of the soul. In a letter of 1905, Housman explained that sports in his poem are presented as 'palliations of misery'. If so, they appear to do a poor job.

A few months before his death, the poet Francis Thompson was invited to watch Lancashire play at Lord's. Suffering badly from tuberculosis after years of severe opium addiction, he did not take up the offer. But it inspired recollections of a match he had seen, nearly thirty years before, between Lancashire and Gloucestershire at Old Trafford in 1878. He used the memory to produce 'At Lord's' – arguably the most celebrated of all cricketing poems. It begins and ends with the same poignant lines, the poem circling back on itself much like the poet does, his mind consumed by the past:

It is little I repair to the matches of the Southron folk,
Though my own red roses there may blow;
It is little I repair to the matches of the Southron folk,
Though the red roses crest the caps, I know.
For the field is full of shades as I near a shadowy coast,
And a ghostly batsman plays to the bowling of a ghost,
And I look through my tears on a soundless-clapping host
    As the run stealers flicker to and fro,
      To and fro:
O my Hornby and my Barlow long ago!

The lines are some of the most nostalgic in the history of English verse. The poet finds himself haunted by old ghosts – what he calls, in an immortal phrase, 'a field full of shades'. And it is a past that is tragically irretrievable; those great Lancashire opening batsmen, A. N. Hornby and Dick Barlow, are nothing but dwindling memories. 'At Lord's' has firmly entered the hall of fame of cricketing literature; historian Eric Midwinter avowed that it is the 'finest and most memorable' piece of cricket verse, the only example of its kind that 'surpasses dependence on its subject-matter and enters the list of classically great poems'.

The poems of Newbolt, Housman and Thompson offer a potent brew of nostalgia and pessimism at the end of the Victorian age. Taken together, they form a dark trio of fin de siècle fantasies. Wrapped up in melancholic shadows, each has its own mood and message, but all three point less confidently to the future than to the beauty of a lost past.

Few figures in English literature are as closely associated with the end of days quite as H. G. Wells – another literary giant who harboured close connections with the cricketing world. His father Joseph had been a professional, playing eight matches for Kent and earning his own place in history: in an 1862 match against Sussex, he became the first ever player to take four wickets in successive balls.

With this kind of pedigree, it is perhaps not surprising that cricket found its way into H. G.'s writing. In an 1897 essay, 'The Veteran Cricketer', he paints a warm portrait of an ageing former player. Reduced now to umpiring, he is gruff and grouchy – but still, in the author's eyes, a valuable conduit to a vanished English past:

My ancient cricketer abounds in reminiscence of the glorious days that have gone for ever. He can still recall the last echoes of the 'throwing' controversy that agitated Nyren, when overarm bowling began, and though he never played himself in a beaver hat, he can, he says, recollect seeing matches so played. In those days everyone wore tall hats – the policeman, the milkman, workmen of all sorts. Some people I fancy must have bathed in them and gone to bed wearing them. He recalls the Titans of that and the previous age and particularly delights in the legend of Noah Mann, who held it a light thing to walk twenty miles from Northchapel to Hambledon to practise every Tuesday afternoon, and wander back after dark.

Wells's depiction shares some ground with Thompson's 'At Lord's'; in both, the past is treated with reverence. The 'ancient cricketer' becomes a window across time, resurrecting memories of the Hambledon glory days of over a century before. It is an era that, in all truth, this cricketer could have known nothing about, however ancient he might be – in 1897, no one living would have retained more than the vaguest memories of pre-Victorian England. But the ruminations on John Nyren and Noah Mann are a potent fantasy – a dream of a cricketing paradise taken from an idealised, bygone age. Wells's veteran cricketer represents something that has become familiar in the chronicles of cricket – the belief that the present is a low ebb, and that things were so much better back in the day.

And cricket features, too, in Wells' dystopian masterwork *The War of the Worlds*. Towards the end of the novel, the narrator wanders through a south London cityscape that has been emptied and burned by the Martians. On Putney Hill, he is reunited with an artilleryman whom he had met earlier in the story. They sit together and discuss what the future might hold. The artillery-man predicts that the Martians will kill or enslave the weak. But the strong, he believes, might be able to survive – evading the Martians' clutches, and building their own new community:

> Our district will be London. And we may even be able to keep a watch, and run about in the open when the Martians keep away. Play cricket, perhaps. That's how we shall save the race. Eh? It's a possible thing? But saving the race is nothing in itself. As I say, that's only being rats. It's saving our knowledge and adding to it is the thing.

In this dark vision of a wrecked planet, the dream is that maybe – just maybe – some cricket might, one day, still be played. It is hard not to see something comical in the notion. But to all those who love the game, it also makes perfect sense. Sure, the entire world might have been occupied by aliens. The majority of the human race might have been eliminated. But the faint remaining hope of a bear-able human future is, nevertheless, a cricketing future.

V
MODERNS

Edgbaston, 5 July 2022.

*The delivery from Shardul Thakur was technically a good one –
pitched up but not a half-volley and a foot outside off stump.
Exactly the right areas, at least in theory. It's just that Joe Root
didn't make it look that way.*

*By the time Thakur released the ball, Root was already shifting
himself into a strange position – twisting his bat round so that it
pointed back at the bowler and stepping into a crouched, front-on
pose with his legs either side of the stumps, like he was a goalkeeper
preparing to save a penalty.*

*If Thakur's delivery was from the pages of a coaching manual,
Root's stance most certainly was not.*

*And then, with the most casual of flicks, he launched the ball
over third man for six.*

*'He is an incredible batsman, in the form of his life,' cooed
Michael Atherton in the commentary box, 'showcasing everything
he has to offer.'*

*It had already been around for a while, the ramp shot, or
paddle scoop – occasionally known as the 'Marillier' after
Dougie Marillier, the Zimbabwe batsman credited as its inventor. Seen largely in Twenty20 and one-day cricket, though, there
were few who dared to try it in test matches. But Joe Root was an
exception.*

'One thing I think,' he explained, 'is that as current players of the game we have the ability to rewrite the coaching manual. I don't think we should be scared of it.'

In cricket, it has often been the past that dominates, the seductive terrain of nostalgic dreams. But there is always, too, the pull of the future. Make it new, wrote Ezra Pound, the grand puppet-master of Modernist innovation. Make it new. Make it new. It is a tradition that Root seemed to be channelling – the avant-garde attitude of Picasso, Duchamp, James Joyce, Virginia Woolf – as he scornfully guided Thakur's textbook delivery high into the Edgbaston stands . . .

14

'CRICKET, COUSINS, THE MOVIES':
MODERNIST ARTS AND FICTIONS

Albert Chevallier Tayler was well established as an artist before, in 1906, he started work on the first great cricket painting of the twentieth century. A keen cricketer himself, his back catalogue boasted a range of cricketing subjects. In 1886 he had painted the Eton–Harrow match at Lord's. And in 1905, he produced a dozen watercolour portraits of eminent cricketers, a set that included Lord Harris and W. G. Grace.

In fact, it was Lord Harris himself – as Kent's county chairman – who commissioned what was to become Tayler's most famous work. It would be an action shot of Kent against Lancashire designed to capture the tension and movement of a match. In order to maximise realism, the artist prepared assiduously, arranging sittings with every single member of the Kent team.

In the final painting, Kent spinner Colin Blythe is bowling to Lancashire batsman Johnny Tyldesley:

The image is one of the most celebrated in the history of cricketing art. The dynamic grace of Blythe's bowling action is superbly captured – the front leg braced, the body twisting mid-delivery stride, the bowling arm just about to emerge over his shoulder to release the ball. Altham wrote that Blythe's action 'reflected the sensitive touch and the sense of rhythm of a musician'; this scene honours the technique of one of the game's most elegant spin bowlers.

At the other end, Tyldesley stands stiffly, awaiting his fate. He seems nervous – frozen in a hyper-defensive, no-backlift stance at odds with his formidable reputation as one of the era's finest top-order batsmen. An element of understandable Kentish bias is manifest. They had, after all, commissioned the painting after winning the county championship that summer. Not only that, but in this particular game against Lancashire, they had won by an innings and 195 runs. Tyldesley had made only 19 and 4 – Blythe winkling him out, in the first innings, on the way to a five-wicket haul.

Another feature of the painting – one that heightens Kent's dominance – came, in fact, from a technical challenge. Tayler wanted to make sure he delivered clear representations of the Kent players, but he also wanted to get them all in. This led to a compression of the action. Unlike many paintings of cricket matches, the view is not from the boundary. Instead, we are right there in the middle of the pitch, in a sort of leg slip position. The viewer is not a passive spectator, but a close fielder – we become one of the Kent team, braced and ready for a catch.

And the Kent fielders are aggressively placed. Close catchers surround Tyldesley in all directions. As well as a slip, a gully and a silly mid-on, there is a silly point (fast bowler Arthur Fielder) who appears to be psychotically close – confident, clearly, that he is not about to get a ball in the face. In addition, the ring of outfielders – at mid-off, cover and point – seem a lot nearer than they need to be. This is Kent going in for the kill, with no fewer than eight of their players perched in catching positions.

The backdrop is a beautiful English summer's day. A pale blue sky is wreathed with cotton-wool clouds. The Bell Harry Tower of Canterbury cathedral is just visible in the distance. The chalk-white façade of the St Lawrence ground pavilion looms like a colonial palace. All in all, it is an archetypal image – perhaps even *the* archetypal image – of cricket's Golden Age, that pre-war peak when the game was supposedly at its most brilliant and beautiful. The aura of innocence it radiates is inseparable from the darkness that followed. Blythe – killed, in November 1917, by shrapnel at the age of thirty-eight – was one of nearly three hundred first-class cricketers who did not survive the Great War.

From the beginning, the painting was well received. It is notable, though, that by the time it was finished in 1907, Henri Matisse had already been opening up new possibilities of colour expression in works like *Bonheur de Vivre*; Pablo Picasso, meanwhile, was finishing the proto-cubist masterpiece *Les Demoiselles d'Avignon*. Tayler's *Kent v. Lancashire 1906* shares little with the experimental enterprises of early Modernism. In an extended study of the painting, cricket historian Jonathan Rice noted that Tayler 'believed in depicting real scenes as faithfully as he could, but these scenes were usually tinged with a romance, a sense of England at its purest and best, that marks him out from some of his contemporaries'.

He was, in other words, a nostalgic painter – more interested in accessing an idealised Englishness than in pushing artistic boundaries. As Rice goes on to explain, Tayler's painting aimed to preserve time-honoured Victorian values, the sacred cows of Muscular Christianity and *mens sana in corpore sano*: 'The sun is shining, the skies are filled with fluffy, friendly clouds and the crowds in their best clothes and their best behaviour are sure that all is for the best in this best of all possible worlds.' The piece is refined and beautiful, but in the traditional

Victorian style: a twentieth-century work, with a nineteenth-century temperament.

Reflecting on a copy of the painting that hangs above the pavilion bar at Canterbury, writer Duncan Hamilton was moved to ponder how cricket is perennially torn between change and tradition:

> As I look out of choice at what Tayler painted – irritating the thirsty men who are trying to elbow a way through me towards the bar – the sight of it draws one thing more tightly into focus. No sport so urgently feels the tug of war between modernity and tradition than cricket. It is – and perhaps always will be – in a struggle with itself over whether the game in its modern form is relevant and really matters to the public . . . Cricket is constantly more revolutionary than gradually evolutionary in creating new competitions or laws. But for all this remodelling cricket still has a cultural nostalgia about it, which contributes to its perpetual charm and inspires devotion.

Tayler was a nostalgic, in a cricketing era that has – perhaps more than any other – become layered with a haze of nostalgia. His remarkable painting of Kent and Lancashire at Canterbury not only evokes cricket's beauty, drama and grace; it also reminds us that, however much we might push to make it new, the game will always be borne back ceaselessly into the past.

But despite the wistfulness, there are richer links than one might think between cricket and Modernist innovation. James Joyce, for a start, was a lifelong cricket fan. In his memoir, *My Brother's Keeper*, brother Stanislaus recalls James' childhood love for the game:

> He disliked football but liked cricket, and though too young to be even in the junior eleven, he promised to be a useful bat.

He still took an eager interest in the game when he was at Belvedere, and eagerly studied the feats of Ranji and Fry, Trumper and Spofforth.

Cricket makes an appearance in every one of Joyce's major works. In 'An Encounter', from *Dubliners*, two truant boys are pelted with stones in the street because one of them 'wore the silver badge of a cricket club in his cap'. The game is charged with politicised significance in the divided culture of Dublin – linked with British rule, and a warning sign of unionist sympathies.

Elsewhere in Joyce, cricket has idyllic overtones. In *A Portrait of the Artist as a Young Man*, a practice session is lyrically described: 'The fellows were practising long shies and bowling lobs and slow twisters. In the soft grey silence he could hear the bump of the balls: and from here and from there through the quiet air the sound of the cricket bats: pick, pack, pock, puck: like drops of water in a fountain falling softly in the brimming bowl.' In *Ulysses*, Leopold Bloom's delight in a sunny day inspires thoughts of cricket: 'Heavenly weather really. If life was always like that. Cricket weather. Sit around under sunshades. Over after over. Out. They can't play it here. Duck for six wickets. Still Captain Culler broke a window in the Kildare street club with a slog to square leg.'

But by far the strangest use of cricket appears in *Finnegans Wake*. One remarkable passage, towards the end of the book, reads like a cricketing crossword puzzle – a bewildering collage of allusions that range from the obvious to the oblique:

She had to spofforth, she had to kicker, too thick of the wick of her pixy's loomph, wide lickering jessup the smooky shiminey. And her duffed coverpoint of a wickedy batter, whenever she druv behind her stumps for a tyddlesly wink through his tunnil- clefft bagslops after the rising bounder's yorkers, as he studd and stoddard and trutted and trumpered, to see had lordherry's

blackham's red bobby abbels, it tickled her innings to consort
pitch at kicksolock in the morm. Tipatonguing him on in her
pigeony linguish, with a flick at the bails for lubrication, to
scorch her faster, faster. Ye hek, ye hok, ye hucky hiremonger!
Magrath he's my pegger, he is, for bricking up all my old kent
road. He'll win your toss, flog your old tom's bowling and I darr
ye, barrackybuller, to break his duck! He's posh. I lob him . . .

As anyone who has read his letters to Nora Barnacle will know,
Joyce was not exactly allergic to risqué territory. And cricket has
a playfully erotic purpose here, the language teeming with innuendo and slang words for sex. As Joyce scholar Ron Malings
noted, 'It is no secret that the many cricketing names and expressions . . . serve to describe an exercise in copulation.'
In a 1937 notebook of extracts and clippings, Virginia Woolf
included a newspaper story from 6 October of that year. It was a
report on a speech given by Molly Hide, captain of the England
women's cricket team. WOMEN'S CRICKET 'HERE TO STAY', ran
the headline. 'No Games Against Men'. Hide was quoted delivering an impassioned defence of the women's game: 'I know there
are a large number of people who thoroughly disagree with
women playing cricket . . . I wonder how many of them have ever
watched a women's cricket match? If they watched they would
be sure that the game is losing nothing by the way it is played by
women.'
Hide was a genius of twentieth-century English cricket, in
the earliest days of women's international matches. She played
in the first ever women's test, at Brisbane in December 1934. A
few years later, she became the second-ever captain of the
women's test team, as she developed a reputation for mental
toughness and high expectations. Teammate Netta Rheinberg
hailed her as the personification of women's cricket – a bold
champion at a time when scorn towards the women's game was
still rife. 'It was not simply the classical batting that elevated

Molly Hide above the rest,' wrote sports historian Roy Case. 'For she could drive the ball beautifully, astonishing many a cynical male spectator.'

It is no wonder that Virginia Woolf saved the story of Hide's speech – not only did she follow cricket, she had played the game herself as a youth. Talking of childhood with her sister, the painter and interior designer Vanessa Bell, she once explained, 'Vanessa and I were what we call tomboys; that is, we played cricket, scrambled over rocks, climbed trees, were said not to care for clothes and so on.' And there is photographic proof of these childhood cricketing exploits:

Virginia – on the left – clutches the ball protectively, a somewhat glazed expression on her face. It is tempting to surmise that she is in the midst of some precocious childhood dream of creativity. She stares at the camera – self-conscious, perhaps, about the fact she is being photographed. Vanessa, meanwhile, cuts a very different figure. She is absorbed in her own work – eyes on the ground in front of her, a straight bat fastidiously gripped, as she offers up a pretty accomplished forward defensive stroke.

Cricket was a feature of their childhood at Talland House, the family's Cornish summer residence in St Ives. Games were set up in the garden, rather in the style of the family Grace. Their father Leslie Stephen recalled, 'We made what we called a "lawn tennis" ground on the most level bit, where the children delighted in playing small cricket every evening.' An even earlier photo shows Virginia alertly crouched as wicket keeper, while her little brother Adrian bats:

These photos make one thing clear: cricket was in Virginia Woolf's blood from a very early age. The second was taken in 1886, when she was only four years old.

Cricket plays a role in several of Woolf's novels. In *Jacob's Room*, from 1922, Fanny Elmer associates the game with the transience of youth: 'And for ever the beauty of young men seems to be set in smoke, however lustily they chase footballs, or drive cricket balls, dance, run, or stride along roads.' In *The Waves*, published in 1931, Louis, an Australian immigrant to England, links cricket with a vision of Englishness that he yearns for: 'Now we move out of this cool temple, into the yellow playing-fields . . . And, as it is a half-holiday (the Duke's birthday) we will settle among the long grasses, while they play cricket. Could I be "they" I would choose it; I would buckle on my pads and stride across the playing-field at the head of the batsmen.' *To the Lighthouse*, 1927, is laced with family cricketing scenes – the '"How's that? How's that?" of the children playing cricket' – that recall the author's own childhood contests.

But it is in *Mrs Dalloway*, 1925, that cricket is most vividly present. The game appears several times in the novel, linked to a range of different characters. Suffering from shell shock, First World War veteran Septimus Smith wanders through London in a state of suicidal distraction. Desperate to divert him from dark thoughts, his wife Lucrezia attempts to interest him in a group of passing cricketers:

Away from people – they must get away from people, he said (jumping up), right away over there, where there were chairs beneath a tree and the long slope of the park dipped like a length of green stuff with a ceiling cloth of blue and pink smoke high above, and there was a rampart of far irregular houses hazed in smoke, the traffic hummed in a circle, and on the right, dun-coloured animals stretched long necks over the Zoo palings, barking, howling. There they sat down under a tree.

'Look,' she implored him, pointing at a little troop of boys carrying cricket stumps, and one shuffled, spun round on his heel and shuffled, as if he were acting a clown at the music hall.

'Look,' she implored him, for Dr Holmes had told her to make him notice real things, go to a music hall, play cricket—that was the very game, Dr Holmes said, a nice out-of-door game, the very game for her husband.

Cricket is pictured as therapy, prescribed as medical treatment – a wholesome outdoor pastime that might, Lucrezia hopes, bring Septimus back to good health. Haunted by the horrors of the war, her husband does not hear. 'Look,' she repeats, time after time; but he gives no reply.

Peter Walsh is another character haunted by the past. He has returned to London to file for divorce and wants to remarry; but he has never fully recovered from Clarissa Dalloway's refusal of his marriage proposal many years before. As he reflects on that affair – and the prospect of attending Clarissa's party that night – he buys a newspaper to check the cricket scores:

But cricket was no mere game. Cricket was important. He could never help reading about cricket. He read the scores in the stop press first, then how it was a hot day; then about a murder case. Having done things millions of times enriched them, though it might be said to take the surface off. The past enriched, and experience, and having cared for one or two people, and so having acquired the power which the young lack, of cutting short, doing what one likes, not caring a rap what people say and coming and going without any very great expectations (he left his paper on the table and moved off), which however (and he looked for his hat and coat) was not altogether true of him, not to-night, for here he was starting to go to a party, at his age, with the belief upon him that he was about to have an experience. But what?

Cricket brings him comfort amid the tangle of his thoughts and the tumult of the city; it is the first thing he looks for in the pages of his paper. *Cricket was no mere game*, he insists to himself ... the claim revives the old Victorian mantra, Tom

Brown's belief that cricket is an institution, a philosophy, a conduit to civilised life. It is a bold proposition. But it does not stay with Peter for more than a moment. His mind quickly shifts to other things, like the imminent party and the thought of seeing Clarissa again.

In the final section of the novel, once the party has begun, Clarissa floats around the house to greet her various guests. It turns out that one of them, Lord Gayton, has spent the day at the cricket:

> But she must speak to that couple, said Clarissa, Lord Gayton and Nancy Blow.
>
> Not that they added perceptibly to the noise of the party. They were not talking (perceptibly) as they stood side by side by the yellow curtains. They would soon be off elsewhere, together; and never had very much to say in any circumstances. They looked; that was all. That was enough. They looked so clean, so sound, she with an apricot bloom of powder and paint, but he scrubbed, rinsed, with the eyes of a bird, so that no ball could pass him or stroke surprise him. He struck, he leapt, accurately, on the spot. Ponies' mouths quivered at the end of his reins. He had his honours, ancestral monuments, banners hanging in the church at home. He had his duties; his tenants; a mother and sisters; had been all day at Lord's, and that was what they were talking about – cricket, cousins, the movies – when Mrs. Dalloway came up. Lord Gayton liked her most awfully. So did Miss Blow. She had such charming manners.
>
> 'It is angelic – it is delicious of you to have come!' she said. She loved Lord's; she loved youth, and Nancy, dressed at enormous expense by the greatest artists in Paris, stood there looking as if her body had merely put forth, of its own accord, a green frill.

The substance of the conversation – 'cricket, cousins, the movies' – provides a snapshot into the small talk of 1920s London society.

Clarissa's reply, 'She loved Lord's', immediately merges with her admiration of Nancy's stylish beauty. Cricket – like the movies, like fashion – is something for people to stand around and talk about, an essential piece of the fabric of contemporary urban life.

'One of these days I will write about London, and how it takes up the private life and carries it on, without any effort.' So wrote Woolf, in a diary entry of 26 May 1924. At the time, she was in the early stages of writing *Mrs Dalloway* – still at that point titled *The Hours*. And it was, indeed, to become a story that captures 'life; London; this moment of June' – the texture of the city, on one particular day. As the characters go about their lives, cricket is a key part of that texture, a feature in the city's sound and movement – what Clarissa Dalloway, on the way to buy her flowers, describes as 'a beating, a stirring of galloping ponies, tapping of cricket bats; Lord's, Ascot, Ranelagh and all the rest of it; wrapped in the soft mesh of the grey-blue morning air.'

It took a long time for Henry Stockley to become fully recognised as a significant British artist of the naïve and primitive tradition. Throughout his life, his reputation was held back by a cocktail of prejudice and class snobbery. After growing up in poverty – his family home had neither a toilet nor running water – he had no formal artistic training. For over thirty years, he worked for London Transport as a bus driver; his early works, lacking proper equipment and canvas, were painted on anything he was able to get his hands on.

Art patron Lucy Wertheim discovered him by chance. Her description of their first meeting brings to life the extent of his eccentricity:

> I was sitting at my table discussing some matter with a client when my attention was taken up by an artist at the other end of the gallery. He was a man of about forty who had just unrolled a bundle of paintings and laid them on the floor against the

wall . . . His efforts were executed on pieces of linoleum and old bits of linen and though somewhat crude there was a striking quality about them that distracted my attention from the business I had on hand.

When I saw the artist stoop down, collect his paintings and begin to roll them into a bundle again . . . I went over to the other end of the gallery to have a word with the man himself. He said he was a bus driver who devoted all his spare moments to painting. He had pinched from his wife some old linen pillow slips and ground his own paint and the results were contained in the bundle.

The upshot of that meeting was an exhibition of Stockley's oil illustrations from Bunyan's *The Pilgrim's Progress*, in 1932, which were received by critics with a combination of fascination and snootiness. 'He has a sense of design,' ran a piece in the *Daily News*, 'and such enthusiasm that the public will find this untrained but observant painter's work very interesting.' The headline to the story was simply BUS DRIVER'S PAINTINGS. His humble origins and modest day job were an albatross round his neck. He became invariably known as 'Busdriver' Stockley.

The connection between Stockley and cricket is underacknowledged. In the same year as his *Pilgrim's Progress* exhibition, he also produced an extraordinary pair of paintings, the first of which is *The Boy Cricketers*.

Its idealised pastoral setting recalls the engravings of William Blake – another visionary artist, shunned by the establishment – to whom Stockley has been compared. And Blake's spirit feels present in the vigour emanating from the schoolboy cricketers. Two outfielders seem to sway, as if dancing. The bowler prepares to deliver the ball with a balletic skip. The wide-eyed batsman waits, the bill of his cap rakishly spun to the side. A heap of jackets, so close to the action, suggests informal, spontaneous play. The backdrop to the scene is a swirling sky of indigo, silver and burgundy that manages to be both beautiful and vaguely threatening.

Its companion piece is *The Girl Cricketers*. The resemblance to Blake is strong here, too; one girl throws the ball to another who wields a bat with one hand, much like the boys in Blake's 'Ecchoing Green'. Once more, the children's elation and movement are vividly present. But this time, the whole scene is wrapped in a deep gloom. The sky is a brooding fog of purple. The ground is cast in thick shadow; the last vestiges of daylight look like they are about to disappear. A tree looms over the children, its branches stretched out in ominous symmetry, like a crucifix. While the boys seemed to have been playing on a sun-kissed afternoon, these girls play in a sinister fire of apocalyptic twilight.

The precise reasons why Stockley chose to make two separate images of cricketing boys and cricketing girls are unclear. But his enigmatic paintings present a vision of cricket that feels a very long way from the machinery of the establishment. In 1932 – the year these paintings were made – the captain of the England cricket team was Douglas Jardine, not only the most controversial in English cricket history, but also – to this day – the figure who most potently stirs allegations of privileged entitlement. That coming winter would see Jardine push sportsmanship to its absolute limit in an effort to muffle Don Bradman and win the Ashes. His cold demeanour was linked to his public-school background, his rarefied lifestyle responsible for a supercilious, cutthroat character. 'All Australians are uneducated, and an unruly mob,' he once sniped.

Stockley's paintings feel like a resistance to such a world – an effort to recapture an early Romantic vision of cricket as a game of rural spaces, open greens and liberated, childhood play. Just maybe, the glowering doomsday-red of Stockley's sky was meant to express the futility of such an effort. Or maybe it was another Blakean touch, with the world of happy childhood innocence threatened by its dark contrary of experience. Whatever the answer, he was not the only artist of this era who fashioned images of cricket compellingly distinct from the status and glamour of Lord's.

'I saw the industrial scene and I was affected by it. I tried to paint it. All the time I tried to paint the industrial scene as well as I could. It wasn't easy. I wanted to get a certain effect on the canvas. I couldn't describe it, but I knew when I'd got it. Well, a camera could have done the scene straight off. That was no use to me. I wanted to get an industrial scene and be satisfied with the picture.' These are the words of L. S. Lowry, the twentieth century's greatest painter of the industrial north.

His scenes of crowds pouring into football matches are well known and justly celebrated. Rather less attention, though, has been paid to the cricketing scenes he would occasionally paint, such as *The Cricket Match* of 1938:

All the key features of Lowry's distinctive style are apparent: the 'matchstick men' figures, the industrial buildings, the urban blight, the plain colour palette of white, blue, red and yellow. A group of children play cricket in what appears to be a midwinter scene. The white ground would suggest snow – except, by this stage in his career, Lowry had established white as the default backdrop to his paintings, a signature element of his aesthetic. What might be snow might, instead, merely be the soot and haze of a polluted landscape. In this instance, the dead trees – their spindly branches stretching up into a concrete-coloured sky – reveal that it must be a winter setting. The summertime green so synonymous with cricketing activity is nowhere to be seen. Though some of the players stand bravely in shorts, many wear hats and gloves, implying cold conditions.

Numerous other details deepen the bleak atmosphere. Bits of broken-up wood – even a semi-submerged wheel – are scattered around the makeshift pitch. The windows of the buildings in the background are spoiled with holes; in some cases, there is no glass at all, just a gaping void. Toxic smoke spills from chimneys. In the foreground, ragged fence palings emerge from a pool of stagnant water.

This is cricket, in 1930s Salford, a snapshot of working-class poverty that existed in a different universe to any Douglas Jardine paradigm of public-school privilege. The group of adults smoking pipes and talking, over by a broken wall on the left, have sometimes been read as unemployed locals, complaining to each other about their lot. And the cricket game itself is hardly a polished affair. It is difficult to tell what the wickets are made from, but they are clearly not proper sets of stumps – heaps of earth, perhaps, or bundles of clothes. A chaotic feel prevails; a couple of the children are turned away from the action towards the grown-ups, as if more interested in their gossip.

But despite the drab locale, the playing children manage to convey a joy that echoes Stockley and also, in turn, William

Blake. Unphased by the ragged squalor and poverty of their surroundings, they cheerfully get on with their game. Commenting on these children-cricketers, art critic Simon Hucker has suggested, 'They are cyphers of the life you have, before all the cares and woes start. They stand for freedom and happiness and play.' There is an echo here of Thomas Gray's schoolboy cricketers, strangers yet to pain, playing on regardless of their doom. Perhaps the adults over by the wall are a sombre reminder of their fate.

Lowry was not, in fact, a cricket fan. It was his close friend Alick Leggat – president, for many years, of Lancashire County Cricket Club – who taught him the fielding positions and encouraged him to depict the game. In total, Lowry was to produce five cricketing scenes. Another was *A Cricket Match* from 1952:

A massive, five-storey factory dominates the picture. Art historian Charlotte Goodhew, collections manager at the MCC, has observed, 'The faceless players, reduced to mismatched coloured shirts and black workers' boots, are dwarfed by the industrial landscape. The looming clocktower, a symbol of the daily grind, watches over rows of terraced houses. These stylised, characterful dwellings, in turn seem to watch the match (and the viewer), overwriting the barrier between paint and life.' The jaunty aura of the youthful cricketers again sits in contrast to the dinginess of the scene, a gloomy backdrop of black smoke, dark walls, blank windows and sunless skies.

Lowry's cricketing art was brought together in a single exhibition, curated by Goodhew, for the first time in 2023. 'Sometimes he's sneered upon down in London,' said Michael Atherton, commenting on the display in the writing room at Lord's. 'They think he's a bit provincial, a bit sentimental. But I think if you're from that region, you recognise both the candour and compassion . . . it's a difficult, post-industrial scene, often in decline, and I think you see that coming out in Lowry's work.' Goodhew states that Lowry used his 'artistic language to comment on society, to comment on working-class people playing cricket in the industrial north in the twentieth century'.

Lowry's paintings – urban, grimy, unromantic – could not appear to be much more different from the sunlit idealism of Albert Chevallier Tayler's 1906 magnum opus. But even in the Lowry scenes, an element of nostalgia just might be perceptible. As his biographer Allen Andrews has noted, 'All the people in the crowd scenes in his pictures . . . wore the old-fashioned clothes, the shawls and the caps and big boots, of a bygone age.' This, says Andrews, is *not* a mid-century aesthetic, as Lowry himself claimed, but a much earlier one; 'Lowry's true period,' he explains, 'was the time before the Great War'. If this is right, Lowry's cricket paintings are, once again, products of the English imagination that draw on ghosts of the past. This time, though, they offer something a long way from any idealised Golden Age, as he fuses past and present to form half bleak, half hopeful images of carefree cricket in ramshackle urban wastelands.

15

'DROPPERS, I CALL THEM. SPEDEGUE'S DROPPERS':
EARLY TWENTIETH-CENTURY TALES

'I was in the school cricket team two years and in the school football team one . . . At cricket I was a fast bowler – the equivalent
of a baseball pitcher. We had a great team my year, not losing a
school match.'

These are the words of Pelham Grenville Wodehouse, looking
back on the cricketing feats of his boyhood at Dulwich College.
The great novelist's love for cricket has become a well-known
part of Wodehousian folklore. One of his most legendary characters, Jeeves – sagacious valet to Bertie Wooster – was named after
the Warwickshire and England bowler, Percy Jeeves. 'It must
have been in 1913,' he later recalled, 'that I paid a visit to my
parents in Cheltenham and went to see Warwickshire play
Gloucestershire on the Cheltenham College ground. I suppose
Jeeves's bowling must have impressed me, for I remembered him
in 1916 when I was in New York and starting the Jeeves and
Bertie saga, and it was just the name I wanted.' Wodehouse's own
nickname, 'Plum', was one he came to cherish after discovering
that the great Middlesex and England batsman, Pelham Warner,
went by the same moniker.

The author's zeal for the game is apparent throughout his work
– but it is most richly present in two early novels, *Mike* (1909) and
Psmith in the City (1910). The first is a schoolboy tale that, in many
ways, sits firmly in the tradition of *Tom Brown*. Wodehouse even
references Hughes' novel; during a fight between Mike and another

schoolboy, the former 'threw away his advantages, much as Tom Brown did at the beginning of his fight with Slogger Williams'.

But Wodehouse's taste for levity and wit sets him well apart from the earnest tone of his predecessor. He even went so far as to satirise Hughes in an early short story called 'The Tom Brown Question'. In it, a stranger on a train strikes up conversation with the narrator, who is in the middle of reading *Tom Brown's School Days*. The stranger makes a bold claim – that the novel's second half was written by an impostor. And he cites the portrayal of the cricket match as evidence:

> 'Do you remember that match? You do? Very well. You recall how Tom wins the toss on a plumb wicket?'
>
> 'Yes.'
>
> 'Then with the usual liberality of young hands (I quote from the book) he put the MCC in first. Now, my dear sir, I ask you, would a school captain do that? I am young, says one of Gilbert's characters, the Grand Duke, I think, but, he adds, I am not so young as that. Tom may have been young, but would he, could he have been young enough to put his opponents in on a true wicket, when he had won the toss? Would the Tom Brown of part one have done such a thing?'
>
> 'Never,' I shouted, with enthusiasm.

Moreover, Brown's decision to give the talentless George Arthur a game – 'for no other reason than that he thought a first eleven cap would prove a valuable tonic to an unspeakable personal friend of his' – proves that the text cannot possibly be genuine. The stranger explains that the book's second half was, in fact, written by a kind of Victorian moral police – the 'Secret Society for Putting Wholesome Literature Within the Reach of Every Boy, And Seeing That He Gets It' – who replaced violence and vice with a story that would 'suit the rules of our Society'.

This gibe at Hughes' high-minded sanctimony was a sign that Wodehouse's agenda would always be more about fun and mischief than po-faced moralising. And *Mike* is precisely that – a sunlit comedy, chronicling the exploits of ultra-talented batsman Mike Jackson at two fictional public schools, Wrykyn and Sedleigh.

The protagonist is the youngest brother in a cricketing dynasty. The novel's opening announces how central cricket is to the Jackson home:

> It was a morning in the middle of April, and the Jackson family were consequently breakfasting in comparative silence. The cricket season had not begun, and except during the cricket season they were in the habit of devoting their powerful minds at breakfast almost exclusively to the task of victualling against the labours of the day. In May, June, July, and August the silence was broken. The three grown-up Jacksons played regularly in first-class cricket, and there was always keen competition among their brothers and sisters for the copy of the *Sportsman* which was to be found on the hall table with the letters.

There is an echo here of the brothers Grace: the Jacksons even have a net in their own garden, together with a professional, Saunders, who has been hired to train them up. But there may also be a nod to Wodehouse's own upbringing. He was one of four brothers and, although 'Plum' himself was a talented bowler – once, in a school match, taking nine wickets in an innings – his brother Armine was widely considered to be the better player.

Mike Jackson is a straightforward young chap – short on depth, perhaps, and low on academic ambition, but something of an artist with a bat in his hand. He heads off to Sedleigh to embark on a glittering cricket career, vying with his less gifted older brother for a place in the first eleven. Saunders, for one, has no doubt about the level of Mike's potential. 'He'll be playing for England in another eight years,' he prophesies. 'That's what he'll be playing for.'

For cricket fans, *Mike* is quite simply the most delightful reading experience. Wodehouse's rare comic gifts merge with a fondness for cricket that is evident on every page. And for all his lightness of touch, Wodehouse also squares up to some of the controversies of the day. In the opening years of the new century, B. J. T. Bosanquet of Middlesex and England began to test out something new – a method of spin that aimed to deceive the batsman in unprecedented fashion. This was a delivery that looked like a leg break but, thanks to a tweak of fingers and wrist, spun like an off break. Soon dubbed a 'googly', it was a revolution in the art of spin, opening up a whole new vocabulary of guile and trickery.

Bosanquet – nephew of the philosopher Bernard Bosanquet – had been a fast-medium bowler while a boy at Eton, as well as a talented batsman. Years after his retirement, he credited his shift to spin – and the googly's improbable origins – to a childhood game called Twisti-Twosti. 'The object was to bounce the ball on a table,' he explained, 'so that your opponent sitting opposite could not catch it. It soon occurred to me that if one could pitch a ball which broke in a certain direction and with more or less the same delivery make the next ball go in the opposite direction, one would mystify one's opponent.'

Once he applied the concept to cricket, the effects were dramatic, if unreliable. Bosanquet could be an expensive bowler – and if it went wrong, the googly could be a mortifying spectacle, bouncing three or four times before reaching the batsman. But when everything worked, it could be devastating; in the first home Ashes test of 1905, he took eight wickets in the second innings, bowling England to victory more or less on his own. 'The Englishmen,' *Wisden* reported, 'owed everything to Bosanquet.'

Spin bowling would never be the same again. The moral ramifications of the googly, though, drew mixed views. In Australia, some saw it as just another example of English fraud and deceit. The Australian slang term for the delivery – a 'wrong 'un' – was also a slang word for 'criminal', as well as being a homophobic slur.

And in Wodehouse's novel, one of the opposition bowlers is a practitioner of the contentious new method. Mike discusses the threat with his captain, Burgess:

'. . . they've got a slow leg-break man who might be dangerous on a day like this. A boy called de Freece. I don't know of him. He wasn't in the team last year.'

'I know the chap. He played wing three for them at footer against us this year on their ground. He was crocked when they came here. He's a pretty useful chap all round, I believe. Plays racquets for them too.'

'Well, my friend said he had one very dangerous ball, of the Bosanquet type. Looks as if it were going away, and comes in instead.'

'I don't think a lot of that,' said Burgess ruefully. 'One consolation is, though, that that sort of ball is easier to watch on a slow wicket. I must tell the fellows to look out for it.'

'I should. And, above all, win the toss.'

Burgess' response – 'I don't think a lot of that' – implies disapproval of such underhand tactics. After all, the googly's trickery was hardly consistent with the game's supposedly noble ethics. To some, it was not really *cricket* – a worrying deviation from the principled aspirations of Victorian England. Is the googly an illegal delivery? Bosanquet was once asked. 'Oh no,' he replied, with a distinctly Wodehousian roguishness. 'Only immoral.'

In the novel's second half, Mike shifts school and befriends the dapper, monocle-sporting Old Etonian Psmith – one of the most memorable characters in all of Wodehouse's fiction. And their story continues beyond school into *Psmith and the City*, a satire on office life that chronicles the characters' unhappy experiences of the banking world. The novel's final act sees Mike suddenly called up to play against Middlesex at Lord's – requiring him to skip work, and face the sack, but an offer that he is more than happy to snap up. At a cricketing level, it turns out to be a good decision, as Mike hits a magnificent, match-saving century.

But the glory has come at a price. During the match, Mike contemplates his future, now that he has sabotaged a banking career. He yearns to be a cricket professional – but feels he is faced with a problem:

> Could he get taken on? That was the question. It was impossible that he should play for his own county on his residential qualification. He could not appear as a professional in the same team in which his brothers were playing as amateurs.

The notion of playing alongside his amateur brothers, but taking money *himself*, is inconceivable. As biographer Benny Green explains, 'He weighs the chances of staving off genteel destitution by becoming a professional, knowing that such a resort will constitute a social outrage.' But it is, in truth, something of an illusory problem, as Green goes on to note: 'Wodehouse is surely being excessively naïve, and must have known that the old Gentleman–Player distinction of his boyhood was a social rather than a financial one.'

In any case, Mike's money worries do not last long. In the closing pages, Psmith's family offers to pay his way through Cambridge. All of a sudden, the world looks a lot rosier:

> Mike's mind roamed into the future. Cambridge first, and then an open-air life of the sort he had always dreamed of. The Problem of Life seemed to him to be solved. He looked on

down the years, and he could see no troubles there of any kind whatsoever. Reason suggested that there were probably one or two knocking about somewhere, but this was no time to think of them. He examined the future, and found it good.

The problems of Wodehouse's novels tend, like this, to be temporary and fixable. 'As we grow older,' he wrote elsewhere, 'we come to see that the only real and abiding pleasure in life is to give pleasure to other people.' The world of Wodehouse is a world where all is well, where the sun always shines – an escapist dream, detached from life's trials.

A young Wodehouse also played cricket for a team founded by Peter Pan creator J. M. Barrie. These were called the Allahakbarries – a hybrid pun on Barrie's name and on the Arabic phrase '*Allah Akbar*', which he mistakenly believed to mean 'Heaven help us' (a better translation is 'God is great'). It was a kind of all-star literary eleven, packed with writers including Rudyard Kipling, Jerome K. Jerome, A. A. Milne and H. G. Wells.

Barrie himself was a frail and dainty figure – often fielding with a pipe in his mouth – not really much of a cricketer. But he was certainly a keen one, approaching the game's aura of Englishness with all the fascination of a Scotland-born outsider. Barrie's view of cricket was romantic and sentimental – rooted in dreamy ideals of English life. 'A rural cricket match,' he once wrote, 'is surely the loveliest scene in England, and the most disarming sound. The ranks of the unseen dead forever passing along our country lanes, the Englishman falls out for a moment to look over the gate of the cricket-field and smile.'

The team name itself is a hint that the Allahakbarries were not exactly a top-tier outfit, in terms of cricketing skill. Later in life – under the pen name of 'James Anon' – Barrie would mock their ineptitude: 'Charles Whibley threw in unerringly but in the wrong direction. You should have seen Charles Furze as wicket-keeper, but you would have had to be quick about it as Anon has so soon to try someone else . . . the team had no tail, that is to say, they would have done just as well had they begun at the other end.'

At its heart, his team was a motley crew of writers and artists, cobbled together, having a heap of fun. Sporting seriousness was thin on the ground. A much more leisurely focus was paramount. A recurrent rival team, for instance, was Broadway in Worcestershire – 'The scene of contests and suppers of Homeric splendour,' Barrie recalled, 'at which fair ladies looked sympathetic as their heroes told of their deeds of long ago.'

The Broadway skipper was the American barrister A. F. de Navarro. And the team's real mastermind, wrote Barrie, was his wife, legendary actress Mary Anderson:

> . . . behind them stood the far more threatening figure of Worcestershire's loveliest resident, Madame de Navarro, the famous Mary Anderson . . . who never (such is the glory of woman) could follow the game, despite deep study, and always called it 'crickets'. She had however a powerful way of wandering round the field with the Allahakbarries' top scorer, who when he came back would tell Anon sheepishly that he had promised to play for her in the second innings.

The actress oversaw events with an eagle eye; although she herself 'never wielded the willow', she 'watched avidly every ball sent down'.

Barrie detailed these matchups in a privately printed pamphlet that was later republished, after his death, with a foreword by Don Bradman. It was dedicated to 'Our Dear Enemy, Mary de Navarro'. Alongside Barrie's anecdotes were two sketches involving the patroness. In the first, Barrie looks on in despair as his stumps are demolished by an underarm shooter – delivered by none other than de Navarro herself. The second, by cartoonist Bernard Partridge, similarly pokes fun at the team captain:

RESULT OF THE TEST MATCH, 1898.
Drawn by Bernard Partridge

An imperious de Navarro towers over a grumpy-looking, pint-sized, pipe-puffing Barrie. 'The Ladye Marye de Navarro,' runs the caption, 'throweth ye glove to ye puissant Sir James of Kirriemuir, and challengeth him to combat in ye tented field.' Playful as the image might be, its depiction of female empowerment also reflects the illustrator's more serious politics; Partridge produced a range of pro-suffragist cartoons for *Punch* magazine, for whom he worked for over fifty years.

A much more formidable member of the Allahakbarries was Arthur Conan Doyle – who was seen by Barrie as 'the chief exception to [the] depressing rule' that 'the more distinguished as authors his men were the worse they played'. Doyle, in fact, was a fine cricketer. He played for the MCC over the best part of a decade, including ten first-class matches for the club. He once took 7 wickets for 61 runs against Cambridgeshire at Lord's. Only one of his wickets came in a first-class match – but this lone scalp happened to be that of a veteran batsman by the name of William Gilbert Grace.

Doyle commemorated the feat in a poem, 'A Reminiscence of Cricket', in which W. G.'s larger-than-life persona is richly evoked:

Once in my heyday of cricket,
One day I shall ever recall!
I captured that glorious wicket,
The greatest, the grandest of all.

Before me he stands like a vision,
Bearded and burly and brown,
A smile of good-humoured derision
As he waits for the first to come down.

A statue from Thebes or from Knossos,
A Hercules shrouded in white,
Assyrian bull-like colossus,
He stands in his might.

With the beard of a Goth or a Vandal,
His bat hanging ready and free,
His great hairy hands on the handle,
And his menacing eyes upon me.

There is a delightful, writerly touch to the portrayal. Grace is no mere mortal: he is by turns a piece of art, a demigod, and a mythical warrior, preparing to crush Doyle's pathetic offerings. But to the surprise of everyone, including Doyle himself, Grace belted one straight up in the air for the wicketkeeper to snaffle:

I stood with my two eyes fixed on it,
Paralysed, helpless, inert;
There was 'plunk' as the gloves shut upon it,
And he cuddled it up to his shirt.

Out – beyond question or wrangle!
Homeward he lurched to his lunch!
His bat was tucked up at an angle,
His great shoulders curved to a hunch.

Walking he rumbled and grumbled,
Scolding himself and not me;
One glove was off, and he fumbled,
Twisting the other hand free.

Grace's cranky response suggests he was not best pleased to fall victim to such an insipid bowler. 'Understandably perhaps,' notes writer David Rayvern Allen, 'there is no mention of the fact that Grace had made a hundred before he was dismissed.'

Elsewhere, in a tribute to Grace for the *Strand* magazine, Doyle offered a different slant on the dismissal. 'The old man laughed and shook his head at me,' he confessed. 'He was thinking probably that it was the worst ball that ever got his wicket, but he was too polite to say so.' Doyle's characterisation of Grace is reverential:

To those who knew W. G. Grace he was more than a great cricketer. He had many of the characteristics of a great man. There was a masterful generosity and a large direct simplicity and frankness which, combine with his huge frame, swarthy features, bushy beard, and a somewhat lumbering carriage, made an impression which could never be forgotten. In spite of his giant west-of-England build, there was, as it seemed to me, something of the gipsy in his colouring, his vitality, and his quick dark eyes with their wary expression.

As was so often the case in Victorian portrayals, worship merges with an element of myth-making. Doyle aims to convey not just Grace's greatness, but also the aura of mysterious exoticism that he seemed to exude.

Much like Wodehouse, Doyle drew on cricket history in naming his fictional characters. 'Holmes was homely,' he once explained, 'and as for "Sherlock" – well, years ago I made thirty runs against a bowler by the name of Sherlock, and I always had a kindly feeling for that name.' The evidence actually suggests that he took the name from two different players – Francis Shacklock and Mordecai Sherwin of Nottinghamshire. Derbyshire fast bowler William Mycroft, meanwhile, is widely felt to be the inspiration behind the name of Sherlock's brother, Mycroft Holmes.

Despite Doyle's prowess, the adventures of Sherlock Holmes are generally a cricket-free zone. But in 1928, Doyle's best-known cricketing work, 'The Story of Spedegue's Dropper', appeared in the *Strand*. It tells of former cricketer, Walter Scougall, who stumbles on an extraordinary scene one day while walking in the New Forest:

> In a narrow glade there stood two great oaks. They were thirty or forty feet apart, and the glade was spanned by a cord which connected them up. This cord was at least fifty feet above the ground, and it must have entailed no small effort to get it there. At each side of the cord a cricket stump had been placed at the usual distance from each other. A tall, thin young man in spectacles was lobbing balls, of which he seemed to have a good supply, from one end, while at the other end a lad of sixteen, wearing wicket-keeper's gloves, was catching those which missed the wicket. 'Catching' is the right word, for no ball struck the ground. Each was projected high up into the air and passed over the cord, descending at a very sharp angle on to the stumps.

The bowler is Tom Spedegue, an asthmatic club cricketer who has developed what he hopes to be the next true innovation in cricket – a slow delivery, sent ultra-high into the air, that with uncanny accuracy drops straight down onto the batsman's bails.

Scougall has never seen anything like it. He gets talking to Spedegue, who outlines his vision:

> . . . it was my ambition to invent an entirely new ball. I am sure it can be done. Look at Bosanquet and the googly. Just by using his brain he thought of and worked out the idea of concealed screw on the ball. I said to myself that Nature had handicapped me with a weak heart, but not with a weak brain, and that I might think out some new thing which was within the compass of my strength. Droppers, I call them. Spedegue's droppers – that's the name they may have some day.

The nod to Bosanquet is revealing. Spedegue is no athlete; his innovation is a feat of the mind. An age-old point arises about spin bowling – the way in which it involves a mental battle, a psychological clash. More than any other aspect of cricket, it is territory where the intellectual can take precedence over the physical. 'The spin bowler,' explained writer and presenter Amol Rajan, 'cannot extricate his opponent by employing sheer power; his weapons are more cerebral than that, based on subtleties and strategies whose execution can only be effective with extensive practice.'

Meanwhile, it just so happens that the England selection committee of Doyle's tale are searching for something that might offer surprise value against the visiting Australians. When they get wind of Spedegue's bizarre methods, they decide – with some reluctance – to give him a go in the test side.

Spedegue's implausible debut begins disastrously, as nerves take over and the Lord's crowd laughs at what looks like the worst selection in history. But once he settles, the Australians crumble in the face of the weird new threat. Endlessly trained in orthodox methods, they just do not know what to do with an approach so far outside their experience:

The splendid Australian batsmen, those active, clear-eyed men who could smile at our fast bowling and make the best of our slow bowlers seem simple, were absolutely at sea. Here was something of which they had never heard, for which they had never prepared, and which was unlike anything in the history of cricket. Spedegue had got his fifty-foot trajectory to a nicety, bowling over the wicket with a marked curve from the leg. Every ball fell on or near the top of the stumps. He was as accurate as a human howitzer pitching shells.

Spedegue ends up with 7 wickets for 31 runs – winning the match for England – before immediately retiring to protect his health. 'His heart would not stand it,' we are told. 'His doctor declared that this one match had been one too many and that he must stand out in the future. But for good or for bad – for bad, as many think – he has left his mark upon the game for ever.'

At its core, Doyle's story is a lighthearted bit of far-fetched comedy. But there is a darker background too, in the form of the First World War; it is the 'great tragedy' that 'broke [Scougall's] heart for games', and ended his playing career. The trauma of war gives what preceded it an aura of unearthly beauty: the notion of a Golden Age is shaped through the prism of nightmare.

The arrival of the Great War desolated the culture of cricket, with the sport – like all other games – abruptly appearing like a distasteful frivolity. To begin with, county matches continued – but The Times stopped printing cricket scores, and there was a widespread perception that cricketing activity was an unfitting indulgence. Young men should be signing up, not playing sport. A few weeks after war began, W. G. Grace declared it unseemly that 'able-bodied men should be playing day by day and pleasure-seekers look on. There are so many who are young and able and are still hanging back.'

It is no surprise that, in the literature of the post-war years, there is a persistent homesickness for the lost ease of a pre-war past. 'No Lord's this year,' wrote poet E. W. Hornung in 1915, a year that would see his son Oscar killed at Ypres. 'No silken lawn on which/A dignified and dainty throng meanders./The Schools take guard upon a fierier pitch/Somewhere in Flanders.'

Hornung, the brother-in-law of Arthur Conan Doyle, had already made his own contribution to cricketing literature some years earlier in the form of the character of Raffles – a gentleman thief, who also manages to be 'a dangerous bat, a brilliant field, and perhaps the very finest slow bowler of his decade'. Effortlessly brilliant cricketer that he is, stealing stuff is where his passions lie: 'What's the satisfaction of taking a man's wicket,' he explains, 'when you want his spoons?' Raffles offers an intriguing connection between cricket and criminality: 'If you can bowl a bit, your low cunning won't get rusty, and always looking for the weak spot's just the kind of mental exercise one wants. Yes, perhaps there's some affinity between the two things after all.' It is no coincidence that spin bowling – that arcane vehicle of guile and deception – is Raffles' particular speciality.

Siegfried Sassoon is another writer-soldier who pursued a cricketing career more eager than distinguished. Playing for a club called the Blue Mantles, he admitted that he was not exactly a nailed-on certainty for selection: 'To be candid, the cricket was a good deal better than I was; but by being always available if someone "chucked" I often obtained a place in the side at the eleventh hour.' His record was a modest one, though it still became a source of pride. Across the 1910 and 1911 seasons, he averaged nineteen with the bat. 'This,' he wrote, 'I consider quite a creditable record for a poet, and I don't mind saying that it gives me fully as much satisfaction as the royalty statements I have received from the publishers of my verse.'

For Sassoon – as for so many – the war obliterated the happiness of rural English life and left horror in its place. In the chilling poems upon which his reputation rests, cricket makes several appearances. In 'The Subaltern', a soldier's young face stirs memories that echo the opening of Newbolt's 'Vitai Lampada':

> He turned to me with his kind, sleepy gaze
> And fresh face slowly brightening to the grin
> That sets my memory back to summer days,
> With twenty runs to make, and last man in.

But the pleasant childhood memory is immediately crushed by the subaltern's account of life on the front line:

> He told me he'd been having a bloody time
> In trenches, crouching for the crumps to burst,
> While squeaking rats scampered across the slime
> And the grey palsied weather did its worst.

Blue summer skies have gone; cricket has been swapped for an inferno of blood, rats and exploding shells. Similarly, in 'Dreamers', soldiers look back on cricketing memories in the search for crumbs of emotional comfort:

> I see them in foul dug-outs, gnawed by rats,
> And in the ruined trenches, lashed with rain,
> Dreaming of things they did with balls and bats,
> And mocked by hopeless longing to regain
> Bank-holidays, and picture shows, and spats,
> And going to the office in the train.

To dream can be to hope; but dreams are also illusions. Cricket, like the other customs of life – holidays, movies, squabbles, even the mundanity of the daily commute – has passed into the realm of the unreal, a freedom never to be felt again.

The game also appears in Sassoon's *Memoirs of a Fox-Hunting Man*, a semi-autobiographical account of early childhood inspired by Sassoon's own upbringing in Kent. It is a story full of affection for a secluded rural life. When the narrator, George Sherston, is picked for the annual village cricket match, it is a landmark event in his childhood – 'To play in it for the first time in my life,' he explains, 'was an outstanding achievement.' The world of English country cricket is a beautiful bubble, shielded from the darker reality of things. 'How little I knew of the enormous world beyond that valley and those low green hills,' he muses on the morning of the game.

And the match itself – with its white-clad players, timeworn umpires, chiming church clock and village flower show – is a light-filled English utopia. When lunchtime arrives, a feast of Hambledon proportions is on offer: 'Slices of lamb and beef, to say nothing of veal and ham pie and a nice bit of gammon of bacon.' And triumph even awaits young Sherston at the end of the game, as he timidly heads out to bat and somehow manages to scramble the winning runs. It is all a delightful dream – the light before shadow. In the book's final chapter, he is sent out to the front. In the closing pages, the barren waste of no man's land denotes a world drained of hope: 'Down in the craters, the dead water took a dull gleam from the sky. I stared at the tangles of wire and the leaning posts, and there seemed no sort of comfort left in life.'

Cricketing stories of the inter-war years tend to harbour this mixture of light and dark. The game's Golden Age had become a lost paradise of pure English bliss, wrecked forever by war. In this sense – a century after Hazlitt, Mitford and Nyren – dreams of Merrie England were once again alive; still just as fondly cherished, and still just as much of a dream.

It led, in places, to fresh bursts of nationalism. Hugh de Sélincourt's *The Cricket Match* (1924), a quaint tale of a Sussex village team, was hailed by J. M. Barrie as 'the best story about cricket or any other game that has ever been written'. And the editor's preface in the first edition was as stoutly patriotic as anything Pycroft managed. 'Cricket,' wrote the editor, 'is the one and only outdoor game which has remained purely English. Today, in nearly every other field of sport, foreign countries compete with us – often very successfully. But cricket is played by the British alone.'

It was – to say the least – a curious claim to make, after a whole half-century of international cricket. But it is a revealing one, too. Once again, we encounter the insistence that this game *belongs*, somehow, to England; the doubtful but passionately held belief that, in understanding cricket, we will somehow be able to understand the essence of Englishness itself.

It is a belief that has been shared by many cricket writers across the ages – including by the greatest cricket writer of all.

16

'He was ever an artist': A Note on Cardus

'He was not only quixotic,' wrote Duncan Hamilton, 'but infinitely complicated, a puzzle unsolvable no matter how long you tried to unpick it. He had worn a mask over a mask, leaving only the bright wicks of his eyes visible beneath it.'

His mother was a prostitute. He never knew his father. His name, Neville, was not actually his name; he was born John Frederick Cardus in 1888, adopting 'Neville' for reasons that he never made clear. There is even some dispute over his date of birth. Neville Cardus, in short, was a constructed self – a self-made man, in more than one sense of the term.

Born in Rusholme – a working-class Manchester suburb, just a couple of miles from Old Trafford – his love for cricket stretched back to early childhood: he was nine years old when he first went to watch Lancashire play. His youth coincided with the heart of cricket's Golden Age. It was an era to which he would often return, glorifying pre-war heroes like Archie MacLaren, Reggie Spooner and Victor Trumper. But Cardus also had a complicated relationship with cricket's passion for nostalgia. 'I have no patience with the man who is constantly saying that cricket is not what it used to be,' he complained. 'The *Golden Age* is always well behind us. We catch sight of it with young eyes, when we see what we want to see.'

He made his name writing for the *Manchester Guardian* and the pieces he crafted were something new – something that went beyond sporting journalism. His aim was not simply to record events and scores. He was not even primarily interested in the accuracy of his descriptions. Over time, he became notorious for distorting and even inventing elements of his stories. Players would be caricatured and given lines they had never spoken; matches he never saw would be recalled as if he had witnessed every ball. There was, in Cardus, a vexed relationship with the truth. 'I am myself,' he once confessed, 'often at a loss to remember if I am accurately reporting an event or a saying.'

To some extent, it has affected his legacy. He has been accused of being a liar and a charlatan. Even the details of his upbringing have been called into question. His Dickensian, rags-to-riches narrative was recast as a bit of dishonest spin, an effort to give some exotic edge to what was actually a comfortable, if not affluent childhood.

It *is* certainly true that Dickens was his favourite author. He would often compare both himself and the people he met to characters from his novels. 'Discovering Dickens is one of the few really important events that occur in mortal life, like first love,' he once claimed. But how we judge Cardus' frequent departures from the literal truth really depends on how we assess the purpose of cricket writing or, indeed, writing in general.

He aspired to write about cricket in a manner that was not just reportage, but something more poetic – even, one might say, philosophical. The specifics of what happened in a game were, at times, less important to him than the act of capturing the essence of a player's character or the mood and meaning of a particular scene. He openly attacked the 'solemn upholders of prosaic fact'. In the virtuoso hands of Cardus, journalistic cricket writing went deeper than the practicalities of factual record – it became, in a very real sense, literature.

Cardus is a colossus in the history of cricket writing. His influence is all-pervading – the effect he had as powerful, in some ways, as the technical revolution of W. G. Grace's batsmanship. As John Arlott put it, 'Cardus was the first writer to evoke cricket; to create a mythology out of the folk hero players . . . There can never be a greater cricket writer than Neville Cardus. He created it. There is not one of his juniors who has not been affected by him.'

He was able to combine his Dickensian eye for character with a Wordsworthian devotion to nature, the rhythms of the seasons, and the unique beauty of an English summer. One memorable piece – 'On a Fresh Cricket Season' – pictures a player in Maytime, pondering the delights of cricketing days ahead:

> It was at Horsham, our cricketer tells himself, he saw the season die last August. How far away did May seem on that afternoon when the sun burned out and he packed the bag for the last time and said 'Goodbye' to his companions! Did he not wish then with all his heart for Maytime back again? Did he not then ask himself why, when the season's beginning was with him, he had not shouted for joy the day long? Well, a spring morning is here for his delight again. Let him hang on to every minute of it, revel in a delighted sense of the time of the year, tell himself over and over: 'I am getting the best out of the day as it passes; I am missing nothing!'

For Cardus, cricket was not simply a sport – it was a way of being fully alive in summer, in England; properly connected to the pulse and patterns of the land.

He wrote almost exclusively about two subjects: cricket and classical music. To some, it seemed a strange combination – high art colliding with the crude vulgarity of sport. But the merit of this fusion went to the very heart of his philosophy on the game. In important ways, Cardus the music critic explains Cardus the cricket writer. 'Music was what he always wanted . . . to write about,' explained publisher and biographer Rupert Hart-Davis. 'Part of him would prefer to repudiate cricket altogether, but before the musician has time to gain the day, his love of the brave humours of the street reasserts itself, and so the strange dichotomy continues.'

Can sport be art? It is a proposition that is not always taken seriously. The two can seem diametrically opposed – the grand profundity of one utterly unlike the rough aggression of the other. Philosopher David Best bluntly dismissed the idea of any overlap: 'Not only do I contend that no sport is an art form . . . I fail to understand why it should be thought that sport would somehow be endowed with greater respectability if it could be shown to be art.' Sure, a sport might *contain* aesthetic properties; but these are not intrinsic to its meaning, which is always more competitive and functional – whether that be scoring a goal, smashing an ace, potting a ball or hitting some runs.

Not everyone, though, has been so scornful. One figure with a very different view was the historian and writer C. L. R. James, who passionately defended the artistic integrity of cricket. The fact that it is a game was, in his eyes, no reason to think otherwise. 'Cricket is an art,' he proposed, 'not a bastard or a poor relation, but a full member of the community . . . It is a game and we have to compare it with other games. It is an art and we have to compare it with other arts.'

This principle was the lifeblood of Cardus' writing. Like music, cricket is an art. It must be treated as such and written about as such. Here, for instance, is Cardus on one of his heroes, Reggie Spooner:

> Spooner's cricket in spirit was kin with sweet music, and the wind that makes long grasses wave, and the singing of Elisabeth Schumann in Johann Strauss, and the poetry of Herrick. Why do we deny the art of a cricketer, and rank it lower than a vocalist's or a fiddler's? If anybody tells me that R. H. Spooner did not compel a pleasure as aesthetic as any compelled by the most cultivated Italian tenor that ever lived I will write him down as a purist and an ass.

It is not enough to say that Spooner's batting contains *some* artistic merit. One must go further. His batting is, in a very real sense, one of the high arts – absolutely the equal of the greatest music and poetry.

As we read through Cardus' stirring portrayals of great cricketers and famous matches, we find the same point made again and again. Another legend of the Golden Age – K. S. Ranjitsinhji – was an artist of the willow, focused not so much on mere run-scoring than on the poetry of batting itself:

> Who cares about the tussle for championship points if a Ranji be glancing to leg? Even the man who wants Surrey to get beaten cannot find it in his heart to complain if Hobbs scores a hundred . . . only the other day, a great batsman in one of our counties, when he was bowled trying to hook an off-ball, explained his failure in these words: 'Well, you simply can't go on hitting off-balls past mid-off. Any fool is able to do that. One gets tired of doing a thing in the easiest way.' The divine discontent of the artist this, surely. Who that has a soul at all, be he bricklayer or maker of sonnets, is happy just moving along the lines of least resistance: had Ranjitsinhji been content with fat scores made in the fashionable way, he could easily have gone on hitting balls from the middle stump straight to long-on. But he was ever an artist, 'tired of doing things in the easiest way', ever seeking to widen the scope of his craft, experimenting, creating obstacles for the sheer fun of overcoming them.

Ranji's inventive grace embodied the way in which the aesthetics of cricket could overpower the cynical requirements of competition. He aimed to score runs, of course; but all the time, he was aiming for something deeper – to generate pieces of art, with every elegant flick of his bat.

Cardus also felt that cricket was uniquely able to bring something out of English people – an appreciation of the beautiful that the English were inclined to suppress:

Go among the shilling crowds any fine day at the Oval and what do you hear? Little technical jargon, little talk of off-breaks and the position of the left funny-bone in the late cut. Instead, you will hear many delighted cries of 'Beautiful stroke – *beautiful!*' Now the same word 'beautiful' is one which average Englishmen are not in the habit of using; it is, indeed, a word they commonly distrust quite as much as they distrust the word 'art'. The truth is we are as a people prone to be ashamed of living the life aesthetic; we see and feel beauty even in our games, but we rarely confess to it. Yet that 'Beautiful!' which a glorious cover drive by Hobbs will bring warmly from our tongues tells the truth; Hobbs is for us an artist.

Cricket, then, has healing potential – even something educational about it. The benefits it brings, though, are not the moral advances claimed by Victorians like Thomas Hughes and James Pycroft, but something drawn from the imagination. Cricket turns the public into art lovers. It opens up a recognition of beauty otherwise hidden beneath the veneer of English reserve.

'A true batsman,' Cardus wrote, 'should in most of his strokes tell the truth about himself.' And the truth, for Cardus, was never anything so prosaic as the simple facts of the matter. It was always something more creative and visionary. Keats' maxim that *beauty is truth, truth beauty* will have made perfect sense to this most supremely gifted of cricket writers. To judge great players by facts and statistics was a mistake; a higher truth was always at play. For Cardus, Victor Trumper 'was an artist-cricketer; let him live again in the mouths of men whenever Test matches are in action'. Wally Hammond 'was an artist of variable moods'. Don Bradman delivered 'something unexpected, mingled with art and beauty'. Above everything else, it was the art of cricket he valued; and without doubt, Cardus himself was an artist.

17

'WHO WATERED THE WICKET IN MELBOURNE?': POST-WAR PROGRESSIONS

'On the Friday morning when Hitler invaded Poland, I chanced to be in the Long Room at Lord's watching through the windows for the last time for years. Though no spectators were present, a match was being continued . . . As I watched the ghostly movements of the players outside, a beautifully preserved member of Lord's, spats and rolled umbrella, stood near me inspecting the game. We did not speak of course; we had not been introduced. Suddenly two workmen entered the Long Room in green aprons and carrying a bag. They took down the bust of W. G. Grace, put it into the bag and departed with it. The noble lord at my side watched their every movement; then he turned to me. "Did you see, sir?" he asked. I told him I had seen. "That means war," he said.'

More than one analyst has questioned the accuracy of this anecdote, which appears in the autobiography of a certain Neville Cardus. Those seeking a Lord's scorecard for 1 September 1939 – the day of Hitler's invasion – will be hard pushed to find it, as no county match actually took place at the ground that day. But there is a spiritual truth to Cardus' story, if not a factual one. Here is W. G., once again, as a totem of England – a weather gauge of national well-being. Removing his bust from the Long Room, at the home of cricket, could only have meant one thing.

When the war began, there was a concerted effort to keep English cricket going amidst darkening skies. There was no chance of a County Championship and not every ground was available.

The Oval, for instance, had been grimly modified into a prisoner-of-war camp (never to be used, in the end), the outfield defaced by an ugly network of barbed-wire containment pens. And so, in place of official county sides, others were formed – a London Counties eleven, for instance, and a British Empire eleven. Some international cricket was even possible; West Indian and Royal Australian Air Force teams both played matches at Lord's in 1943.

And these wartime games were well attended. That same summer, over 200,000 people watched a total of forty-seven fixtures. Cricket was a morale booster as well as a beacon of hope that some form of normality might still be available, both in the moment and into the future. As former England cricket captain Pelham Warner observed, 'I had the feeling that if Goebbels had been able to broadcast that the war had stopped cricket at Lord's it would have been valuable propaganda for the Germans.'

But the horrors of the war ultimately took their dreadful toll. Well over a hundred English first-class cricketers lost their lives. Five England test players were killed – Maurice Turnbull, Kenneth Farnes, Geoffrey Legge, George Macaulay and Hedley Verity. England's premier paceman, Bill Bowes, was a ghost of his former self after three brutal years as a prisoner of war – his body shrunken, his once-fiery bowling reduced to tame medium pace. In the decimated landscape of post-war England, an ache for familiar comforts sat alongside a knowledge that life would never be the same again.

In Harold Pinter's first full-length play, *The Birthday Party* (1957), Stanley Webber – an ill-tempered, down-and-out lodger – has his drab boarding-house life invaded by two sinister strangers, Goldberg and McCann. Or at least, they claim to be strangers. Whether they actually are or not is one of many murky questions in a play teeming with uncertainties. 'There are no hard distinctions between what is real and what is unreal,' Pinter once wrote, 'nor between what is true and what is false. A thing is not necessarily either true or false; it can be both true and false.'

In the famous interrogation scene from the play's middle act, the duo pepper Stanley with a barrage of disjointed questions. In the midst of jibes at his poverty, apostasy and generally pathetic life, an unexpected allusion appears:

GOLDBERG: No society would touch you. Not even a
   building society.
McCANN: You're a traitor to the cloth.
GOLDBERG: What do you use for pyjamas?
STANLEY: Nothing.
GOLDBERG: You verminate the sheet of your birth.
McCANN: What about the Albigensenist heresy?
GOLDBERG: Who watered the wicket in Melbourne?

Who watered the wicket in Melbourne . . . The reference is not explained by Goldberg or anyone else. It seems to have no relevance to anything that surrounds it. And it is, of course, comprehensible only to cricket fans, a fact leading to the sort of comical misunderstanding that seemed always to delight Pinter. As Michael Henderson has noted, it 'was once translated in a German production as, "Who pissed against the city gate?"'

For all its cryptic weirdness, the line's inclusion in *The Birthday Party* signposts Pinter's deep bonds with cricket. His biographer Michael Billington perceptively observed, 'Cricket – the perfect Pinter game in that it combines individual skill with team loyalty – was his prime passion.' The playwright's boyhood memories of the East End, during the blitz, not only paint a stark picture of fear, murdered neighbours and unlit streets, but they also underline his early zeal for the game. In one hair-raising story, the garden of the family home burst into flames after a bomb fell nearby. 'We were evacuated straight away,' he recalled, 'though not before I took my cricket bat.'

In the late sixties Pinter started playing for the Gaieties and would remain the club's loyal stalwart for the rest of his life. Their patriarch, Arthur Wellard – the veteran Kent all-rounder – had played two pre-war tests for England. Famed as a brutal striker of the ball, Wellard had blasted around a quarter of his twelve thousand first-class runs in sixes. For many years, he jointly held the world record for the most sixes in an over, before Garfield Sobers surpassed him in 1968. As a bowler, he amassed over a hundred five-wicket hauls. He was a class act – who would have played far more than just the two tests, had the war not intervened.

Pinter wrote of him warmly as a gifted storyteller by the club bar, charming teammates with yarns about the great players of yesterday:

> What about Larwood, Arthur? How fast was he? Larwood? He was a bit quick, Larwood. Quickest thing I ever saw. First time I faced him was at Trent Bridge, that was my first season with Somerset. Who's this Larwood? I said, supposed to be a bit pacey, is he? I didn't reckon the stories. He's a bit quick, they said. A bit quick? I said. We'll see about that. I'd faced a few quickies in Kent. Well, I went out there and I got four balls from Larwood and I didn't see any of them. The first I knew about them was Ben Lilley throwing them back. The fifth ball knocked my hob over and I didn't see that one either. I'll tell you, he was a bit quick, Harold Larwood.

'Wisden supports this,' Pinter observes – before noting that Wellard was not just a great raconteur, he was a humble one too. 'What Arthur didn't mention was that in the Notts innings we read: H. Larwood b. Wellard o.'

Pinter himself was a decent cricketer rather than a great one. He could be modest about his abilities. 'Arthur was a stern critic of my batting,' he recalled, 'and with good reason. My skills were limited.' Other stories, though, suggest a sharper competitive edge. Actor and director Harry Burton recalled, 'He believed that when you get your opponents down, you should drive them into the dust. Go for the jugular. Finish them off. When he was out in the middle he rarely spoke to an opponent . . . On the sacred field of combat, banter was sacrilege.' Club journeyman he may have been – but for Pinter, cricket was a serious business.

During the war years, a brief stint in Yorkshire sparked two things in Pinter: lifelong support for Yorkshire Country Cricket Club and a devotion to Len Hutton, who became his cricketing hero. In 1969, Pinter penned a piece for the *Telegraph* – initially called 'Memories of Cricket' – that was later republished as 'Hutton and the Past'. Among a range of recollections, it is his idol who gets the highest praise:

Hutton was never dull. His bat was part of his nervous system. His play was sculptured. His forward defensive stroke was a complete statement. The handle of his bat seemed electric. Always, for me, a sense of his vulnerability, of a very uncommon sensibility. He never just went through the motions, nothing was glibly arrived at. He was never, for me, as some have defined him, simply a 'master technician'. He attended to the particular but rarely lost sight of the context in which it took place.

There is something of Cardus in these insights – the focus on Hutton's transcendence of the technical; the way even his defensive strokes expressed the 'complete statement' of the artist-batsman. There was also, perhaps, something about Hutton the man – the first professional ever to captain England – that spoke to Pinter's own working-class Hackney upbringing.

But Hutton also evoked something else – a sense of beautiful days gone by that even Pinter's essay title, 'Hutton and the Past', clearly calls to mind. Pinter has long been established as the archetypal playwright of brooding, post-war menace, offering bleak visions of humanity detached from meaning – what the literary critic Martin Esslin deemed 'a sense of metaphysical anguish at the absurdity of the human condition'. From this stand-point, cricket gave access to something brighter and more orderly.

Like so many cricket writers before him, Pinter saw the game through plangent sunbeams of nostalgia. His oft-quoted, three-line mini-poem – 'I saw Len Hutton in his prime/Another time/Another time' – is a pearl of sentimentality, expressing heartache for lost glory days, a pinnacle of aliveness long gone. 'Cricket . . . reoccurs in his work as an idyllic metaphor,' according to scholar William Baker, 'part of the memory of placid tranquil times.'

There is also, though, a more uneasy edge to cricket in Pinter's work, something darker and more downcast – a sense that, though the splendour of cricket may exist, it exists elsewhere, with an altogether more unpleasant reality in its place.

In *No Man's Land* (1975), he named his characters after four great cricketers of the Golden Age: George Hirst, the Yorkshire all-rounder; Reggie Spooner, the Lancashire batsman so loved by Cardus; Johnny Briggs, the diminutive Lancashire left-arm spinner; and R. E. 'Tip' Foster, who remains the only man ever to captain England at both cricket and football. Foster and Spooner were gentleman amateurs, Hirst and Briggs were professionals. Briggs's life ended tragically – he succumbed to mental illness, was confined to an asylum and died at the age of thirty-nine. But do such details matter in Pinter's play? Are we supposed to find meaningful links between the characters and their cricketing namesakes – or are these just mischievous red herrings?

The play begins with Spooner, an aspiring writer, in the drawing room of Hirst's grand Hampstead house. They have, it seems, met in the pub that night – although it is also possible that they are old friends. Over the course of a disjointed, drunken conversation, Spooner abruptly moves the topic on to their wives:

SPOONER: Tell me then about your wife.
HIRST: What wife?
SPOONER: How beautiful she was how tender and how true.
   Tell me with what speed she swung in the air, with what velocity she came off the wicket, whether she was responsive to

finger spin, whether you could bowl a shooter with her, or an
offbreak with a legbreak action. In other words, did she google?
Silence.
You will not say. I will tell you then . . . that my wife . . .
had everything. Eyes, a mouth, hair, teeth, buttocks,
breasts, absolutely everything. And legs.

Alongside the absurdist comedy of Hirst's wife as a cricket ball,
there is a suggestive overtone. Spooner's shift into lusty thoughts
about his own wife's body makes it even clearer that the images
here are really innuendo. Cricket denotes sex, in a manner that
recalls nothing so much as the frisky cricketing passage from
Joyce's *Finnegans Wake* we saw earlier.

In this light, there is something seedier in Spooner's lines.
They become a string of dirty jibes. His question, 'Did she
google?', takes on a more barbed meaning. Bosanquet's feat of
cricketing deception becomes code for marital infidelity.

Later on in the play, cricket appears again with very different
connotations. Hirst – by now confident that he and Spooner
have, in fact, been chums since their Oxford days – tries to recall
when they had last seen each other:

When did we last meet? I have a suspicion we last dined together
in '38, at the club. Does that accord with your recollection?
Croxley was there, yes, Wyatt, it all comes back to me, Burston-
Smith. What a bunch. What a night, as I recall. All dead now, of
course. No, no! I'm a fool. I'm an idiot. Our last encounter – I
remember it well. Pavilion at Lord's in '39, against the West Indies,
Hutton and Compton batting superbly, Constantine bowling, war
looming. Surely I'm right? We shared a particularly fine bottle of
port. You look as fit now as you did then. Did you have a good war?

Frayed as Hirst's memory might be, the cricketing memory
here is accurate: Hutton scored 196 at Lord's that summer, with

Compton making 120, as England overhauled the tourists by eight wickets. In Hirst's ageing mind, the game represents youth and pleasure-filled days – a pre-war idyll that has cruelly been obliterated. His morbid question, 'Did you have a good war?', lays bare what replaced it. In Pinter, the sunshine of cricket is always viewed from a position of shadow.

He might never have had the cricketing pedigree of his great contemporary, Samuel Beckett, who remains the only Nobel Laureate ever to have played first-class cricket, but Pinter cannot be understood in isolation from the game. 'Lord's was his personal Eden,' explains Michael Henderson, in a moving tribute to his friend. 'He was enchanted by that meadow where, one beautiful evening, he saw Compton make seventy for Middlesex.' Henderson also recounts how, at the end of every season, the Gaieties XI would gather in a London pub to mark the summer's end, and to hear Pinter recite Francis Thompson's 'At Lord's'. Those nostalgia-drenched lines – with their field full of shades, their run-stealers flickering to and fro – sum up Pinter's view of cricket as a vessel of fond dreams. 'I tend to think that cricket is the greatest thing that God ever created on Earth – certainly greater than sex,' he once claimed. 'Although sex isn't too bad either.'

Alongside plays, Pinter also wrote scripts for several films – one of which was an adaptation of L. P. Hartley's 1953 novel *The Go-Between*. And cricket has an important role in Hartley's tale of ruined childhood innocence. Beginning as it does with the ageing Leo Colston stumbling on his old diary and summoning long-buried ghosts, it is a novel that casts its gaze on both past and present – the snobbery and class conflict of the late Victorian age, and also the traumatised reality of the mid-twentieth century, scarred and wrecked by war.

The story follows Leo's memories of summer as a twelve-year-old boy, in the year 1900, at Brandham Hall, the estate of his wealthy schoolfriend. One pivotal scene involves a cricket match between the hall and the local village. Hartley uses it as an opportunity to probe English class divisions. To begin with, young Leo – called into the squad at the last minute – believes that cricketing team spirit dissolves the boundaries of class:

> I remember walking to the cricket ground with our team, sometimes trying to feel, and sometimes trying not to feel, that I was one of them; and the conviction I had, which comes so quickly to a boy, that nothing in the world mattered except that we should win. I remember how class distinctions melted away and how the butler, the footman, the coachman, the gardener, and the pantry boy seemed completely on an equality with us, and I remember having a sixth sense that enabled me to fore-tell, with some accuracy, how each of them would shape.

It is a rehearsal of a typical Victorian argument. Far from being elitist, or divided, a cricket team is a democratising force. The burdens of class and social roles all 'melt away'. Only the needs of the team matter. But despite his youth, Leo works out that this is far from a true picture – just another Victorian cricketing fiction, in fact, hiding a more complex reality. Class division permeates the hall-versus-locals game.* Mr Maudsley – the infirm lord of the

---

* A similar point about class snobbery is made in *Maurice*, by E. M. Forster – his tragic tale of same-sex love at the beginning of the twentieth century. Written in 1913, Forster never dared to publish the novel during his life, which appeared posthumously in 1971. In the closing chapters, protagonist Maurice Hall – staying at the estate of his friend, and former lover, Clive Durham – is approached by the valet with a cricketing request:

> 'Sir, in Mr Durham's absence the servants feel – we should be so honoured if you should captain us against the Village in the forthcoming Park versus Village match.'
> 'I'm not a cricketer, Simcox. Who's your best bat?'
> 'We have no one better than the under gamekeeper.'
> 'Then make the under gamekeeper captain.'
> Simcox lingered to say, 'Things always go better under a gentleman.'

manor – scratches his way towards a cautious half-century. It is an innings that does not appeal to Leo. 'It wasn't cricket,' he explains, 'that an elderly gnome-like individual with a stringy neck and creaking joints should, by dint of head-work and superior cunning, reverse the proverb that youth will be served. It was an ascendancy of brain over brawn, of which, like a true Englishman, I felt suspicious.'

The association of Englishness with strength and vitality is interesting – recalling, as it does, the age-old notion of cricket as a manly enterprise. And in this match, the muscle comes from local farmer Ted Burgess – who, it just so happens, is conducting a secret affair with Maudsley's daughter. Ted's innings for the village is a much more aggressive spectacle:

It was a very different half-century from Mr Maudsley's, a triumph of luck, not of cunning, for the will, and even the wish to win seemed absent from it. Dimly I felt that the contrast represented something more than the conflict between Hall and village. It was that, but it was also a struggle between order and lawlessness, between obedience to tradition and defiance of it, between social stability and revolution, between one attitude to life and another.

In Leo's mind, the two innings become emblems for competing modes of being. Maudsley's tame, weakly nurdling evokes the stability of tradition and the preservation of the social order. In contrast, Ted's mighty thumps to all corners of the ground express defiance, subversion and a revolutionary spirit.

It is a class battle – between 'tenant and landlord, commoner and peer', as Leo puts it – but it is also something deeper. On this apparently peaceful English green, a kind of existential struggle plays itself out – a war between the forces of order and chaos. And Leo – called onto the field as a substitute – inadvertently decides it. With 'a pang of regret, sharp as a sword-thrust', he takes a diving catch to end Ted's innings and win the match for the hall.

In the end, hierarchies are preserved. The revolutionary spirit is crushed. It is an ominous sign for Ted, whose heretical affair with a woman above his station will lead him, in the end, to disaster.

In one way or another, cricket tends to appear in post-war fiction alongside transgression – as a game of disciplined English conduct, against which sins and indiscretions stand out. In Iris Murdoch's *The Sandcastle* (1957), married schoolmaster Bill Mor – a temperate and inhibited character – has his world shaken up by the free-spirited Rain Carter, a visiting artist at the school. In one scene, the sedate backdrop of a house cricket match is infected by rumours about their affair. Mor's son, Donald – aware of the liaison – is batting; his best friend, Jimmy Carde, is bowling. And when Rain suddenly appears on the boundary, Carde cannot resist a bit of teasing banter:

'Your pappa's poppet!' he said – and he went away down the pitch and whistling 'A nice girl, a decent girl, but one of the rakish kind' and tossing the ball rhythmically up and down.

Unsurprisingly, Donald is rattled. The next ball uproots his middle stump.

Kingsley Amis's novel, *Take a Girl Like You*, also features a schoolmaster – although Patrick Stanforth is a very different character, a sleazy libertine ruled by lust. Amis's comic gifts do not prevent the novel from making an unsettling read. Jenny Bunn – a young and pretty primary-school teacher – endures constant sexual advances from more or less every man she meets. Trapped in a wasps' nest of male desire, her efforts to protect her honour are doomed. In one scene, Patrick invites her to a cricket match at his school. It is a staid backdrop, against which Patrick's seedy personality bubbles to the surface. 'I hit him for two fours in his first over,' he boasts. 'Pity you weren't here to see that. Right off the middle of the bat to the mid-off boundary, same place each time. As good as sex. Sorry. And it wasn't really.' Published in 1960, on the cusp of the sexual revolution, the novel charts the collapse of traditional sexual morality in a modern world of transformed expectations.

Elsewhere in post-war cricketing literature, though, it is an ache for the past that prevails. Perhaps the most famous cricket poem, from this era, is 'Eighty-Five to Win' – a two-hundred-line epic by John Masefield, poet laureate for over thirty years until his death in 1967. It commemorates the Australians' victory at the Oval in 1882 – the match that precipitated the birth of the Ashes. In the opening lines, Masefield presents the Oval ground as a bridge between past and present:

> Though wayward Time be changeful as Man's will,
> We have the game, we have the Oval still,
> And still the Gas-Works mark the Gas-Works End
> And still our sun shines and the rains descend.

The famous gasholders – the first of which was built in the 1840s – become a sign of permanence in a turbulent world. Time might be 'wayward' and 'changeful' and the modern world might be impossible to predict, but cricket offers stability – a comforting sense that, somewhere at least, the flame of the past remains alive, and traditions can be kept safe.

In the final lines, the match is over, and time is moving on. It is only in memory – in the imagination – that the extraordinary events of that day in August 1882 will endure:

> A thunder muttered and a shower fell
> As twilight came with star and Vesper-bell.
> Over the Oval, stamped where Spofforth bowled,
> Reviving grass-blades lifted from the mould.

From Spofforth's footprint in the English soil, a new dimension of cricketing history begins to grow. Eric Midwinter called the poem 'an estimable try . . . at what has perplexed many a poet – producing a Homeric description of a sporting event.'

The perhaps surprising links between cricket and sex were

explored by a number of post-war writers. In *A Season in Sinji* (1967), novelist J. L. Carr – a lifelong cricket lover, who continued playing the game until the age of sixty-seven – told a story of sexual jealousy in which a trio of Royal Air Force cricketers compete for the same woman. In his memoir *Shadows on the Grass*, Simon Raven offered up a scandalously louche cocktail of cricket, sex and booze. And a particularly mischievous vision of cricket's past was conjured by George MacDonald Fraser – who, in his Flashman novels, gave new life to the vicious bully of *Tom Brown's Schooldays*. The novels are framed as Flashman's memoirs, detailing his life as a roistering womaniser and decadent scoundrel throughout the middle of the nineteenth century. In the opening pages of *Flashman's Lady*, a chance alehouse encounter with a certain Tom Brown leads to an improbable opportunity. Flashman is invited to play at Lord's – for a Rugby School 'past and present' eleven against an all-star Kent team.

Flashman's personal musings, about the 'good old sporting days' of his youth, are a delicious parody of traditional cricketing nostalgia. The bright canvas of village-green rural life is perfectly evoked, but with a sting in the tail:

> . . . I see it late in the morning sun, the players in their white top-hats trooping in from the field, with the ripple of applause running round the ropes, and the urchins streaming across to worship, while the old buffers outside the pavilion clap and cry 'Played, well played!' and raise their tankards, and the captain tosses the ball to some round-eyed small boy who'll guard it as a relic for life, and the scorer climbs stiffly down from his eyrie and the shadows lengthen across the idyllic scene, the very picture of merry, sporting old England, with the umpires bundling up the stumps, the birds calling in the tall trees, the gentle even fall stealing over the ground and the pavilion, and the empty benches, and the willow wood-pile behind the sheep pen where Flashy is plunging away on top of the landlord's daughter in the long grass. Aye, cricket was cricket then.

Recast as the setting for Flashman's randy antics, the old vision of Merrie England is drily skewered. Flashman is the incarnated subversion of Victorian moral bombast – the embodiment of cricketing anti-nobility. 'It may strike you,' he confesses, 'that old Flashy's approach to our great summer game wasn't quite that of your school-storybook hero . . . No, not exactly: personal glory and cheap wickets however you could get 'em, and d—n the honour of the side, that was my style, with a few quid picked up in side-bets, and plenty of skirt-chasing afterwards.' The pious Tom Brown swiftly regrets bringing such a rascal into his team. But it pays surprising dividends. Brought on to bowl his 'expresses', he somehow manages to claim the wickets of three Kentish legends – 'Felix', Fuller Pilch and Alfred Mynn – in three successive balls. According to this account, one need look no further for the first hat-trick in cricket history – Flashman was its author. 'That trick's worth a new hat any day, youngster,' Mynn says to him after the game, solemnly presenting him with a boater.

This sort of playfulness towards English cricketing history was given a more surreal edge by Douglas Adams in *Life, the Universe, and Everything* – the third book in his *Hitchhiker's Guide to the Galaxy* series. In the opening pages, Adams' hapless hero Arthur Dent is transported back to Earth through a space-time anomaly – ending up, of all places, at Lord's. Dent – who, in the first book of the series, had seen Earth destroyed to make way for an intergalactic bypass – is initially thrilled by his unlikely arrival back at the home of cricket. 'Tea,' he said, 'cricket,' he added with pleasure, 'mown grass, wooden benches, white linen jackets, beer cans . . .'

But the peaceful scene is swiftly spoiled by a gang of murderous robots – from the planet Krikkit – who arrive wielding cricket bats and lobbing lethal cricket-ball grenades in order to steal away the Ashes. It is hard to work out whether the ensuing story – which follows the Krikkiters' plans to collect stumps and bails for the 'Wikkit Gate' that they need to destroy the universe – is a fond homage to cricket or a send-up. Adams, after all, confessed, 'I am not a great cricket fan. I just came across an article about the history of the Ashes – a cricket stump which was burnt in Melbourne in 1882. I happened to read it in a daydreamy mood and it went from there. There was no deep significance to it.'

With regard to post-war cricketing visual art, there is little to match the work of David Inshaw. A founding member of what became known as the Brotherhood of Ruralists, Inshaw – along with contemporaries such as Peter Blake, Jann Haworth and Graham Ovenden – aimed to push against conceptual and abstract artistic trends in favour of a more traditional, representational approach. 'Our aims,' explained Peter Blake, 'are the continuation of a certain kind of English painting. We admire Samuel Palmer, Stanley Spencer, Thomas Hardy, Elgar, cricket, the English landscape and the Pre-Raphaelites.'

The presence of cricket in Blake's list of artistic influences is interesting – suggesting, as it does, that the game was not merely something the Ruralists enjoyed, but a source of artistic inspiration. And Inshaw turned to the subject of cricket on several occasions. The most famous of these is *The Cricket Game* (1976):

A batsman plays what looks like a glorious cover drive as the fielding side watches on. But it is nature, really, that dominates the image. The cricketers are dwarfed by the surrounding landscape – a verdant blend of trees, rolling hills and lush green grass. Inshaw has always cited Thomas Hardy as a key inspiration. He once said that 'it was Hardy's use of nature and landscape as a metaphor for human emotion that struck a deep chord, and gave me an insight into how I could develop my own work'. And his cricketers notably recall the opening of Hardy's *The Return of the Native*, where tiny human characters traverse the vast, brooding expanse of Egdon Heath. 'The sea changed, the fields changed, the rivers, the villages, and the people changed, yet Egdon remained.' Inshaw's painting expresses a similar point about human transience, and nature's timeless power.

The image also has an elegiac feel. The sun – a blur of warm yellow in the right of the sky – is about to disappear below the horizon. Long shadows stretch across the land, covering much of the outfield. It is evening time – close to the end of the day's play. And alongside the serenity of the scene, an element of tension is evident in the cricketing action. The field is aggressive, with plenty of close fielders – two slips, a leg slip, a silly mid-off, a silly mid-on. If we look closely, too, there is drama to be found in that perfect-looking cover drive, which is not all that it seems. Where is the ball, precisely? It is visible – just about – in front of the wicketkeeper's gloves. It may *look* like a magnificent stroke – the aesthetic centrepiece of the image – but in fact, the batsman has missed it. Perhaps he has even edged it, and we are witnessing the keeper taking a crucial catch, winning the game for the fielding side in the quickly fading light.

Robert Sandelson, former director of the British Art Fair, has noted how the painting 'evokes the soft, early evening light and the fullness of high summer; we feel the perfection of cricket in the landscape'. And with its quietly dramatic action and grand backdrop of English green, the image communicates something powerful about the passage of time and our relationship with the natural world. 'It is the moment held in time,' as Inshaw said of his most famous work, *The Badminton Game*, 'as if you are aware of before and after, as if a film had stopped on a single frame, and you are aware, in that instant, of the emotion of all time.'

Inshaw's paintings are a significant entry in the history of cricketing art. Charged as they are with a mysterious, often sensual energy, they mark him out as something more than a landscape painter in a straightforward sense. Alongside the realism there is always something more dreamlike – some element of the transcendent or the uncanny. Writer and critic Andrew Lambirth has observed, 'Although Inshaw takes nature as his starting point, he is far from a slavish copier of it: he translates and transforms, and at his most successful, he transfigures.' A particular kind of England is evoked in Inshaw's work, an old England of spells, enchantments and charms – a landscape filled with a sense of the numinous, a feeling of magic and wonder.

VI
CRICKET ACROSS THE ARTS

That question posed by Cardus – Why do we deny the art of a cricketer and rank it lower than a vocalist's or a fiddler's? – *is the kind of question that also, in turn, raises others . . .*

Is it possible, for instance, to see something musical *about cricket – about the art of batting, say, or the rhythmical action of a fast bowler? If cricket really is an art, what connections, exactly, might it have to other arts – whether that be music, painting, theatre or dance?*

In the summer of 2001, Mark Butcher was not supposed to have been playing for England. 'The whole thing was an accident, more than anything else,' he later said. 'I only got picked in the squad because everybody else was injured.' Drafted in at the last minute for the first test, he wasn't even able to turn up for training on time; with no thought of being selected, he had arranged to move flats that day. Expectations – against one of the great Australian sides – were low.

Butcher, though, found some form that summer. He scored 38 and 41 in the first test – nothing special, but enough to keep his place. In the second test, his innings of 83 was England's highest score. His team may have been in the process of being dismantled – but Butcher himself was looking like a shrewd pick. His career was granted a surprise new lease of life.

The wheels almost came off when England slumped to a series defeat at Trent Bridge and Butcher, after a poor game, drowned his sorrows in a night of heavy boozing. Head coach Duncan Fletcher was unimpressed. He was almost dropped, but senior players backed him and he remained in the team for the fourth test at Edgbaston where, on the last day, England had been set 315 to win.

The innings of 173 not out that Butcher played that day remains a piece of cricketing art – one of the most inspired in the history of English cricket.

On an uneven pitch – against Glenn McGrath, Jason Gillespie, Brett Lee and Shane Warne – batting was far from easy. At first, these eminent Australian bowlers were survived; but then, as Butcher found his touch, they were imperiously dismissed. Runs seemed to flow from his bat in an endless sequence of succulent cover drives. It was an otherworldly performance, all poise and fluent grace – the innings unfolding with the inevitability of a perfectly crafted musical composition.

And it was music that Butcher turned to, once his cricket career was over – carving out a new calling as a guitarist, vocalist and singer-songwriter. He has always been keen to draw a line between his musical and sporting pursuits. 'It's separate from my life in cricket,' he explained. 'I've always kept it that way. There's no correlation between one and the other.'

But not everyone would agree. Jazz musician Charles Mingus once said, 'Making the simple complicated is commonplace; making the complicated simple, awesomely simple, that's creativity.' Just maybe, that day in 2001, Butcher really was a kind of musician – making everything he did look so simple, plucking perfect pulls and flicks and cover drives out of the air like some sequence of haunting, beautiful chords . . .

18

'Hello . . . you in London . . . name's Charters': Cricket in Film and Television

The year of 1895 was W.G. Grace's Indian summer – the great, late flowering of his genius. He would turn forty-seven and many believed, with some justice, that his best days were behind him. The lithe shape of his youth had long been traded for something distinctly plumper. The previous year, his batting average had been below thirty, and in two consecutive recent English summers – 1891 and 1892 – he had failed to score a single century. Grace was starting to look like a declining force, an ageing master whose light was beginning to dim.

But that year, he produced something magical. Amidst the cold weather and green tops of the early season, he became the first batsman ever to score a thousand runs before the end of May – amassing four centuries, including two double hundreds. His score of 288 against Gloucestershire – his highest for nearly two decades – was also his hundredth hundred, a pioneering feat in the game's history. No other batsman had ever scored even half that many.

The great man had secured his reputation long before. This, though, was something else – proof of divinity, from a man approaching his fiftieth birthday.

But this era-defining year in English cricket was also an era-defining year in the history of British film. Photographer Birt Acres and electrician Robert W. Paul had been collaborating on a new piece of equipment – the 'Paul–Acres camera' – the very first, in Britain, to use 35mm film. And in February 1895 – outside Acres' home in Chipping Barnet – the duo made their own piece of history.

The test film was titled *Incident Outside Clovelly Cottage*. The full plot is not known. Only a few frames of the project remain. There is a woman, in bonnet and black dress, pushing a pram past a front door. And there is a man, dressed in a cap and all in white; when he first appears, he is clambering over the porch banister, before the fragment cuts to him walking away past the front window. The actor is believed to be camera operator Harry Short, a friend of Paul's. And there is something familiar about those all-white clothes . . .

. . . here, in the earliest film ever made in England, is a man dressed in cricket whites.

What a thing to find at the very birth of this new art form, in these blurred, broken glimpses into late Victorian suburbia. Later that year, Edward Lawson – organiser of Grace's testimonials – would extol 'those out-of-door sports and pursuits, which – free from any element of cruelty, greed or coarseness – most and best develop out British traits of manliness, good temper, fair play, and the healthy training of mind and body.' And here cricket sits, the crown jewel of Victorian character-building sport, centre stage at the dawn of a new creative outlet for the English imagination.

Harry Short may well have been wearing cricket whites for purely practical purposes, because the bright clothes would show up better. But the aptness of the link is hard to shift. A rich relationship, between film and English cricket, would blossom over the years to follow.

Alfred Hitchcock's 1938 movie, *The Lady Vanishes* – a heady brew of melodrama, mystery thriller and slapstick comedy – has received abundant accolades over the years. According to film critic Philip French, it is 'one of the greatest train movies from the genre's golden era, challenged only in the master's oeuvre by

North By Northwest for the title of best comedy thriller ever made'. Legendary director Francois Truffaut admired the film for its 'first-rate screenplay'. Another of its attributes has, though, been given less attention: it was one of the first movies to offer a significant role to the game of cricket.

The opening scenes present two dapper English gentlemen – Charters and Caldicott – marooned in a hotel on the continent. They are desperate to get back home, though the reason is not initially clear. It is only when Charters grabs a hotel phone – with an open line to London – that we learn the cause of their urgency:

> CHARTERS: Hello? Hello . . . you in London . . . name's
> Charters. I don't suppose you know me. Well, you needn't
> worry . . . Tell me . . . what's happening to England? . . .
> Blowing a gale? No, you don't follow me, sir. I'm enquiring
> about the test match in Manchester. Cricket, sir,
> cricket! . . . What, you *don't know*? You can't be in England
> and not know the test score . . . [to CALDICOTT] Fellow
> says he doesn't know.
> CALDICOTT: Course he does.
> CHARTERS: Hello, can't you find out? Nonsense, it won't
> take a second. Well, if you won't, you won't!

'Wasting my time,' he mutters, after slamming down the receiver. 'The fellow's an ignoramus.' Charters and Caldicott are cricket nuts – and they have tickets for the Old Trafford test match.

The duo's obsession is a running joke throughout the film. 'Nothing but baseball,' Caldicott complains, as they scan a copy of the *Herald Tribune*. 'You know. We used to call it rounders. Children play it, with a rubber ball and a stick. Not a word about cricket. Americans have got no sense of proportion.'

At the train station, Charters thoughtfully inspects the skies. 'I hope the weather's like this in Manchester,' he muses. 'Perfect wicket for our fellows.'

Later, in the restaurant car, he grabs some sugar cubes in order to illustrate a point. 'There's nothing moot about it, it simply wasn't out, that's all. But for the umpire's blunder, he'd probably still be batting,' he grumbles, before snatching the sugar bowl. 'I'll show you: look here. I saw the whole thing. Now then, there's Hammond, there's the bowler, there's the umpire.' Disaster strikes when a fellow passenger asks for the sugar.

The two characters embody a long-standing association between cricket and English gentlemanliness. Charters – an Oxford man – sports a bow tie for much of the film and frequently puffs a pipe. Both are fond of tweed jackets. Early in the film, their modesty is comically put to the test when they are forced to share a room with the hotel maid. In short, they are carica-tures of a particular kind of English traditionalism with which cricket was clearly deemed a perfect fit. 'I should challenge the Englishness of any man,' wrote Cardus, 'who could walk down a country lane, come unexpectedly on a cricket match, and not lean over the fence and watch for a while.' Charters and Caldicott are English archetypes; as such, it is only right that their passion is for cricket.

Another of their John Bull traits is a healthy dose of stiff upper lip. In the film's final act, when the train comes under attack from gangsters, the duo respond with preternatural calm – as if they have been asked to help out with the dishes – while grabbing hold of guns and firing away at the enemy. 'We'll never get to the match now,' Caldicott evenly reflects, as their carriage is blasted with gunshots. In the final minutes, it seems – for a moment – like all their concerns about missing the cricket were groundless. With the baddies defeated, their train arrives at last in London. 'Ample time to catch the 6.50 to Manchester after all,' Charters notes with a smile, before their faces suddenly drop. A newspaper seller wields a placard with shattering news: TEST MATCH ABANDONED. FLOODS.

This link between cricket and English character is taken further in *The Final Test* (1953) – one of the few films, in cinema history, to take cricket as its central subject. Scripted by Terence Rattigan, the story revolves around an ageing cricketer – Sam Palmer – who is playing his last game for England. A string of England legends – including Len Hutton, Denis Compton, Alec Bedser and Jim Laker – make cameo appearances that amply demonstrate how cricketing talent does not automatically translate into acting. Actual test footage is spliced into the mid-match scenes, with John Arlott providing the commentary. And from the opening credits – which appear on a backdrop of Three Lions crests – a patriotic mood is set.

The film begins with an American visitor, Senator Baumbacher, arriving in London with one aim in mind – to learn more about the 'British way of life'. Within moments, he is baffled by bleak headlines greeting him in the newspaper stands – LITTLE HOPE FOR ENGLAND, ENGLAND MAY COLLAPSE TODAY. 'Well . . .' he sighs, frowning and shaking his head. It is with some relief that he hears a more cheerful view from a station porter, in conversation with a taxi driver:

PORTER: Well, I don't know, I still think England have got a sort of a chance.
SENATOR [approaching]: Ah, thank heaven, you at least have not been bitten by this bug of defeatism.
PORTER: I beg your pardon, sir?
SENATOR: You said, you still think that England have a chance?
PORTER: Oh well, if it doesn't rain, I think we'll pull through.
SENATOR: Ah, you mean the harvest?
PORTER: No, sir, I mean the Oval wicket. We've 560 odd runs to make in the first innings.
SENATOR: Be so good, sir, as to inform me what the blazes you're talking about?

The cabbie steps in to help. 'Cricket, guv'nor,' he clarifies. 'The final test. England versus Australia at the Oval.'

It is an explanation that shocks the senator. 'Cricket,' he replies in amazement. 'Now that is illuminating. I've heard these stories about the passionate excitement cricket arouses over here, but I never did realise it could drive a grave financial crisis off the national headlines.' But as the porter points out, a financial crisis is nothing compared to the drama of an Ashes test. 'You see,' he explains, 'since the war we've had quite a few of these financial crises. One a year on average. And we only get the Aussies over here once in four.'

Detecting a perfect opportunity to learn more about the British way of life, the senator promptly heads off to the Oval – only to find his confusion deepening once he arrives.

'Going to be an exciting day?' he asks the spectator in the next seat.

'I hope not,' is the peevish reply. 'All I want is to see the boys piling up the runs quietly and not getting out. I don't want any *excitement*, thanks.'

In *The Lady Vanishes*, cricket is wedded to a firmly public-school, gentlemanly tradition. But in *The Final Test*, the game is shown to have a much broader social appeal. A number of scenes take place in the local pub – where groups of patrons, under the care of Cora the barmaid, gather round the radio to listen to the action. Here is cricket, in the English imagination, as a game of the people – bringing together fans from all walks of life, in a society where class divisions are still deeply felt.

The post-war years were the final throes of the amateur/professional distinction. The annual 'Gentlemen v. Players' fixture would remain in place until 1963. When the match was finally abolished, some traditionalists – such as E. W. Swanton – were sad to see it go, but to many others, like Fred Trueman, it was long overdue. 'I was all for the abolition of amateurs,' he wrote in his memoirs. 'It meant there would be no more, "Sir" or "Call me Mister so-and-so". No more "fancy caps". We were now all of the same cricketing flesh and blood and no one was afforded privileges based on their status.'

The lingering social tensions of status and class conflict play a significant role in *The Final Test*. Palmer himself is a working-class professional made good. Romantically involved with Cora, he worries that she might seem too common in the eyes of his son, Reggie – who has been privately educated and is aspiring to Oxford. But there is a more pressing problem. Reggie – girlish, literary and obsessed with writing poetry – has no interest whatsoever in cricket.

The main story revolves round Reggie choosing to visit an eminent poet, Alexander Whitehead, rather than watch his dad playing his last-ever game. It leads to a central irony that dominates the film's final section: Whitehead turns out to be a cricket obsessive, whose number-one hero is Sam Palmer. When Reggie reveals that he has come all the way to visit him instead of taking his seat at the Oval, Whitehead reacts with astonishment. 'More important to see *me*?' he gasps. 'Are you out of your senses?'

Off they rush to catch the rest of the day's play. And on the way, Whitehead – driving with the speed of a man who has a cricket match to reach – is hostile to his companion's talk of poetry. 'Tell me, Mr Whitehead, do you prefer Keats to Wordsworth?' Reggie hopefully asks, only to be met with a brusque reply: 'My dear boy, you mustn't expect me to talk about literature when there's a test match on. My brain doesn't function properly. Ask me if I prefer your father to Don Bradman, and I'll give you the answer.' A distinctly Cardus-esque philosophy is endorsed. The distinction between cricket and high art – at first so clear – is exposed as a delusion. 'Great artist, your father,' claims Whitehead, to Reggie's disbelief.

It is perhaps no coincidence that both *The Lady Vanishes* and *The Final Test* are comedies at heart. The codes, traditions and eccentricities of cricket offer a perfect opportunity to send up

ECHOING GREENS

English manners. The game has also featured in a string of popular sitcoms over the years. As writer Jon Hotten has observed, cricket 'fits the format perfectly because it can be used so easily to reveal character and also as a metaphor for class, which is – or at least was – the subject of most sitcoms'.

One episode from the fourth season of *Dad's Army*, first broadcast in 1970, saw Captain Mainwaring's men play a cricket match against a team of air raid protection wardens. Preparations unfold in a barrage of slapstick, satire and creaky innuendo. Mainwaring himself – after claiming to be a 'passable opening bat' – leads a disastrous net practice session. Wicketkeeping duties are claimed by the geriatric Lance Corporal Jones, who recalls, 'Do you know, I once kept wicket in the rear of the great Ranjitsinhji, sir? He was a fine cricketer, sir. An Indian gentleman, sir. He was a fine, upstanding man till I whipped his bails off.'

As always with *Dad's Army*, the levity of the script provides a counterpoint to the wartime backdrop. 'Well, it will be good to hear willow striking leather again, Wilson,' says Mainwaring philosophically, as his team take the field. 'We are walking out here as free men to play a friendly British game. That's what we are fighting for, you know.' Wilson's response is typically sardonic: 'Yes, of course sir. Yes, yes. Amongst other things.' The comically inept Home Guard team look destined for defeat, until an injury to the opposition star bowler – a cameo turn from Fred Trueman – allows them to scrabble an improbable one-wicket win. But as they celebrate in the closing moments, a reminder of a darker world surfaces – the blaring of air-raid sirens. 'Here they come again,' says Mainwaring, looking wearily to the skies. 'Right, men. Get to your posts as quickly as you can.'

Trueman was delighted to appear in what he described as 'one of the all-time great sitcoms', seeing the opportunity as one of the 'great bonuses' of fame. '*Dad's Army* was a very British pleasure,' he explained in his memoirs, 'depicting a simple, fresh and innocent Britain that did once exist.'

Elsewhere in British sitcom history, though, it is a motley crew of characters who speak up for cricket. The Major in *Fawlty Towers* is both one of the most memorable and most controversial of all TV cricket fans – his lacing of cricketing references ('Evening, Fawlty! Hampshire won') with flashes of casual racism leading to the cancellation of repeat showings. In one episode of *In Sickness and in Health*, xenophobic crank Alf Garnett rages at the television during an England v. Pakistan test match, screaming violent cheers at Ian Botham ('Go on, whack him one, go on! Go on, Ian, clout him!').

Perhaps the most anarchic use of cricket in sitcom history came in a 1984 episode of *The Young Ones* – when the characters, bored out of their minds on the summer break, decide to play a game inside their flat. Rick – played by Rik Mayall – is forced to play as the stumps. Unhinged punk maniac Vyvyan is swiftly judged to be the winner, after smacking Rick on the head with the ball. 'What's my prize?' he asks. The answer, of course is the Ashes: 'All you've got to do is burn the stumps, and they're yours.' Vyv promptly pulls out a matchbox and sets Rick on fire. It would be hard to imagine a purer subversion of cricket's aspirations towards refinement and good taste.

The Monty Python team turned their madcap attention to cricket several times, aiming similarly savage digs at the old moral claims of Victorian England. One sketch begins with Graham Chapman posing as a reporter outside Lord's. 'The headquarters of these urban idiots is here, in St John's Wood,' he explains. 'Inside, they can enjoy the company of other idiots, and watch special performances of ritual idioting.' John Cleese provides the commentary from a desk crammed with bottles of booze. Cricket's slowness is ridiculed: 'So far today we have had five hours' batting from England and already they are nought for nought.' The sketch culminates with the players being replaced with bits of furniture and household equipment. 'Now, the green chesterfield has taken guard and, ah, Iceland are putting on their spin-dryer to bowl,' observes Cleese. 'The spin-dryer moving back to its mark . . . it runs up to the wicket . . . bowls to the table . . . a little bit short, but it's coming in a bit there and it's hit him on the pad! There's an appeal and the table is out, leg before wicket! That is England out for one!'

A rather more poignant cricketing tale was told in *Ever Decreasing Circles*. The sitcom was one of the most popular to emerge in the mid-1980s, and followed the plight of uptight, obsessive Martin Bryce, played by Richard Briers, and the ongoing envy he directed towards charismatic neighbour Paul, played by Peter Egan. In 'The Cricket Match', from series two, Martin – captain of the local team – is desperate to avoid picking Paul, a former Cambridge Blue, but ultimately has no choice after a last-minute injury. There is a current of sadness – what Hotten has perceptively called a 'quiet, unacknowledged and deep-running despair' – in the way Martin helplessly watches Paul amass a brilliant, match-winning century. 'It was the most beautiful innings I have ever seen in my life,' he confesses afterwards in a trembling voice. 'I would give anything to play an innings like that, just once.' His wife has little comfort to offer beyond asking, 'Would you like a packet of crisps?'

Ever Decreasing Circles was one of a string of British sitcoms to take the petty politics of middle England as its focus; but screenwriter and playwright Richard Harris's *Outside Edge*, running for three series in the mid-nineties, was the only show to revolve around a cricket team. An adaptation of Harris's stage play, first performed in 1979, the tone is set from the first episode's opening shot – zooming in, as it does, on a ring of identical redbrick houses in a suburban cul-de-sac. Waking up in one of them is Roger Dervish – captain of the Brent Park eleven. The initial bedroom scene appears, at first, to be a picture of romantic intimacy – perhaps even erotic promise. 'What are you thinking?' says wife Miriam seductively, giggling and giving her husband a cuddle. Roger, though, has other things on his mind. 'I'm thinking that, in six hours from now, I shall be leading my team against the strongest line-up in West Surrey. I'm thinking that, last year, I scored thirty-seven not out against the buggers.'

Roger (played by Robert Daws) treats Miriam (played by Brenda Blethyn) with a nightmarish level of chauvinist disdain. While she irons his whites in the kitchen, he practises outside among the garden gnomes, all of whom are decorated in full cricket gear. He snipes at her constantly, blaming her for every new setback: as a representative of English village cricket, he is a nasty piece of work. Diffident and long-suffering, Miriam does everything for him – packing the boot of the car while he studies notes for the game, and even fastening his seat belt. It is something of a relief when the feisty Maggie Costello – played by Josie Lawrence – encourages her to rebel.

Outside Edge places cricket in the culture of middle-class, suburban English life that has been a rich vehicle for comedy over the years – by turns cosy, comfortable, banal and small-minded. But it is not the only setting in which cricket has reared its head. *The Shout* (1978), directed by Jerzy Skolimowski, is a strange, dream-like horror movie featuring an impressive cast that includes John Hurt, Tim Curry, Susannah York and Alan Bates. Set in the gardens of a lunatic asylum, it features a team of patients playing against the local village – the peaceful English green backdrop, and cricket's mood of quiet decorum, disturbingly assailed by the patients' deranged behaviour.

Tim Curry – scorer for the visitors – is forced to listen to his opposite number's menacing tale about a man who can kill people with a single shout. Meanwhile, the match proceeds in a mixture of orthodox cricket and bouts of lunacy. At one point, a bowler's rejected appeal moves a patient to smash a window and scream 'Out! Out!', leading the whole fielding team to do likewise; on the boundary, a wheelchair-bound patient breaks into

Shakespeare – 'Out, out, brief candle!' – and gleefully claps his hands while being trundled along by a nurse. It all makes for an unsettling watch – English cricket as a bad dream, its village-green ideals deformed into a sinister nightmare. In the closing scene, a thunderstorm arrives and the patients run for cover, lapsing into howls of fear – one of them even stripping off his clothes and smearing himself in streaks of cow pat, as he unleashes a succession of bestial screams.

Cricket is put to far more wholesome use in *P'Tang Yang Kipperbang* (1982), a lighthearted coming-of-age comedy set in the years immediately following the Second World War. Alan Duckworth – 'Quack Quack' to friends – is an awkward, cricket-obsessed schoolboy infatuated with his aloof classmate, Ann Lawton. He channels his adolescent insecurities into daydreams of heroic cricketing feats – with commentary provided by John Arlott. In the opening minutes, Alan's journey to school quickly becomes an imagined Ashes battle:

> Bedser snatches the ball out of the air . . . polishes it on that not inconsiderable chest of his and prepares, this giant of a man, to bowl yet again to Don Bradman. But Bradman, 63, and Australia a dismaying 235 for 1 . . . here he comes . . . gathering pace, gathering strength, pounding, pounding powerfully up to the wicket and he bowls . . .

The fantasy crumbles when he trips on the kerb and sends his schoolbooks flying. 'Bradman yet again hooks him convulsively for four,' concludes Arlott, as Alan glumly gathers his things, 'and Bedser, shoulders dropping, grimaces philosophically at no one in particular.'

When he is cast as the lothario figure in the school play, Alan is gifted a golden opportunity to secure the kiss of his dreams. But at the last minute, his courage fails him – and to the derision of the audience, he resorts to shaking Ann's hand instead. At the very end of the film she asks him why. And in an effort to explain, he turns to cricket:

> It's like cricketers. Well, I mean, it *isn't* like cricketers – Cyril Washbrook or Denis Compton or any of them. They face the bowler . . . and there are thousands of people watching. Their families and friends, all the Australian fielders, the umpires, John Arlott and thousands of total strangers . . . but they don't care. Just keep their eye on the ball and play their stroke. I don't know how they do it. I couldn't.

An unexpected but cogent link is made – it is, perhaps, an under-appreciated truth that the self-belief of a skilled seducer resembles the self-belief of a master batsman.

Elsewhere, cricket is imbued with a much more political significance. One of the most eloquent representations of cricket in British cinema is *Playing Away* – a 1987 comedy-drama about a Brixton team of West Indians playing a fixture against a parochial village side. Norman Beaton stars as the captain of the Brixton team – the Conquistadors. It is a film that taps directly into the racial divisions of 1980s England, divisions that were sharply felt in a cricketing culture that was, at the same time, both vibrantly multi-racial and riddled with vicious prejudice.

In 1980, Roland Butcher had become the first black cricketer to play for England. Despite the growing diversity of the game, though, black English cricketers often had to endure appalling racist abuse. Fast bowler David 'Syd' Lawrence remembers – at his first-ever away game for Gloucestershire in 1982 – opening his hotel room to find a banana skin on the floor. It had been left there by one of his own teammates. 'I just sat in that room thinking: I'm a cricketer, what makes me different?' he would later reveal. 'Why would somebody want to do that, just because of the colour of my skin?' In the middle of his playing days, Phil deFreitas was sent death threats from the far-right National Front party. 'I received

[them] two or three times, saying, "If you play for England, we will shoot you,"' he disclosed. 'So, can you imagine me driving down to London? I'm in a hotel two days before a Test match at Lord's, and I'm thinking, Do I play or don't I? Am I going to have a sniper?'

Playing Away interrogates this climate of discrimination by dropping West Indian immigrant culture into the cloistered bigotry of rural middle-England. A brass band greets the team's arrival in the fictional village of Sneddington for a match billed as the culmination of 'Third World Week'. It is a relentlessly twee setting of half-timbered houses, bunting, cucumber sandwiches and tea in china cups. The clash of cultures leads to some awkward interactions. At a reception for the visitors – while a string quartet plays on the lawn – one of the Sneddingtonians flaunts the merits of a cleaner. 'Oh, yes, she comes in and does, sort of, well, pretty much anything, you know. Bit of ironing . . . bit of washing up.'

'Yeah,' comes the reply. 'Have you ever been to Brixton?'

Polite greetings and friendly pints in the village pub gradually degenerate into hostility. With the match planned for the following day, the Conquistadors are all put up by various locals. Several stay with Derek, the smug Sneddington captain, who foists upon them a series of condescending quips. 'Just have a glance through that,' he says, presenting a copy of Clayton Goodwin's *West Indians at the Wicket* (which he has been reading in preparation). 'You'll find Ramadhin, Valentine, Gibbs. Great spinners. You see, I don't understand why all of a sudden you chaps want to be speed merchants.'

Later in the evening, things take a much more sinister turn. The daughter of Willie-Boy, the Conquistador captain, is given a lift by a trio of oafish locals. After driving her out into the middle of nowhere, they threaten to rape her before at last setting her free. Meanwhile – worried about her disappearance – her dad gets drunk and makes the mistake of stumbling into the other pub in the village. This, by implication, is a whites-only joint where a moustachioed gentleman stares at Willie-Boy in horror through his monocle while the barman refuses him a drink, claiming not to understand his accent. When the match begins, the visitors only have ten players and one of the Sneddington team remarks, to general laughter, 'I reckon they got hungry and ate the other one last night.'

In short, *Playing Away* is a comedy with very dark overtones – loaded with a blunt message about the deep-set racism of rural England. The Sneddington players and locals are presented in unpleasant fashion – nasty, snobbish and narrow-minded, at war with each other just as much as their guests. 'These people have difficulties of their own,' reflects Conquistador vice-captain Jeff at the end, as the team bundle themselves into the minibus back home. One senses that they have little desire to repeat the visit.

Another stirring cricketing tale – which also confronts England's racial divides – is *Wondrous Oblivion* (2003), written and directed by Paul Morrison. Set in 1960s' south London, it follows the fortunes of David Wiseman – a cricket-loving school-boy with Jewish immigrant parents. There are echoes of Alan Duckworth, from *P'Tang Yang Kipperbang*, in the way he dream-ily hoards cigarette cards of cricket legends and fantasises about his own epic achievements. In real life, though, David is a bungling catastrophe of a player – equally inept with bat, with ball and in the field. He yearns to be in the school team but, to his dismay, he is consigned to the role of scorer. 'You've a head for numbers, at least,' observes the master in charge, as David glumly updates the scoreboard.

His fortunes change when new neighbours arrive next door – a family from Jamaica, the Samuels, whose first act is to put up a cricket net in the garden. Father Dennis – bursting with hope about a new life in England – begins to coach his daughters. One day, David plucks up the courage to ask if he can join in and his cricketing journey well and truly begins. Dennis is an expert coach who wisely encourages his young charges, and overflows with love for the game of cricket. 'This man is like Moses to me.

He's a political theorist and the best cricket writer in the world,' he at one point explains, reverentially showing them a copy of C. L. R. James's *Beyond a Boundary*. After reading a brief passage, he gets even more animated: 'You see that? We are talking about an *art form*.' Under Dennis's wing, David soon becomes one of his school team's star batsmen.

From the outset, though, the Samuels are on the receiving end of vile racist abuse. The morning after their arrival, a pile of manure is dumped on their doorstep. Neighbours gather to gossip, scheme and sneer. The Wisemans – as fellow immigrants – are pressured to rid the neighbourhood of the unwanted newcomers and become the target of abuse when they do not do so. It is a grim procession of bullying and bigotry. Anonymous threatening letters are posted through letterboxes, David's mother is spat at and his father is sent death threats. Things reach their nadir when a local goon breaks into the Samuels' garden at night and sets the cricket net on fire, nearly killing them all while they sleep. It is a chilling reminder that, for immigrant families, the streets of London could be every bit as hostile and dangerous as the backwater villages of England.

Only at the very end of the film is there a return to a more hopeful mood. In a show of local solidarity, the Samuels are gifted a new cricket net for their garden by some neighbouring families. Dennis invites David to play in a match he has organised – a 'little picnic thing . . . a very special do' – and even though it clashes with the school Junior Challenge Cup, David accepts. It turns out to be a good decision. Once the game begins, while David is batting, two old friends of Dennis's turn up – a pair of smartly dressed gents named Frank Worrell and Garfield Sobers. The latter, still in his suit and tie, strolls onto the pitch to make an appearance as a guest bowler. David nervously misses the first one – before hitting him for a glorious, cover-driven four. 'Too good for me, man,' says Sobers, with a beaming smile.

Another famous document of the English immigrant experience is *Bend it Like Beckham* (2002) – a film which takes football as its focus, but which also gives cricket a notable supporting role. The plot revolves around Jess Kaur Bhamra – a precocious, seventeen-year-old footballer, whose conservative Sikh parents are fiercely hostile to the idea of her playing. It is, they explain, simply not consistent with the expectations they hold for their daughter: she must study, get married and fulfil the expectations of a wife. 'What family,' her mother complains, 'will want a daughter-in-law who can run around kicking a football all day but can't make round chapatis?'

There is, though, a second reason for their caution. Her dad, Mohaan, was a keen cricketer in his youth. And his experience as an immigrant to England was crushing. 'When I was a teenager in Nairobi,' he explains to Jess's coach, 'I was the best fast bowler in our school. Our team even won the East African Cup. But when I came to this country – nothing. I was not allowed to play in any of the teams. Those bloody *goras* [white people] in the club houses made fun of my turban and sent me off packing.' Put simply, he does not want Jess to have the same experience he did. 'I don't want you to build up Jasminda's hopes. She will only end up disappointed like me.'

Jess's own efforts to explain that things might have moved on do not carry much weight. 'Dad, it's all changing now,' she ventures, in an effort to bring her parents round. 'Look at Nasser Hussain. He's captain of the England cricket team – and he's Asian.' But her mother instantly brushes this aside. Not all immigrant communities, she claims, have the same values. 'Hussain is a Muslim name,' she explains. 'Their families are different.'

It is all looking rather bleak for Jess's footballing hopes. The film ends, though, with an abrupt change of heart. Mohaan ultimately decides that his daughter must not fold in the face of prejudice like he did. 'When those bloody English cricket players threw me out of their club like a dog, I never complained,' he says. 'On the contrary, I vowed that I will never play again. Who suffered? Me. But I don't want Jessy to suffer. I don't want her to make the same mistakes that her father made of accepting life, accepting situations. I want her to fight. And I want her to win.' Off she goes to America on her football scholarship, after all.

Not only that, but in the very final moments of the film, a game of cricket is shown taking place on the green of a Hounslow street. It is Mohaan, playing cricket once more, for the first time in years. Perhaps a more hopeful future lies ahead. As the camera pans up over the rows of suburban houses, there is a tentative sense that – at the beginning of a new century – things might slowly be moving in the right direction.

19

'You never know whether he's gone': The Music of Cricket

We do not have full details of the songs that golden-voiced wicket-keeper Tom Sueter sang to his teammates in the Hambledon clubroom. But the fact that he did so – and that it moved John Nyren to 'rapture' – helps to highlight an under-acknowledged link between music and cricket. One need only glance at the abundance of cricketer-musicians over the years – a roll call that includes not only Mark Butcher, but Brett Lee, Shane Watson, Alastair Cook, Curtly Ambrose, Richie Richardson, Harbhajan Singh, Henry Olonga, A. B. de Villiers and even keen piano player Don Bradman – to accept that some kind of spiritual affinity must be at work.

In other words, it is not just in the work of Neville Cardus that these two art forms discover common ground. Cricket and music, in fact, are cousins – distant cousins perhaps, not alike on the surface, but nevertheless tied together by deep-set threads of connection. 'Cricket songs are as old as the game itself,' observes David Rayvern Allen, in his pioneering study of the field. 'A lot of the earliest songs must have been lost in the days of illiteracy, when the game's lack of status meant that the few who were equipped to convey to paper the jocular rhymes of the shepherds in the Weald often did not do so.'

Once we reach the seventeenth century, music was already being written about that risqué relation of cricket, stoolball. Henry Purcell wrote songs for Thomas D'Urfey's *Comical History of Don*

263

Quixote, first performed in London in 1694. As was so often the case, the game is linked with romantic shenanigans: 'Come all, great, small, Short, tall, away to Stool-Ball . . . Down in a Dale on a Summers day, All the Lads, and Lasses, met to be merry, A Match for Kisses at Stool-Ball play . . . Then went the Glasses round, Then went the Lasses down, Each Lad did his Sweet Heart own, And on the Grass did fling her.' Elsewhere, D'Urfey wrote lyrics on cricket too – such as in his 1693 play, *The Richmond Heiress*, where one song includes the lines 'Hur was the prettiest Fellows, trum, trum, trum,/At Bandy once and Cricket, trum, trum trum trum.'

Another of the earliest pieces of cricket music is the 'Radnage Cricket Song' – believed to have originated in Buckinghamshire in the seventeenth or eighteenth century. It is a warm tribute to the game but also, at the same time, something more intriguing – with the lyrics suggesting a link to romance, stoolball-style:

Well played my pretty partner, be sure to bat upright
And when she comes, with a hop hop hop
We'll cut her out of sight
To cricket we will go, will go
To cricket we will go
Well played my pretty partner
See how she tips the bail
And if we keep them to a length
I'm sure we will not fail . . .

The words hover between two meanings – either sporting camaraderie or something much racier, depending on your point of view. Here is cricket, in the English imagination, as flirting, seduction and sex.

By the arrival of the Victorian era, cricket songs of many different kinds were becoming widespread. Nicholas Wanostrocht – author of *Felix on the Bat* – was, among his many other talents, a fine musician, and would often conduct an amateur band at

Canterbury during breaks in play. Elsewhere – such as in 'The Cricketers' by composer Kent Sutton – the lyrics echo some of Victorian England's more jingoistic tendencies:

In Canada they have la crosse,
The yankee has his baseball
Australia has her 'boating'
And the Scotsmen of course 'football'
The Frenchman likes his 'fencing foils'
The Spaniard his 'bull baiting'
The German his 'gymnastics'
And in Norway they love 'skating'
But to my mind there's none can beat . . .

. . . other games, from around the world, might well have their merits; but it is, of course, the English game of cricket that sits atop the pile.

The Victorian belief in cricket as an educational tool was expressed in the many school cricket songs of the era. The Tonbridge School song mingled loyalty to the empire with sprinklings of Latin: 'O'er Britain's wide empire, 'neath many a star, Alumni of Tonbridge are scatter'd afar; And this is the bond that the wand'rers unites, The thought of our *Ergo ludamus!*'

The Reverend Edward Thring, headmaster of Uppingham, composed several songs for his school – songs that summoned the ideals of England's rural past ('Whilst cricket we play each summer day, 'Tis Merry England still') and the fickleness of its weather ('Jolly sun we do implore thee, Stay with us the whole year round'). In the 'Eton Cricket Song', Arthur Campbell Ainger – a master at the college – fashioned lyrics that stressed the game's superiority over all others: 'You may talk of your tennis, your rackets, and fives, the skill they demand and the pleasure they bring; but you're bound to admit in the course of your lives, they all have their merits but Cricket is King.'

Peter Warlock was the author of over a hundred songs for voice and piano before his suicide, in 1930, at the age of just thirty-six. The year before his death, he wrote the music for 'The Cricketers of Hambledon' – with accompanying words by poet and frequent collaborator Bruce Blunt. It was inspired by a 1929 match played on Broadhalfpenny Down – a midwinter match, unusually, played on New Year's Day between the Hampshire Eskimos and an 'Invalids' team of ex-soldiers who had been wounded in the Great War.

The match was hardly a classic. Perhaps the January weather was to blame. The Invalids were bundled out for 89, with the Eskimos making only 78 in reply, before everyone piled into The Bat & Ball inn for much-needed warming ales. Blunt's lyrics, in any case, focus not so much on the game as on the legends of the club's glory days:

> I'll make a song of Hambledon, and sing it at 'The George',
> Of balls that flew from Beldham's bat like sparks from
>   Fennex's forge;
> The centuries of Aylward, and a thousand-guineas bet,
> And Sueter keeping wicket to the thunderbolts of Brett.
> Then up with every glass and we'll sing a toast in chorus:
> 'The cricketers of Hambledon who played the game before
>   us,
> The stalwarts of the olden time who rolled a lonely down,
> And made the king of games for men, with Hambledon the
>   crown.

'Silver Billy' Beldham, William Fennex (who worked as a black-smith – hence the 'forge'), James Aylward, Tom Sueter, Thomas Brett – and also, later in the song, John Small and Richard Nyren – are all lionised as gods to be toasted. The proposal that they created the 'king of games for men' abides by the time-honoured tradition that cricket is not just the best, but also the manliest of games.

In the melée of post-Second World War Britain's social, sexual, political and musical revolutions, one might have expected cricket to feature very little. The game's connotations of formality and refinement seem squarely at odds with rock music's subversive irruptions and spirit of rebellion. But cricket has, in fact, had an influence on what might look – from a certain angle – like surprising territory. Some of rock's most legendary figures – Eric Clapton, the Rolling Stones' Mick Jagger and Led Zeppelin's Jimmy Page, to name just a few – have been keen cricket fans. A set of photos even exists of a young Page, padded up in full cricket whites, playing a range of shots using his guitar as a cricket bat.

They are compelling images – the roistering rock star, cigarette in the side of the mouth, flaunting the cultured aesthetics of cricketing tradition. Cricket never appeared in any Led Zeppelin songs. But in Page's passion for folk music, alternate tunings, old Celtic ballads and English folklore, there is perhaps a concealed explanation of his affection for the game.

Few figures in rock history have absorbed cricket into their art as memorably as Ray Davies, frontman and songwriter for The Kinks. He has spoken about his passion for the game on more than one occasion. 'One of my best days,' he revealed in a 2019 interview, 'was going to the MCC and seeing the Chappell brothers play. They had a party in my hotel that night and I became the only rock star ever to complain about cricketers making too much noise. I had to be up for a flight in the morning and they were getting pissed at the end of the corridor. Mike Brearley was the England captain and I gave him a right telling-off.'

As biographer Johnny Rogan observed, 'Davies mined a strain of Englishness like no other songwriter from his generation.' And cricket formed part of his distinctly English tableau. The lyrics for 'Do you remember Walter?' – from The Kinks' sixth album, *The Kinks Are the Village Green Preservation Society* (1968) – summon up scenes of youthful happiness. And as was the case for so many artists and writers – from Francis Thompson to Albert

Chevallier Tayler to Harold Pinter – the game of cricket sits right at the core of this nostalgia, with its recollections of childhood cricket in the 'thunder and the rain'.

It is a song drenched in melancholy, highlighting how our friendships cannot last for ever. People change, life moves on. The only comfort comes from the fact that we can, at least, preserve life's fleeting joys in memory. 'Yes, people often change,' run the song's final lines. 'But memories of people can remain.'

It was in 1975, though, that the greatest of all cricket songs would appear. By this point, folk-rock singer-songwriter Roy Harper was a well-established figure on the British music scene – limited in commercial success, but highly respected by his peers. Led Zeppelin even penned him a tribute, 'Hats off to (Roy) Harper', on their folk-tinged third album. And in the middle of Harper's sixth album, *HQ*, sits 'When an Old Cricketer Leaves the Crease' – a work that, almost half a century later, remains unrivalled as the most legendary cricket song in music history.

It is dedicated to Geoffrey Boycott and John Snow – both of whom are referenced in the lyrics, which place the song firmly in the tradition of cricketing nostalgia.

Once again, the emphasis is on the passing of time – but there is also something more at work. The old cricketer leaving the crease is a metaphor for death itself – an image of someone physically departing, but still present in memory. The song is not just about cricket, but also about grief – how we are haunted by loved ones whose worldly innings have ended. When someone dies, are they really gone? Or are they still there – a ghostly 'twelfth man' alongside us on the pitch – as we continue to play our own game of life? Maybe. Or maybe that is just the ale talking.

Reflecting on the song, Harper has explained how his early life inspired its composition. 'My childhood memories of the heroic stature of the footballers and cricketers of the day,' he revealed, 'invoke the sounds that went along with them.' This shimmering treasure of echoing guitar and aching vocals remains one of his best-known works – and has been persistently revered over the years, in both cricketing and musical domains. DJ John Peel requested that the song be broadcast when he died. Presenter and DJ Tony Blackburn heralded it as the pop song of the 1970s. All in all, it is difficult to dispute David Rayvern Allen's claim that 'it is, in essence, *the* cricket song'.

By the time Harper's song was released, the landscape of British popular music had already long been enriched by the music of the Caribbean. It had been back in 1950 that Lord Beginner sang 'Victory Calypso', celebrating the West Indies' triumph over England at Lord's. The chorus hails the brilliant spin bowling pair – those 'two little pals of mine', Sonny Ramadhin and Alf Valentine, who had taken eighteen wickets between them in the match.

The West Indies went on to win the series 3-1 – their first ever series victory in England, and a watershed moment in their cricketing history.

Lord Beginner had come to England on the *Empire Windrush* boat in the summer of 1948. Alongside him on the same journey was the man who wrote 'Victory Calypso' – Aldwyn Roberts, better known as Lord Kitchener. Perhaps the greatest calypsonian of all, it is difficult to overstate Kitchener's importance to the post-war musical climate – not just as a songwriter, but as an icon of the immigrant experience. His famous performance of 'London is the Place for Me' at Tilbury Docks, immediately after disembarking, underlined his sense of a transformed identity. Yes, he was a West Indian; but now that he was in England, he was also an Englishman. The English people, he sings, treat you 'like a millionaire' . . .

The lines convey an optimism about English hospitality that would, sadly, stand in stark contrast to the prejudice many of the Windrush generation went on to suffer. Elsewhere – such as in the disturbing 'If You're Brown' – Kitchener would bluntly record the racism he witnessed in London. 'Every door,' he grieves, 'is shut in your face.'

The Kitchener cricketing calypsos of the 1950s were crucial

expressions of the immigrant identity – proudly West Indian, at the same time as being patriotically English. At Trent Bridge in 1953, Alec Bedser – at the peak of his powers – cut through the Australian batting to take 7 for 55 in the first innings and 7 for 45 in the second. Thanks to two days of rain, Australia escaped with a draw – but to this day, Bedser's figures remain the best ever in a Trent Bridge test. Kitchener commemorated the feat in his 'Alec Bedser calypso'. Similarly, when Frank 'Typhoon' Tyson bowled England to victory down under eighteen months later, Kitchener wanted to honour the victory in his music. The result was an Ashes calypso, in which he joyfully proclaimed that 'we came back with victory'.

The 'we', here, is significant, as Kitchener affirms the right of immigrants in England to celebrate an Ashes victory along with any other Englishman. His music remains a defiant expression of creative joy in the face of what was, all too often, a hostile culture. 'After the match,' he recalled after the West Indies' 1950 Lord's victory, 'I took my guitar and called a few West Indians, and I went round the cricket field singing and dancing. That was a song I made up. So, while we're dancing up come a policeman and arrested me.'

10cc was one of countless British bands whose sound was shaped by Caribbean music. The chorus to their reggae-influenced hit single, 'Dreadlock Holiday' – *I don't like cricket, I love it* – remains, perhaps, the most famous cricket-related line in popular music; although the song is, in truth, less about cricket than it might first appear. The lyrics were inspired by frontman Eric Stewart's holiday encounter:

> Justin Hayward (from the Moody Blues) and I had both gone on holiday with our families to Barbados . . . Justin and I were on a para-sailing raft in the middle of the ocean and I was strapped into this parachute gear. I was towed behind a speed-boat at high speed. I took off and waved goodbye to Justin. He was then left on the raft with three black guys, one Jamaican

and two from Barbados. The Jamaican guy said to Justin, 'I like your silver chain, man. I'll give you a dollar for it.'

Justin replied, 'Come on, it's worth a lot more than that and it's a present from my mother.'

And this guy said, 'If this was Jamaica, I would cut your hand off for that.'

I came back and asked Justin if he wanted to have a go. He said, 'No, let's get off this raft as quick as we can, I have had some problems.' When we got back to England, I relayed the story to Graham [Gouldman, 10cc bassist] and we wrote a song around it.

The story that 'Dreadlock Holiday' tells is one of violence. A tourist walks the streets of Jamaica and finds himself menaced by a quartet of locals. The famous chorus is simply a tactical manoeuvre – an effort, by declaring a love for cricket, to escape being mugged.

At one level, the song takes aim at white tourists wandering the Jamaican streets trying to look cool – 'Concentratin' on truckin' right', as the opening line puts it. But at the same time, it does not exactly veer clear of racial stereotyping. Threatening black youths bully a vulnerable white victim: 'I looked round in a state of fright, I saw four faces, one mad, A brother from the gutter, They looked me up and down a bit, And turned to each other'. The weed-smoking Jamaican trope also rears its head: while the narrator sips piña coladas by the pool, a local asks him 'Would you like something harder? . . . My harvest is the best.' It is, in other words, a song that in some ways has not aged well. But such concerns hardly held it back at the time – 'Dreadlock Holiday' went to No. 1 in the summer of 1978.

Elsewhere in cricket music, a place has been found for novelty and comedy. 'N-N-Nineteen not out' – a 1985 hit for The Commentators – features Rory Bremner delivering an array of cricketing impressions to a musical backdrop. The 1985 debut album from Birkenhead indie band, Half Man Half Biscuit, includes the improbably titled 'Fuckin' Hell, it's Fred Titmus' – a (to say the least) unconventional ode to the legendary Middlesex all-rounder, though one based on invention rather than a real encounter ('I have never met Fred Titmus,' explained frontman Nigel Blackwell, 'let alone greeted him in such an overfamiliar way'). The Duckworth Lewis Method – founded by Neil Hannon of The Divine Comedy and Thomas Walsh of Pugwash – are perhaps the only band in history not only to write songs about cricket, but to base their entire existence on the game. Their eponymous 2009 album is a feast of waggish cricket-related offerings, with tracks such as 'The Coin Toss', 'Gentlemen and Players', 'The Nightwatchman', 'Test Match Special' and 'Rain Stops Play'.

Cricket has shown no signs of disappearing from music in the twenty-first century. It has, in particular, tended to surface when musicians have wanted to express something about the character of English culture. Roots Manuva – once dubbed the 'voice of urban Britain' by *The Times* – made a cricket-themed video for his 2008 single, 'Again and Again'. Filmed on a sun-drenched Kew Green, there are echoes of the cricket match from *Playing Away* as Manuva wanders out to the crease, rapping to the camera, his bat handle sporting the colours of the Jamaican flag. The song does not take cricket as its subject, but the lyrics feel, in places, like declarations of vibrant identity designed to counteract the anodyne climate of affluent suburbia: 'I'm back at the drawing board, And I'm sketching out two plans with two crystal balls, I see the future and the culture looks corroded, Lose that chap, man. Better do this: just pause it . . .'

Mike Skinner of The Streets has aimed, in his music, to capture a particular kind of urban working-class everydayness; he has variously been labelled the 'English Eminem', the 'poet of British suburbia' and the 'garage laureate of clubland and kebabs'. And cricket has recurrently featured in his work. 'Not Addicted' – from his second album, *A Grand Don't Come for Free* – details

someone struggling with a gambling habit. Initially they squan-
der their money on the football, before deciding that they will bet
to 'lose the cricket'. Elsewhere, Skinner's 2014 single 'Not
Cricket' – a largely instrumental track – keeps its cricket-related
significances closer to its chest.

And in 2011, Skinner recorded a cricketing piece of a different
kind. The previous winter had seen one of the great accomplishments in English cricket history – England had gone to Australia
and, for the first time in a quarter of a century, they had successfully defended the Ashes. Not only that, but they had breezed it.
The 3-1 scoreline was comfortable but it was the nature of
England's victories – all three of them by an innings – that really
emphasised their dominance.

An Australian side still reeling from the recent retirement
of legends (Shane Warne, Glenn McGrath, Matthew Hayden,
Justin Langer, Adam Gilchrist, Brett Lee) was steamrollered by an
England team, led by Andrew Strauss, at the peak of their powers.
Across the series, Alastair Cook scored 766 runs at an average of
127 – the most Ashes runs by any English batsman for over eighty
years. After England's final test win, UK journalist Paul Newman
summed it up in unforgiving fashion: 'The Sydney Cricket
Ground, that most famous of all Australian sporting stages, stood
as a monument to English excellence yesterday as this humbled,
chastened and – yes – humiliated nation came to terms with the
reality that their era of greatness has finally come to a crushing
end while another takes hold. The era of English dominance.'

Mike Skinner commemorated the feat in a short video called
'An English Corner'. In it, he recites lines from a *Guardian* report
by Mike Selvey on England's Ashes triumph:

> They came in their thousands to form an English corner of a
> foreign field for the climax, a day of days in the history of the
> England team and another one of abject misery for a once-
> proud Australian team fallen on hard times. Not even the snap

showers washing in to interrupt play, and a flatness to the team on the field, could deny them a third overwhelming victory which came, by an innings and 83 runs, at 11:56, four minutes before the Shipping Forecast, and just as Billy the Barmy Trumpeter was playing a poignant 'Last Post' for the demise of Australian cricket.

The video plays Skinner's reverb-drenched voice against a backdrop of humdrum, in-front-of-the-TV homeliness – we see a mug and crumb-dusted saucer, a leather sofa, an empty box of beer. There are some droll sound effects (the line 'a once-proud Australian team fallen on hard times' is followed by a burst of canned laughter). And at the end, it is all implied to be a beautiful dream – a sleeping Skinner opening his eyes and asking, 'Where am I?'

Selvey, for one, was delighted by the tribute. 'Mike Skinner's video short . . . is just flattering really,' he observed. 'Actually makes it sound readable. My kids will think I'm seriously cool now.'

'THIS MOMENT OF HUMAN KINDNESS': ICONIC CRICKET PHOTOGRAPHS

The fielding side do not look like the most dynamic outfit. The slip and the point are arthritically crouched, as if bestriding a pit latrine. One feels that, if the ball came at them, it would simply knock them over. Square leg watches timidly – as though they are contemplating the possibility of making a run for it. The fine leg, closest to the camera, is locked in a slothful stance, more like a bored bystander than a keenly motivated sportsperson. The facing batsman, too, emanates a lamppost-like stiffness. The closest we get to vim is the bowler – who stands with arms spread, at the end of his run-up, in an apparent effort to look mean before he delivers the ball.

As cricketing images go, it is a relatively unprepossessing scene. Nonetheless, it is an image of towering significance – one of the most groundbreaking, in fact, in the entire history of the game. Because this is the earliest cricket photograph.

It was taken on 25 July 1857 by Roger Fenton, who, four years earlier, had founded the Photographic Society of London – later the Royal Photographic Society. Intriguingly, the match's location was the Artillery Ground in Islington – a historic spot which, a century before, had been one of the great cricket grounds of England. In Fenton's photo – one of six he took that day of Hunsdonbury Cricket Club against the Royal Artillery team – it is a low-key venue, a quiet green watched by a modest group of spectators.

One might, perhaps, have expected the original cricket photograph – at such a famous site – to offer a more dramatic spectacle. But there are particular reasons why this was never likely. The players will not have really been in action because they had to pose for the ten seconds or so of exposure time. In these early stages of a new art, it was not possible to take an 'action photo': for many years to come, capturing movement would prove to be photography's biggest challenge. It was not exactly a happy experience for the people being photographed. Put simply, the fielders in Fenton's photo look stuck in place, because they were stuck in place; they look bored, because they were bored.

In *Stroke of Genius* – a study of the great Australian batsman, Victor Trumper – Gideon Haigh has detailed the difficulties faced by Victorian photographers. On the day he captured his pioneering image, Fenton will have been struggling with various things at once:

... unable to freeze the action with his camera, he had to curtail it by request; unable to ford the boundary, he had to make the best of his distance. Some effort was made at simulating action: the batsman stooped over his blade; the fielders faced toward the centre. But the chief activity around this photograph would have been Fenton's: first coating the plate with emulsion in his portable darkroom, hurrying to insert it in the holder, exposing it for five to ten seconds, then hastening to process the negative in its silver bath before the emulsion dried, all the while trying not to inhale too much ether vapour from the collodion, and this on a summer's day to boot.

Nineteenth-century photography was a complex business: awkward, arduous, and beset with technical obstacles. One obvious hindrance was that, unlike other visual arts, photography had only one canvas to work with: that of reality itself. Even as technology developed and exposure times shortened, the challenge of capturing a constantly moving world remained. The sorts of creative techniques that painters could draw on were not available in the same way. For photographers, artistic planning had its limits: with reality, you can never quite know what to expect. As Haigh puts it, 'Traditional forms of painting, drawing, printmaking and sculpture had evolved an intricate visual language to convey motion.' Photography, in contrast, 'was condemned to repeat reality, in all its unpredictability'.

But this apparent deficiency is also an advantage. In dealing with the 'unpredictability' of reality, photography has a unique capacity to catch fleeting moments and unexpectedly revealing details. The point was stressed in 1952 by the legendary photographer, Henri Cartier-Bresson:

Of all the means of expression, photography is the only one that fixes forever the precise and transitory instant. We photographers deal in things which are continually vanishing, and when they have vanished, there is no contrivance on Earth which can make them come back again. We cannot develop and print a memory. The writer has time to reflect. He can accept and reject, accept again; and before committing his thoughts to paper he is able to tie the several relevant elements together . . . But for photographers, what has gone, has gone forever. From that fact stem the anxieties and strength of our profession. We cannot do our story over again, once we've got back to the hotel. Our task is to perceive reality, almost simultaneously recording it in the sketchbook which is our camera.

The spontaneous aspects of the art might be a challenge – but within the spontaneous, something magical can be found, a pearl plucked from the flux and ferment of the everyday.

An excellent example is a photograph from 1926, depicting the great England openers, Jack Hobbs and Herbert Sutcliffe, walking out to bat:

At first there is the harmony, the symmetry. Their step is perfectly in tune. Both of the gloved left hands swing forward at the same height. Even the bats are tilted at the same angle. From a casual glance, it looks almost like a doubling of the same image, like some early ancestor of a Warhol print. Several photos of the pair walking out to the crease have the same mirror-like feel – as if they are twins, doppelgängers, psychically joined to each other via some mysterious sixth sense.

The only difference, perhaps, is in their faces. Hobbs – on the left – seems more relaxed. His face is almost sleepy, a soft smile perceptible underneath his half-closed eyes. He looks like he could be heading off to the post office or the pub, rather than into the pressure cooker of a test match. In contrast, Sutcliffe's face has a more brooding quality. There is a smile there of sorts – but also something heavier, more intense about the eyes. The forehead is locked in a pensive frown. It is a look not so much of relaxation as one of cold determination.

This all seems, intriguingly, to reflect the divergent aspects of their characters. Hobbs was famously genial, known for his acts of charity and his affable temperament. John Arlott praised him as 'the kindest, gentlest, most generous of men' – even suggesting that 'there was something almost Christ-like about him'. He was blessed with a sanguine disposition – remarkably capable of brushing problems aside and staying cheerful under pressure. As his biographer Leo McKinstry notes, 'He was warm and optimistic, not given to introspection or moralising . . . to him, cricket was more than just his profession; it was also a source of profound pleasure.' The smile on Hobbs's face, in the 1926 photo, might be a smile in a moment – but it also expresses something of Hobbs the man. He was inclined to see the good in things: a glass half-full character, grateful for what life offered him. 'It has been a wonderful life,' he explained in his memoirs. 'I have enjoyed every bit of it.'

Sutcliffe was not quite the same. He certainly shared Hobbs' gift for calm under pressure; but he also had less placid traits. Although capable of glorious stroke play, he was more of a self-made batsman – not quite blessed with Hobbs's heavenly levels of natural talent, but determined to make the most of what he had. As his Yorkshire and England teammate Bill Bowes once said, 'His personality had the same characteristics as his batting. He was reliable. He was the first to admit that he had not the same ability as Jack Hobbs, Wally Hammond or Sir Len Hutton, but he had concentration and the will to harness his ability.'

He was nothing if not meticulous. He paid careful attention to the details of everything, from the nuances of his batting technique to the particulars of his personal appearance. His dapper look in the 1926 photo – hair faultlessly brilliantined to the scalp – is a sign of this scrupulous character. 'Sutcliffe exuded polish,' notes his biographer Alan Hill, 'possessing . . . the sleekest hairdo in international cricket. His dark head gleamed in the sunshine. His appearance at the crease, from the elegant buckskin boots to the perfectly groomed and neatly parted hair, was as immaculate as his batting defence.' A sober and temperate man, he was able to abstain from alcohol and cigarettes for long periods when the mood took him. 'His mind always seemed to rule his body,' observed former Yorkshire president Sir Kenneth Parkinson. For Sutcliffe, control was all-important. As he once himself put it, 'I like to keep a mastery of these things.'

With the rapidly moving developments in photographic technology, entirely new ways of seeing sport became possible. For a very long time, the fine details of sporting action had fundamentally been mysterious to spectators. Watching from a hundred yards away, there is only so much someone can really see. But the camera brought fresh insights – the power to see Cartier-Bresson's 'precise and transitory instant', dramatic snapshots taken in the white heat of sporting battle.

And across cricket history, there are few mid-match images more dramatic than that of Harold Larwood – bowling to Australia captain Bill Woodfull – at Brisbane in 1933:

Almost a century later, it remains a thrilling picture – though the mood of the thrill may vary, perhaps, depend on your view of the bodyline saga. Woodfull's body position is not from any textbook. Head turned away from Larwood, towards the keeper, it is more of a desperate duck than a controlled or measured response. Larwood himself, in contrast, looks poised at the end of his follow through – light on his feet, like a ballet dancer, calmly watching on. But to contemporary eyes, the most compelling thing is the field. Here is the brutal menace of bodyline captured on film – a tight ring of men surrounding the batsman on the leg side, a full half-dozen of them, from a hyper-close silly mid-on round to a fine leg slip. The zoomed-in lens almost makes the viewer a close fielder, waiting for a catch. The visceral threat is brought savagely to life.

And Woodfull, of course, had good reason to be anxious. In the previous test match at Adelaide, he could easily have died. In his biography of Larwood, Duncan Hamilton details the incident:

The sixth delivery of Larwood's second over caught him on the back foot . . . the ball took Woodfull near the heart and tore the skin. He dropped his bat and pressed both of his gloved hands against his chest, half-stooping as if he'd taken a bullet. He unbuttoned his shirt to inspect the damage. The mark was already red, like a port-wine stain. The booing lasted for three minutes.

But it was not the injury itself that caused the most serious bad feeling. After all, a bodyline field had not actually been set for that particular ball. What most upset Woodfull was the response of the England team – and in particular Douglas Jardine, as captain, who did little beyond shouting out, 'Well bowled, Harold!' Later in the day, England tour manager Pelham Warner entered the Australian dressing room to offer sympathies but was greeted with contempt. Woodfull's laconic jibe has become the stuff of legend: 'I don't want to see you, Mr Warner. There are two teams out there. One is trying to play cricket and the other is not.'

Relations soured further the following day, when wicket-keeper Bert Oldfield top-edged a Larwood delivery into his own head. The result was a fractured skull – and a deepening sense that the English approach was unethical, nasty and dangerous. Once again, a bodyline field had not been deployed at the time, but the hostile mood was now fixed. 'Bodyline bowling has assumed such proportions as to menace the best interests of the game,' ran the Australian cricket board's cable to London during the fifth day's play.

England ended up winning the Ashes, but to many, they had sacrificed the game's soul in order to do so. The England players – most of all Jardine and also, less fairly, Larwood – became pariahs down under. The doubts about leg theory, though, did not only come from Australian shores. Jack Hobbs – who had retired from England duties two years earlier – had been quiet on the subject during the tour. But once it was all over, he made his feelings clear. 'Bodyline bowling is contrary to the spirit of cricket,' he wrote in the *Star* on 6 May 1933, the very day that the England team arrived back home.

Jardine would continue as captain for another year. Larwood, meanwhile, never played for England again.

The scale of the sins committed during the winter of 1932-33 remains one of the great debates of cricket history. But for many, forty-three years later, there was a form of spiritual comeuppance visited upon the England team. In advance of the West Indies' visit in 1976, Tony Greig gave a notorious interview in which he questioned the resilience of his opponents' character:

You must remember that the West Indians, these guys, if they get on top are magnificent cricketers. But if they're down, they grovel, and I intend . . . to make them grovel.

These words – with their obvious connotations of submission to white authority – had an unseemly feel, to say the least. As West Indian fast bowler Michael Holding said, 'It was an extremely insensitive remark to make about a largely black team.' It had been intended as pre-series mind games by Greig – an effort to get into the heads of a side that was already beginning to establish itself as the dominant force in world cricket. But it did not work. Or – to put it another way – it worked all too well. As Holding would later explain, 'We needed no further motivation.'

The first two tests were drawn. But as that famous summer of endless, sun-bleached days wore on, the country started to feel less like the dampish green of England and more like the parched heat of the Caribbean. And in the third test at Old Trafford, the West Indies trio of Andy Roberts, Michael Holding and Wayne Daniel were to produce one of most terrifying examples of fast bowling ever seen.

Playing for England that summer was Brian Close. He had been recalled to the team at the age of forty-five. It was, in many ways, an unexpected return after nine years away from test-match front lines; Greig had pushed for it, to give his batting line-up some extra grit. And against bowling like this, grit would be sorely needed.

England had been skittled out in in the first innings for seventy-one. After Gordon Greenidge and Viv Richards both made hundreds, England were left in a hopeless position – either score 551 to win or bat for over two days to save the game. They were, in truth, playing only for pride. And the West Indian bowlers – with no restrictions on bouncers – settled on a policy of all-out brutality.

Close, in particular – opening the batting with captain John Edrich – was peppered with countless short deliveries. And the photos of Close's innings are unforgettable testaments to cricket as a life or death battle. His batting technique, rather like that of Woodfull's all those years before, was not exactly orthodox.

In one extraordinary image, the ball appears shockingly near to his head, almost singeing the remains of his hair. But Close does not look worried. His face, in fact, wears an expression of bewildering calm – as if he is bending down not to evade a potentially lethal cricket ball, but to examine some kind of insect or rare flower he has just spotted on the grass.

Ball after ball whizzed past his chin. On more than one occasion, he survived by letting the ball hammer into his body. After each blow, he would walk back and forth along the popping crease, not catching anyone's eye, shaking himself off, as if repulsing the unwanted attention of a wasp. One particular bullet to the ribcage did, for a moment, make his knees buckle but, gritting his teeth, he didn't even rub the spot. It all made for gruesome viewing. At one point, his Somerset teammate Viv Richards approached to check if he was okay. Viv was gruffly told, 'Fuck off.'

In the end, Close made 20 from 108 balls. It was not enough to win the match; but it did win him new status as a fearless iron man of British sport. 'Watching him play out there this evening,' said Edrich, 'made you proud to be an Englishman.' Close instantly took an elevated place in the English cultural imagination – not because of the runs he had scored, but because of the character he had shown. It turned out to be the last test match he played, but it did not matter. He was an icon. A cult hero. His name became a byword for bravery of all kinds. Even Eric Morecombe would honour him in a teasing one-liner: 'I always know it's summer when I hear the sound of leather on Brian Close.'

The photographs of Woodfull and Close both capture the game of cricket at its most ruthless. They are windows into a harsh and hostile world – the cold-blooded battlefield of top-level international sport. On other occasions, though, cricket photographs have captured a very different aspect of the game – one that harks back to the Victorian claims about the moral force of cricket. James Pycroft may have been guilty of some serious airbrushing when he said that the game was a panegyric on the English character; but some images *do* exist that seem to give support to such bold claims. If we look in the right places, we find photos expressing a belief that cricket really can be a moral example – depicting not drive and aggression, but the nobility of the sport's soul.

And there is one cricketing photograph, in particular – arguably the most famous of the twenty-first century – that, to many, embodies cricket's ethics in their purest form.

The story of the 2005 Edgbaston test has been told a thousand times. The match has become something more than a match – a kind of fairy tale or fireside fable, a cornerstone in the storybook magic of Ashes history. But its most famous image is not from the match itself – not even those frantic final moments of action. Kasprowicz's panicked parry; the flick of the ball off his glove; keeper Geraint Jones's nimble leap; the stagey verdict of Billy Bowden's crooked finger; the ice-cool genius of Richie Benaud's commentary ('Jones! . . . *Bowden!*'). All these details, happening within just a few seconds of each other, have firmly entered the topmost tier of cricketing mythology. But just after it all, something happened that felt more profound.

This was a moment of spectacular compassion from Andrew Flintoff:

Part of the story is the act itself – to think so quickly of the fallen opponent, in the immediate wake of victory. But the photo, taken by Tom Jenkins of the *Guardian*, would not be so famous if it were not for the expression on Flintoff's face. He looks tearful – almost grief-stricken. Everything about his body language vibrates with empathy. As he commiserates with Lee, praising him for his innings, it is obvious that he is not just going through the motions of a post-match handshake. It is a moment of real emotion, and this is why it is so affecting. Flintoff is not just a sportsman here. He is a moral teacher, a living embodiment of big-hearted grace.

Tim Ewbank, in his biography of Flintoff, acclaims the significance of the picture as an emblem of sport at its best. 'This supreme act of sportsmanship,' he writes, 'became the sporting image of the summer, and the photograph of this moment of human kindness and decency was reprinted time and again in newspapers and magazines. It said much about the spirit in which the series was played, and it said even more about Flintoff the man.'

But Flintoff himself was keen to downplay what he had done. He was quick to point out that there was an element of chance to all the publicity. Steve Harmison, he explained, actually shook Lee's hand before he did – but no one took that photo and so the moment has been forgotten.

In Flintoff's view, the attention was – if anything – worrying. So much hype, about a simple act of courtesy, suggests that we must be living in a time when courtesy is in short supply. 'I think sport is in a sad state of affairs,' he said, 'when a gesture like that gets so much airtime. It's just something you should really do. Has sportsmanship reached such a low level that someone putting an arm around an opponent or shaking his hand has become national news?' There was nothing special about what he did – at least, not in the eyes of the man himself. He was just trying to be a good bloke.

When Roger Fenton captured cricket for the first time back in 1857, there were very few photographs in existence. It is hard, now, even to imagine such a world – a world where the only way to see something, unless it had been drawn or painted, was to witness it first-hand with your own eyes. Our own world is over-whelmed with images; often someone's very first thought, when anything happens, is to record it on a phone. It is almost as if, were it not for the photo, the event somehow would not be real. In 1977, the writer Susan Sontag observed, 'Today, everything exists to end in a photograph'; it is a statement that becomes truer with each passing year.

Alongside this, though, a kind of carelessness has grown about the destiny of these images. There is a transience to the photos we constantly take; they are so omnipresent they become replace-able. Entrepreneur and academic Kalev Leetaru has noted, 'The typical college student today is more preoccupied with finding the easiest way to capture an important moment and share it with his or her friends in realtime than worrying about preserving that image for historians to access hundreds of years from now.'

Perhaps the age of the iconic photo is coming to an end. We are flooded by so many, that the worth of each one is weakened. But within this visual labyrinth, in recent years, there is one cricketing photo that stands out above all others.

The Headingley test of 2019 is another Ashes battle that has passed from match into myth. England's resurrection from the dead provided, like all the best stories, a treasure trove of quirks and memorable details, a divine comedy of unbearable sporting tension. Alongside Stokes' mighty hitting, there was the Marcus Harris dropped catch in the deep; the surreal saga of Jack Leach cleaning his glasses; the crowd-delighting run-out fumble of Nathan Lyon; the plumb l.b.w. appeal, in the dying moments, with no reviews left. Thirty-eight years earlier, Ian Botham and Bob Willis combined to produce what many had thought to be the ultimate in Ashes sporting drama. Stokes and Leach were somehow managing not just to match it, but to surpass it.

And Stokes' moment of triumph – straight after walloping the ball to the fence for the winning runs – was captured in an image taken by Gareth Copley that continues to adorn posters, billboards, magazines, websites, and even T-shirts:

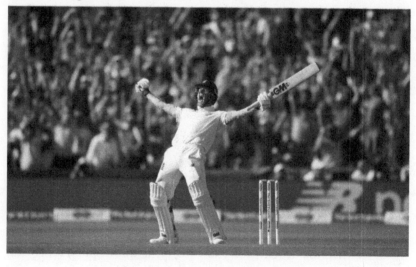

There is something not just heroic, but mythological about the pose. Bat clutched in one hand, inked arms spread wide, he resembles a swashbuckling warrior of the ancient world. There are faint echoes of the Wellington Monument in London's Hyde Park, the bronze statue of a strutting Achilles clutching shield and sword. And in the heart of the picture, there is Stokes' howl of joy – a cricketing barbaric yawp, pouring out all the pent-up emotion of the duel. The crowd in the distance, out of focus, are nothing more than a blur of celebration – daubs of leaping light around their triumphant hero. It is one of the purest images of sporting passion that has been captured this century; a fitting testament to what Alastair Cook hailed as 'The most extraordinary innings ever played by an Englishman.'

21

'THE VIOLENCE OF REALITY': FRANCIS BACON AND THE DARKNESS OF CRICKET

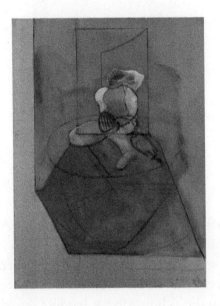

It is, in many ways, a typical Francis Bacon – a grotesque blur of misshapen body parts and amputated limbs. The central figure crouches upon a raised steel-grey platform or table, in front of a wall of angry orange – the outline of an open door visible behind him.

But alongside the Baconian mix of the troubling and the monstrous, there is another, more surprising element. The figure is quite clearly wearing cricket pads.

The painting, *'Figure with Cricket Pad'*, c. 1982, is one of several by Bacon that feature a cricketer. In fact, the game was something of an under-acknowledged preoccupation for the artist. Art critic Alastair Smart labelled him an 'avid cricket fan'. And in the latter part of his career, he repeatedly supplied his figures with pads round their legs. As his biographers Mark Stevens and Annalyn Swan have explained, cricket was one of his 'obsession[s] of the early 1980s'.

Another of Bacon's pad-wearing forms appears in *Study of the Human Body, 1981–2*:

This, if anything, is even more unsettling. A naked torso – severed above the hips – is topped by two bulbous, buttock-like spheres. The right thigh ripples with rolls of folded fat, like a joint of pork. Stevens and Swan deemed the figure to be 'highly coloured, and static' – but with the left foot raised, there is a hint of motion. The disembodied legs appear to be in the process of running a quick single – right off the precipice of the precarious platform on which they stand.

A range of claims have been made about what inspired the painting. Poet and art critic Edward Lucie-Smith made an intriguing suggestion about the body's identity:

It is true that I don't like a good deal of the very late work, particularly the series showing dwarfish figures dressed for the game of cricket. It was only after [Bacon's] death that I learned that these were supposedly inspired by Francis's fascination with the swaggering, ultimately butch cricket hero of that period, Ian Botham. Well, I suppose I can't blame him for lusting after Botham, who when young was testosterone on two legs, and very much aware of the fact.

The notion that Bacon's painting might portray the Beefy crown jewels is certainly eyebrow-raising. If so, the painting becomes – at least in part – an eroticised celebration of Botham's masculinity, for all the image's disturbing qualities. It is an unusual specimen in the mass of tributes to Botham as a cricketing icon and national treasure.

But this is not the only available reading. Canadian writer Barry Joule – a friend of Bacon's – claimed he sat for the cricketing paintings. Not only that, he offered a reason for why the torso has no head. According to Joule, the original version *did* have a head – his own. It was Joule's discomfort at being so recognisably exposed that led Bacon, in a fit of pique, to amend the image:

> Francis, annoyed at me complaining of a fairly good likeness of myself naked in the cricket portrait, at the last minute chopped off – i.e. painted out – my head . . . casually yet sarcastically informing a stunned me the next day: 'There, now I think you look much better this way – just the essentials here . . . and absolutely no head to worry about. I hope you are happy now.' So, somewhat dejected, I found myself headless.

In a further plot twist, Joule also quipped that David Gower had been considered as a model. This was certainly the view of art critic David Sylvester, who put it to Bacon, in an interview, that the image must have been taken 'from a book of photographs of David Gower which I've seen in your studio'.

Bacon did not deny it, though his account of the painting was typically enigmatic. 'Well, I have often seen cricket,' he replied, 'and when I did this image I suddenly said, "Well, I don't know why, but I think it's going to strengthen it very much and make it look very much more real if it has cricket pads on it. I can't tell you why."'

Bacon's pad-wearing figures have received mixed reactions. While not considered the summit of his achievement, their reputation has grown over time. Scottish artist Peter Doig (whose 2012 painting, *Paragrand*, features a game of beachside cricket) took a while to appreciate their power. 'He is certainly the best ever painter to use orange,' Doig said, 'although when I first saw the cricket paintings, I found them repulsive. The stumpiness of them. In the end, I think the colour is electrifying, and he uses it in a way to draw you into the picture so that you almost no longer are aware of it being a colour.'

But Bacon's images – unique and startling – represent something more than a surprising entry in the history of cricketing art. They are gateways into a dramatically darker vision of the game, transforming our sense of how it might be perceived in the imagination. In these distorted, melted, limbless figures, we see cricket at the furthest possible distance from the idealised world of pastoral beauty and English village greens. The cricket pad is dislocated from its traditional aesthetic and thrown into a world of nightmare. Pads, after all, are meant to protect; but Bacon's tormented cricketers are stripped and vulnerable. Art writer Paul Carey-Kent wrote that Bacon uses cricket pads 'as a means of further alienating the distorted body, even as they might pretend to protect it'.

Bacon famously embraced an attitude of sardonic nihilism. His philosophy of life was morbid and desolate. 'Man now realises he is an accident, a completely futile being,' he once claimed. He was consistently hostile to the analysis of his own art – but he did once say, about his work, 'It's to do with an attempt to remake the violence of reality itself.' This is the kind of world into which he drags the game of cricket: a world of violence and screams of despair.

What kind of light, exactly, do Bacon's paintings shine on the darkness of cricket? Alongside the cosy nostalgia and the claims about cricket's noble spirit, the game has always harboured a more shadowy side. And this is not limited to the abundant presence of skulduggery and corruption through its history. For cricket is also a game of psychological darkness – uniquely so, according to many analysts and former players. Perhaps Bacon's disturbing cricketer figures are a reminder of the rupturing effect it can have on the individual. 'Cricket,' Peter Roebuck once wrote, 'is a game played in the mind', and this pressure can have drastic consequences.

Arthur Shrewsbury was one of the great batsmen of the Victorian age – the first ever player to score a thousand runs in test matches and, in many people's eyes, second in stature only to W. G. Grace himself. 'Arthur Shrewsbury must be acknowledged as the greatest professional batsman of his age,' Grace once said. When asked to pick his first-choice player, the answer was simple: 'Give me Arthur.' (This would be the title of the Shrewsbury biography by Peter Wynne-Thomas.)

Even in his later playing years, Shrewsbury's excellence as a batsman was undiminished: in his final season, the summer of 1902, he topped the first-class averages at the age of forty-seven. But by this point, his mental health was in steep decline. He had developed an acute hypochondria – complaining about pains in his kidneys, struggling to walk and fruitlessly consulting with various doctors. In February 1903, he entered a nursing home in London for further medical tests. But no one could find anything wrong with him. The sickness, it seemed, was not in his body. It was in his head. Peter Wynne-Thomas has detailed what took place on 12 May of that year:

> At about eight o'clock, Shrewsbury went upstairs to his bedroom, asking his girlfriend, Gertrude Scott, to make him a cup of cocoa. From the kitchen, Miss Scott heard a

sharp noise and shouted up the stairs to ask if anything was amiss, but Shrewsbury replied: 'Nothing.' A minute later she heard a distinct pistol shot and ran upstairs to find Shrewsbury bleeding from a wound in his head. Miss Scott rushed next door and fetched the neighbour, John Arnold, who came to the house and went up to Shrewsbury's bedroom. He stayed with the cricketer whilst Dr Knight of Carlton was summoned. By the time the doctor arrived Shrewsbury was dead. It was then discovered that he had first shot himself in the chest, but when that did not prove fatal, fired a second time at his head.

It is impossible to know what precise role cricket might have played in Shrewsbury's suicide. *Wisden* recorded that he died from an 'illness which he could not be induced to believe curable'; at the same time, it suggested that 'the knowledge that his career in the cricket field was over had quite unhinged his mind'.

Shrewsbury's suicide is, sadly, hardly an isolated case in the history of cricket. One of his foremost opening partners, A. E. Stoddart, also committed suicide in 1915. A string of others – Cyril Buxton, Albert Trott, Harold Gimblett, Cyril Bland and David Bairstow, to name just a few – suffered the same fate. Cricketers are more likely to commit suicide than players of any other professional sport. It is difficult to avoid the conclusion that something is at work in the game, something hazardous and malign. The list of prominent English cricketers of more recent years, who have struggled with their mental health, is staggering: Marcus Trescothick, Jonathan Trott, Phil Tufnell, Graham Thorpe, Matthew Hoggard, Steve Harmison, Monty Panesar, Andrew Flintoff, Ben Stokes.

'How far is the nature of cricket itself responsible for harming those who play it?' asked Michael Atherton in *The Times*. Are the plentiful stories of depression and self-harm just a coincidence, a statistical anomaly of some kind? Or is the game, somehow, at fault? In Atherton's view, aspects of cricket's architecture can have a psychologically toxic impact:

> . . . the nature of the game itself is cruel: the time spent wait-ing, pondering and then failing; the brutal way that all the preparation can be cut short, especially for batsmen who, with the prospect of being given out, Mike Brearley has written, must face a kind of death on a daily basis. There are short, enjoyable summer months followed, for county cricketers, by long, lonely winters.

Another former cricketer, Ed Cowan, has suggested something else. The kind of person drawn towards cricket in the first place might be part of the problem: 'The game, buried in statistics, may attract the analytically inclined – the sort of person who wants to obsess about technique and dwell on statistical compari-sons to justify his worth to the team. Perhaps it attracts a certain kind of high achiever.'

The deepest research into this territory has been conducted by cricket writer David Frith. He produced a whole book, *Silence of the Heart*, on the subject of cricket suicides. In the foreword, he asks similar questions about whether we should seek out the answers in cricketers, or in cricket itself:

> Does cricket, more than any other game, actually *attract* the susceptible by virtue of its wicked, teasing uncertainties, its long, drawn-out routine, its compulsive, all-consuming commitment? Or conversely, by its sometimes cruel and frustrating pattern, does it gradually *transform* unwary cricket-loving boys into brooding, insecure and ultimately self-destructive men when the best days are past?

There is, in Frith's wording, a disquieting suggestion that the toxicity of cricket is – in some way – part of its appeal. The game is brutal, unpredictable, exhausting; as such, perhaps it draws those who are seduced by such things.

It is a precarious claim. After all, it could be said that any sport at the top level is psychologically challenging, even harmful. The pressures of intense competition can take their toll, providing a potential recipe for mental health decay. Frith, though, argues there is something uniquely tough about cricket. The game has its own brand of ruthlessness:

> It is the uncertainty that excites or, more usually, erodes. As any serious batsman takes guard, whether he be a Bradman or a colt on trial, he knows that first ball could get him, bringing with it humiliation. It matters less when personal success is the norm. But it is *uncertainty*, day in and day out, that plays a sinister beat on the soul. Not for the cricketer the assurance known to golfers: that however much a mess the first or the second hold might have been, there will be eighteen altogether, and time for recovery. The footballer, barring a broken leg, knows he should have ninety minutes' play, with the chance of a good second half to offset a poor first. In tennis you can always come back in a five-setter from being two sets down. Even in boxing, men rise from the canvas to land a knockout blow.

Cricket is a game of uncertainty, of no second chances. It shares all the pressures of other sports, and brings along its own snares, traps and quagmires.

Perhaps, then, Bacon's ominous art is a window into the darkness of cricket – a vision of the game on a very different plane to the comfortable image of white-clad figures on a sunlit English green. It is a reminder that cricket might not, in fact, be the route to civilised dignity that James Pycroft and Thomas Hughes once claimed. It might, instead, be a road to pain and disappointment. Of all team games, it can lay claim to being the most brooding and introspective. You may well have teammates around you

– but in the end you are on your own, with only your own thoughts for company. It is a vulnerable place to be. 'It might be called a team game,' wrote John Arlott, 'but no one is so lonely as a batsman facing a bowler supported by ten fieldsmen and observed by two umpires to ensure that his error does not go unpunished.'

VII
FUTURES

14 July 2019. Lord's.

Jofra Archer had only made his England debut two months earlier. But already, he had been heralded as a sensation – the next global superstar of English cricket.

Barbados-born, he had played a handful of games for the West Indies Under-19 team; under the old rules, he would not yet have been playing for England. These, though, were new rules. The seven-year qualification period had been reduced to three. And Archer's rare level of talent – a liquid run-up reminiscent of Michael Holding, vindaloo-heat pace and a dazzling range of deliveries including chin-menacing bouncers, off-cutters, leg-cutters, slower balls and toe-crushing yorkers – led to clamours for his inclusion.

'He's got to be in,' said Andrew Flintoff. 'Who would I get rid of? Anyone. He's brilliant.'

Something new had been brewing in English cricket – not just new qualification rules, but a new philosophy: one of fearless-ness, innovation and all-out aggression. After many years of underpowered performances, the England one-day unit had finally dragged itself into the twenty-first century. Back in 2007, England were hitting an average of 1.6 sixes per game – the lowest average in international cricket. By 2018, this had become 5.6 per game. The team Archer had joined was a juiced-up,

musclebound outfit – a team to be afraid of. His dynamic bowling perfectly expressed that this was not the old, tame England,
but a very different beast.

And here he was, at the home of cricket – about to bowl the
Super Over at the end of the World Cup final.

The match had already delivered enough drama to reach legendary status. At 196 for 4 – chasing 241 – England had been cruising
to victory, before doing their best to self-destruct. In the end they
only just scrabbled to parity – thanks largely to an instantly notorious stroke of luck, in the final over, when the ball deflected off Ben
Stokes' bat for four overthrows. After fifty overs each, there was
nothing between the teams. One extra over each, to settle things.

Super Overs had been around for a while in T20 cricket. But it was
the first time they had been seen in a one-day international. And this
was Lord's. The World Cup final. There could be no bigger occasion.

England went first. Stokes and Jos Buttler managed to scramble
fifteen runs off Trent Boult. Sixteen to win for New Zealand. If the
scores were tied, that would be no good, as a 'boundary count' rule
would be deployed, on which England were well ahead.

And bowling the Super Over for England? Jofra Archer, in just
his fourteenth international match. 'It was an easy decision,' said
captain Eoin Morgan. 'We just asked him to do what he's been
doing since he became a professional cricketer. He's a guy with the
world at his feet.'

Things did not start well. In such circumstances, nerves were
understandable. Bowling from round the wicket, to the left-handed
James Neesham, the silky run-up looked stilted and the ball seemed
to slip from the side of his hand . . . it came out all wrong. A dud
delivery well out of the batsman's reach. Wide ball. Fifteen required.

The next was much better – a trademark Jofra yorker, right up in
the blockhole. Neesham squeezed his bat down on it – not much of
a shot, really: a scratchy, mistimed drive. But it dribbled past
Archer towards long-off; with the field set back, they ran two.

Then came what looked like disaster. Archer tried another yorker – but he didn't get it right and Neesham launched him high into the Mound Stand for six. Surely this was the decisive moment. New Zealand needed just seven runs from four balls. One Kiwi hand was on the trophy.

Neesham tried the same shot – a brutal swing to mid-wicket – off the next ball and then again off the one after that. But he didn't connect properly with either. Three runs, now, from two deliveries. At this point, very few people would have put any money on England. A spark of inspiration was needed from somewhere.

And somehow Archer found it. With Neesham geared up for a big, match-winning drive, he conjured a surprise short delivery. The batsman could only offer a cross-batted hack, edging the ball onto his own shoe. Just a single. Two runs needed. One ball to go. Film director Jim Jarmusch once said, 'The beauty of life is in small details, not in big events.' Well, here was a big event, that much was clear enough. And the small details would mean everything.

What followed had a dreamlike feel, the margin between victory and defeat so absurdly tiny that it defied belief. Archer's final delivery was not, in fact, a very good one – overpitched, and veering down the leg side. But it seemed to take Guptill by surprise, cramping him for room. He mustered an off-balance push out towards mid-wicket. They needed two – but with Jason Roy swooping in, it would be tight . . . it was an iffy throw, but Buttler managed to grab the ball, swivel, and smash down the stumps . . .

Guptill was two yards out. England had won the World Cup.

As the cheers echoed round Lord's, there was a sense not only of a match won, but an era fulfilled. This was the culmination of a revolutionised England, an embrace of contemporary cricket in all its forms – speed, aggression, vitality, invention. One might have imagined the New Zealanders to be bitter. But their response was impeccable. Captain Kane Williamson's capacity for benevolence was dazzling. 'It's one of those games which, no doubt, you'll look back on and really have appreciated being involved in it,' he said. 'We had a huge amount of fun along the way.'

A more graceful and generous response could not be imagined. Patience, fortitude and self-denial; the various bumps of order, obedience and good humour, with an unruffled temper . . . those were the virtues, the English virtues, that James Pycroft had assigned to cricket 170 years before. And here they all were, perfectly manifested. Except they came not from England, but the other side of the world . . .

22

'A LARGE-SCALE, HIGH-ENERGY RIOT': CRICKET IN THE TWENTY-FIRST CENTURY IMAGINATION

'Each night he added to the pattern of his fancies until drowsiness closed down upon some vivid scene with an oblivious embrace. For a while these reveries provided an outlet for his imagination; they were a satisfactory hint of the unreality of reality, a promise that the rock of the world was founded securely on a fairy's wing.'

Fitzgerald's lines, from *The Great Gatsby*, sum up Jay Gatsby's addiction to fantasy. Perpetually pursuing ideals that will never come to pass, he lives instead in a world of dreams. Truth, for Gatsby, is an imaginative phenomenon – playing itself out in one place only, the bright dreamscape of his own mind.

The unreality of reality . . . it is a phrase that has a good deal of relevance to cricket and the English imagination. For years, for decades, for centuries, extraordinary claims have been made for cricket – not just that it was invented in England, not just that it has been played by the English, but that it is an actual expression of Englishness itself. In the culture, the aesthetics and the iconography of the game – so the argument goes – the meaning of England can somewhere be found.

As these chapters have revealed, the claim has always been more imaginary than real – an unreality on to which, for various reasons, people have tried to cling. In the twenty-first century, the legitimacy of the *Englishness* of cricket feels more doubtful than ever. In our fast-paced, global, multimedia, technicolour world of

T20, the IPL and The Hundred – where instant gratification is expected and test-match cricket itself is increasingly under threat – the old, cosy ideals of cricket on an English green quickly start to look like fusty, head-in-the-clouds stuff, nothing more than sad delusions for out-of-touch dinosaurs.

So, what of cricket in the twenty-first-century imagination? Some of the century's most interesting cricketing literature has looked head-on at the vagaries and complexities of nationhood. Irish writer Joseph O'Neill's 2008 novel *Netherland*, for instance, tells the story of London-based Dutch banker Hans van den Broek, who relocates to New York and finds himself playing cricket for a vigorously international local team of West Indians, Sri Lankans, Indians and Pakistanis. In a city reeling from the 9/11 attacks, cricket offers community for residents feeling unsettled and destabilised, outsiders in their own dwelling place: 'That summer of 2002, when out of loneliness I played after years of not playing, and in the summer that followed, I was the only white man I saw on the cricket fields of New York.'

Zaffar Kunial has written a range of deft and moving cricket poems that stand alongside the very finest cricketing verse of any era. Born and raised in Birmingham, close to the Edgbaston cricket ground, he has chronicled his identity as a child of Pakistani parents growing up in the Midlands. 'England's Moeen Ali went to my school,' he writes, in a poem simply titled 'England'. 'His dad's from Dadyal. Mine's up in the village over the bridge.'

Kunial's most recent collection, *England's Green* – shortlisted for the T. S. Eliot prize in 2022 – shrewdly explores the boundaries of Englishness and national character. At one level, the title is a clear allusion to Blake's 'Jerusalem', with its closing vision of 'England's green and pleasant land' – and all its attached associations of singalong English patriotism. But it also nods towards the green flag of Pakistan, as Kunial seeks to square his own identity with a family heritage he sometimes struggles to grasp. 'When we were left home one Christmas day, it was because/I wouldn't wear a paper crown from a cracker and Dad/exploded. To him the green hat was a country, unfolded – a flag I didn't see.'

Nathan Leamon – analyst for the England cricket team, in various guises, for over a decade – centred his 2018 novel, *The Test*, around the action of an Ashes match. Following the fortunes of stand-in captain James McCall, as he battles to save the game, the story examines the pressures of top-level professional cricket – not just the intensity of competition itself, but the effects such a lifestyle can have on mental health and on family. 'You have a home, but you don't live there,' McCall reflects. 'The deep connections, to place and loved ones, and to the normal rhythms of life; the connections that nourish you and ground you. They wither.' Struggling as he does with both a failing marriage and alcohol addiction, the character of McCall is a notable embodiment of cricket's darker side – a confirmation of Francis Bacon's bleak vision.

Cricket is also central to *24 for 3*, a novella by Jennie Walker – the pen name of poet Charles Boyle. The story follows an unnamed married woman as she negotiates relationships between three men – her husband, her stepson and her secret lover. As the five days of an England–India test match unfold around her, she finds herself drawing parallels between cricket and elements of her personal life.

Aspects of the game serve as metaphors for romantic relations. 'Unlikely partnerships may flourish,' she explains, 'as between a top-order batsman and an incompetent one who may on rare occasions play out of his skin and frustrate the bowlers, who believe he has no right to survive.' The consequences of her affair are compared to the second innings of a test: 'You can't wipe the slate clean: whatever mistakes you've made before still count and have to be made up for before you can really start again.' When she finds out that, in test matches, each team bats twice, she remarks, 'Oh, so it's like that play by Samuel Beckett,' before adding, 'except that you can see the Beckett in one evening.'

Like that play by Samuel Beckett . . . this, of course, is a play in which – according to critic Vivian Mercer's famous assessment – 'nothing happens, twice'. One of the quirkier theories about *Waiting for Godot* has always been that the two tramps, Vladimir and Estragon, are actually two batsmen waiting to go out to bat. From this unconventional angle, their helpless uncertainty is the uncertainty of when the next wicket might fall. 'Come on Gogo,' says Vladimir at one point, 'return the ball, can't you, once in a way?' Maybe, just maybe, there is something in the fact that the tree where they wait is, of all things, a willow . . .

Beckett and Pinter's shared passion for cricket was tackled by Shomit Dutta in his recent play, *Stumped* – a two-hander in which the playwrights are imagined playing a match together for the Gaieties XI. 'Could the radical, dramatic innovation of Harold Pinter or Samuel Beckett have happened,' asked Rachel Halliburton, in her *Times* review of the play, 'if it had not been for their obsession with Britain's most traditional sport? Both men's genius, after all, was marked by plays in which little happened, where violence was distilled into subtle codes and in which waiting was an existential virtue – a novelty in theatre but not so much on the cricket pitch.'

It is an intriguing claim. Might their preoccupation with uneventful narratives – with the phenomenon of *waiting* – have links, somewhere, to their love of cricket? Perhaps, for Pinter and Beckett's masterpieces of dramatic art, we really do have cricket to thank. 'An innings is like a life or part in a play,' Dutta has said. 'Its end is certainly like a death.'

In visual art, the most notable cricketing piece of recent years is surely Sacha Jafri's commemoration of England's 2019 World Cup win:

Jafri's painting pays homage to several things at once – not just the famous Super Over victory, but also Lord's cricket ground and London more broadly. Alongside the Lord's pitch and pavilion, a range of famous landmarks are visible, including the Houses of Parliament, the O2 Arena and the London Eye. The Oval gasholders even make an appearance, in the top right-hand corner.

But the image is not exactly traditional. Jafri pays his respects to the game's institutions – with the MCC headquarters, that supreme historic nexus of cricketing power, in the very heart of the scene. But other aspects – the kaleidoscopic bursts of colour, the merging of the figurative with the abstract, what journalist Josh Sims has labelled 'a large-scale high-energy riot of colour and form' – express something else, a vibrant celebration of contemporaneity. This is a thoroughly twenty-first-century picture – looking forwards as much as it looks back. As arts writer Jane Hughes has put it, we see 'London – painted by countless artists over the centuries – but freshly interpreted by Jafri in a passionate, exhilarating fashion that conveys the energy and atmosphere of the contemporary city'.

Jafri once described his work as an effort to link 'us back to our cultural and ancestral past, our more empathetic and conscious present, and our inspired and hopeful future'. And the electrified energy of his 2019 painting comes, in part, from this double-edged approach to cricketing history. He shows no interest in any staid, nostalgic vision: the graceful, decorous, while-flannelled aesthetic of soft sunlight on the village green is nowhere to be seen. In contrast, he offers an eruption of energy and light – a window into the flamboyant texture of modern urban life.

The glitzy effervescence also expresses something about the pace and the frenetic thrill of contemporary cricket. The high-octane drama of the 2019 World Cup final is conveyed in a manner impossible for a more traditional or 'orthodox' picture. And Jafri's polychrome London is saturated with history, but also feels open to the future – a place of inclusivity and opti-mism; containing every kind of person, every kind of experi-ence, every kind of possibility. It is a transcendent city – the sort of London that writer Peter Ackroyd described as going 'beyond any boundary or convention. It contains every wish or word ever spoken, every action or gesture ever made, every harsh or noble statement ever expressed. It is illimitable. It is Infinite London.'

'Cricket, that ever changeful, changeless game' . . . those words of poet and novelist Edmund Blunden convey something of English cricket's spiritual quandary – the way it has always been caught in a battle between the beauty of its past and the inevitable transformations of its future. Maybe Jafri's painting – in its dual embrace of history and innovation – might point the way beyond what Duncan Hamilton dubbed cricket's 'tug-of-war between modernity and tradition'. Maybe the future of cricket, in the English imagination, could harness a defence of the past that escapes narrow-minded nostalgia and seizes the possibilities of the future. Maybe, just maybe. *Tomorrow we will run faster, stretch out our arms farther . . . and then one fine morning . . .*

ACKNOWLEDGEMENTS

I want to begin by thanking two people who have been essential to the realisation of this book – my agent, Tim Bates, for his invaluable support and guidance; and my publisher, Andreas Campomar, for a range of astute suggestions that helped to give the book direction and drive. Thank you also to Holly Blood at Constable for her wonderfully patient and adroit help at every turn.

Thank you to the collections team at the MCC, for allowing me to visit the extraordinary array of treasures in the Lord's collection. In particular, I am immensely grateful to Neil Robinson and Charlotte Goodhew, both for the time they so generously took to answer my queries, and for the gift of their world-class expertise.

Several friends and colleagues have offered indispensable advice. Ed Farley has been a beacon of cricketing acumen and alehouse insight, lending me some hard-to-find tomes as well as kindly reading several draft chapters. Thank you also to Nigel Mortimer, for his matchless medieval expertise; to Dom Sullivan and Tim Beard, for some valuable promptings towards cricketing literature; and to Richard Osborne, for his unrivalled wisdom and eloquence on the genius of Cardus.

To my old opening partner, Robert Gevertz, I wish you the very best of health, for many long years to come.

A special word must be reserved for the eminent membership

of Gladstone Smalls: Christian Dickman, Gid Habel, Richard Tacon, Ed Vainker, and Duncan White.

To my mother and father, I owe the gift of childhood cricketing support from the very beginning. Somewhere, I hope, my father is reading; somewhere beyond the boundary.

As always, the deepest thanks are to my wife Nouska, and my two daughters, Manon and Hermione, for love and support beyond what any imagination can hold.

BIBLIOGRAPHY

Ackroyd, Peter, *London: The Biography* (London: Vintage, 2001)

Adams, Douglas, *Life, the Universe, and Everything* (London: Pan Macmillan, 1982)

Adburgham, Alison, A Punch *History of Manners and Modes* (London: Hutchinson, 1961)

Allen, David Rayvern, *A Song for Cricket* (London: Pelham Books, 1981)

Allen, David Rayvern with Doggart, Hubert, eds, 'A *Breathless Hush . . .': The MCC Anthology of Cricket Verse* (London: Methuen, 2004)

Allen, Dean, 'England's "Golden Age": Imperial Cricket and Late Victorian Society', *Sport in Society* 15:2 (March 2012) 209-226

Altham, H. S., *A History of Cricket* Vol. I (London: George Allen & Unwin, 1962)

Amis, Kingsley *Take a Girl Like You* (London: Penguin, 1962)

Andrews, Allen, *The Life of L. S. Lowry* (London: Jupiter Books, 1977)

Anon., *A Rod for Tunbridge Beaus, Bundl'd up at the Request of the Tunbridge Ladies, to Jirk Fools into more Wit, and Clowns into more Manners. A Burlesque Poem* (London, 1701)

Anon., 'The Dream of the Rood', *A Choice of Anglo-Saxon Verse* ed. Richard Hamer (London: Faber and Faber, 2006) 163-75

Arlott, John and Cardus, Neville, *The Noblest Game: A Book of Fine Cricket Prints* (London; Toronto; Wellington; Sydney: George G. Harrap & Co., 1969)

Arlott, John and Eagar, Patrick, *An Eye for Cricket* (London: Hodder & Stoughton, 1979)

Arlott, John and Trueman, Fred, *Arlott & Trueman on Cricket* (London: British Broadcasting Corporation, 1977)

Ashton, John, *Social England Under the Regency* Vol. I (London: Ward and Downey, 1890)

Austen, Jane, *Northanger Abbey* (London: Penguin, 2003)

Bailey, Peter, *Leisure and class in Victorian England* (London: Routledge & Kegan Paul, 1978)

Baker, William, *Harold Pinter* (New York; London: Continuum International, 2008)

Baldwin, Barry, 'A Classical Cricketing Classic' in *Vates* 3 (Spring 2011) 24-29

Barrie, J. M., *J. M. Barrie's Allahakbarries C. C.* (London: James Barrie Publishers, 1950)

Barrie, J. M., *The Greenwood Hat, Being a Memoir of James Anon, 1885–1887* (London: Peter Davies Ltd, 1937)

Bateman, Anthony, *Cricket, Literature and Culture: Symbolising the Nation, Destabilising Empire* (London; New York: Routledge, 2009)

Bateman, Anthony, 'Cricket Pastoral and Englishness', *The Cambridge Companion to Cricket* (Cambridge: Cambridge University Press) 11-25

Beckett, Samuel, *The Complete Dramatic Works* (London: Faber and Faber, 1986)

Best, David, 'Art and Sport', *The Journal of Aesthetic Education*, Vol. 14, No. 2 (April 1980) 69-80

Billington, Michael, *The Life and Work of Harold Pinter* (London: Faber and Faber, 1996)

Birkin, Andrew, *J. M. Barrie and the Lost Boys* (New Haven; London: Yale University Press, 1979)

Birley, Derek, *A Social History of English Cricket* (London: Aurum Press, 1999)

Blake, William, *Complete Writings*, ed. Geoffrey Keynes (Oxford; New York: Oxford University Press, 1966)

Blake, William, *Songs of Innocence and of Experience*, ed. Robert N. Essick (San Marino: Huntingdon Library, 2008)

Blake, William, *The Complete Poetry & Prose of William Blake*, ed. David V. Erdman (New York: Anchor Books, 1988)

Blunden, Edmund, *Cricket Country* (London: Collins, 1944)

Blunt, Bruce and Warlock, Peter, *The Cricketers of Hambledon: Song with Chorus for Voice & Piano* (London: Augener, 1929)

Boase, T. S. R., *English Art 1100–1216* (Oxford: Clarendon Press, 1953)

Bold, Alan, 'John Bellany: A Portrait of the Artist', *John Bellany: Paintings, Watercolours and Drawings 1964–1986* (Broxburn: Alan Press, 1986)

Booth, Martin, *The Doctor, The Detective and Arthur Conan Doyle: A Biography of Arthur Conan Doyle* (London: Hodder and Stoughton, 1997)

Border, Allan, *Cricket As I See It* (Sydney; Melbourne; Auckland; London: Allen & Unwin, 2014)

Botham, Ian, *Head On: Botham – The Autobiography* (London: Ebury Press, 2007)

Box, Charles, *Cricket, Its Theory and Practice from its Origin to the Present Day* (London: Frederick Warne & Co., 1868)

Box, Charles, *The English Game of Cricket* (London: The Field, 1877)

Brearley, Mike, *Spirit of Cricket: Reflections on Play and Life* (London: Constable, 2020)

Brookes, Christopher, *English Cricket: The Game and its Players through the Ages* (London: Weidenfield and Nicolson, 1978)

Burnby, John, *The Kentish Cricketers: A Poem, Being a Reply to a Late Publication of a Parody on the Ballad of Chevy Chace; intituled, Surry Triumphant: or, the Kentish Men's Defeat* (Canterbury: T. Smith and Son, 1773)

Buss, R. W., 'Buss's Statement', Walter Dexter and J. W. T. Ley, *The Origin of Pickwick* (London: Chapman and Hall, 1936)

Byron, George Gordon, Lord, *Complete Poetical Works* (Oxford: Oxford University Press, 1970)

Cardus, Neville, *Autobiography* (London: Faber and Faber, 1947)

Cardus, Neville, *Cardus on Cricket* (London: Souvenir Press, 1976)

Cardus, Neville, *Days in the Sun* (London: Rupert Hart-Davis, 1948)

Cardus, Neville, *English Cricket* (London: Collins, 1947)

Cardus, Neville, *The Summer Game* (London: Rupert Hart-Davis, 1948)

Carr, J. L., *A Season in Sinji* (London: Quartet Books, 1976)

Cartier-Bresson, Henri, *The Decisive Moment: Photography by Henri Cartier-Bresson* (Göttingen: Steidl, 2014)

Case, Roy, *The Pebble in My Shoe: An Anthology of Women's Cricket* (Bloomington: AuthorHouse, 2018)

Chaucer, Geoffrey, *The Riverside Chaucer* ed. Larry D. Benson (Oxford: Oxford University Press, 2008)

Collier, J.P., ed., *The Political Decameron, or Ten Conversations on English Poets and Poetry* (Edinburgh: Constable and Co., 1820)

Collins, Wilkie and Dickens, Charles, *The Lazy Tour of Two Idle Apprentices* (London: Chapman & Hall, 1905)

Collins, Wilkie, *The Woman in White* (London: Penguin, 2012)

Colman, George, *The Heir at Law: A Comedy in Five Acts* (Dublin: T. Burnside, 1798)

Coster, Graham, ed., *A Field of Tents and Waving Colours: Neville Cardus Writing on Cricket* (London: Safe Haven Books, 2019)

Dellor, Ralph and Lamb, Stephen, *History of Cricket* (Stroud: Green Umbrella Publishing, 2006)

de Sélincourt, Hugh, *The Cricket Match* (London: Stanley Paul & Co., 1990)

Dickens, Charles, *Barnaby Rudge* (London: Vintage, 2010)

Dickens, Charles, *David Copperfield* (London: Vintage, 2008)

Dickens, Charles, *Martin Chuzzlewit* (London: Vintage, 2010)

Dickens, Charles, *Oliver Twist* (London: Vintage, 2007)

Dickens, Charles, *The Mystery of Edwin Drood* (London: Vintage, 2009)

Dickens, Charles, *The Old Curiosity Shop* (London: Vintage, 2010)

Dickens, Charles, *The Pickwick Papers* (London: Vintage, 2009)

Dickens, Charles, *The Pickwick Papers* (London: Chapman & Hall, 1837)

Dickens, Mamie, *My Father as I Recall Him* (London: Roxburghe Press, 1897)

Donaldson, Frances *P. G. Wodehouse: A Biography* (London: Weidenfeld and Nicolson, 1982)

Doyle, Arthur Conan, 'The Adventure of Spedegue's Dropper', *The Strand Magazine* (October 1928) 315-25

Duncombe, John, *Surry Triumphant: or the Kentish-Mens Defeat. A New Ballad; Being a Parody on Chevy-Chace* (London: J. Johnson, 1773)

D'Urfey, Thomas, *The Comical History of Don Quixote* (London: J. Darby, 1729)

D'Urfey, Thomas, *The Richmond Heiress* (London: Samuel Briscoe, 1693)

Eisler, Benita, *Byron: Child of Passion, Fool of Fame* (London: Hamish Hamilton, 1999)

Eliot, T. S., *Collected Poems 1909–1962* (London: Faber and Faber, 1963)

Esslin, Martin, *The Theatre of the Absurd* (New York, Anchor Books, 1961)

Ewbank, Tim, *Andrew Flintoff: The Biography* (London: John Blake Publishing, 2006)

Farson, Daniel, *The Gilded Gutter Life of Francis Bacon* (London: Vintage, 1994)

Fitzgerald, R. A., *Wickets in the West: or, The Twelve in America* (London: Tinsley Brothers, 1873)

Forster, E. M., *Maurice* (London: Penguin, 1972)

Forster, John, *The Life of Charles Dickens* Vol. I (Boston: James R. Osgood & Co., 1875)

Fraser, George MacDonald, *Flashman's Lady* (London: HarperCollins, 1981)

Frith, David, *Bodyline Autopsy: The Full Story of the Most Sensational Test Cricket Series: Australia v England 1932–33* (Sydney: ABC Books, 2002)

Frith, David, *Silence of the Heart: Cricket Suicides* (Edinburgh; London: Mainstream Publishing, 2001)

Goldwin, William, *Musae Juveniles* (London: A. Baldwin, 1706)

Goodwin, Clayton, *West Indians at the Wicket* (London: Macmillan Caribbean, 1986)

Grace, W. G., *Cricketing Reminiscences and Personal Recollections* (London: James Bowden, 1899)

Gray, Thomas, *Selected Poems* (London: Bloomsbury, 1997)

Green, Benny, *P. G. Wodehouse: A Literary Biography* (Oxford: Oxford University Press, 1981)

Grosskurth, Phyllis, *Byron: The Flawed Angel* (London: Hodder & Stoughton, 1997)

Guttmann, Allen, *Women's Sports: A History* (New York: Columbia University Press, 1991)

Haigh, Gideon, *Stroke of Genius: Victor Trumper and the Shot that Changed Cricket* (London: Simon & Schuster, 2016)

Halford, Brian, *The Real Jeeves: The Cricketer Who Gave His Life for His Country and His Name to a Legend* (Durrington: Pitch Publishing, 2013)

Hamilton, Duncan, *A Last English Summer* (London: Quercus, 2010)

Hamilton, Duncan, *Harold Larwood* (London: Quercus, 2009)

Hamilton, Duncan, *The Great Romantic: Cricket and the Golden Age of Neville Cardus* (London: Hodder & Stoughton, 2019)

Hardy, Thomas, *Collected Poems* (London: Wordsworth Editions, 1994)

Hardy, Thomas, *Jude the Obscure* (London: Penguin, 2003)

Hardy, Thomas, *Life's Little Ironies* (London: Osgood, McIlvaine & Co., 1894)

Hardy, Thomas, *The Return of the Native* (London: Penguin, 1999)

Hartley, L. P., *The Go-Between* (London: Penguin, 2000)

Hazlitt, William, 'Merry England' In *Sketches and Essays; and Winterslow (Essays Written There)* (London: Bell & Daldy, 1872)

Henderson, Michael, 'An English hero for the ages: Ian Botham at 60', *New Statesman* (27 November–3 December 2015) 32-3

Henderson, Michael, *That Will Be England Gone: The Last Summer of Cricket* (London: Constable, 2020)

Herbert, Mary Sidney, *The Collected Works of Mary Sidney Herbert, Countess of Pembroke: Poems, Translations and Correspondence* (Oxford: Clarendon Press, 1998)

Hill, Alan, *Herbert Sutcliffe: Cricket Maestro* (Stroud: Stadia, 2007)

Hobbs, Jack, *My Life Story* (London: 'The Star' Publications, 1935)

Hoefnagel, Dick, 'The Gads Hill "Higham" Cricket Club', *Dickensian* 81:3 (Autumn 1985) 145-7

Holding, Michael, *No Holding Back* (London: Weidenfeld & Nicholson, 2010)

Hornung, E. W., *The Complete Raffles: The Exploits of a Gentleman Thief* (Dundee: Thebes Publishing, 2017)

Hotten, Jon, *The Meaning of Cricket* (London: Yellow Jersey, 2016)

Housman, A. E., *A Shropshire Lad and Other Poems: The Collected Poems of A.E. Housman* (London: Penguin, 2010)

Housman, A. E., *The Letters of A. E. Housman* Vol. I, ed. Archie Burnett (Oxford: Clarendon Press, 2007)

Howat, Gerald, *Village Cricket* (Newton Abbot: David & Charles, 1980)

Hughes, Thomas, *Tom Brown's School Days: by an Old Boy* (London: Macmillan and Co., 1889)

Hughes, William R., *A Week's Tramp in Dickens-Land* (London: Chapman & Hall, 1891)

Jafri, Sacha, *Sacha Jafri* (London: YBP Publishing Press, 2008)

James, C. L. R., *Beyond a Boundary* (London: Vintage, 2019)

Joyce, James, *Dubliners* (London: Penguin, 2000)

Joyce, James, *Finnegans Wake* (London: Faber and Faber, 1939)

Joyce, James, *A Portrait of the Artist as a Young Man* (London: Penguin, 2003)

Joyce, James, *Ulysses* (London: Penguin, 2000)

Joyce, Stanislaus, *My Brother's Keeper* ed. Richard Ellmann (London; Boston: Faber and Faber, 1958)

Keats, John, *Selected Letters* (Oxford: Oxford University Press, 2009)

Kunial, Zaffar, *England's Green* (London: Faber and Faber, 2022)

Kunial, Zaffar, *Six: Cricket Poems* (London: Faber and Faber, 2019)

Kutner, Jon and Leigh, Spencer, *1000 UK Number One Hits* (London: Omnibus Press, 2005)

Lambirth, Andrew, *David Inshaw* (London: Unicorn Press, 2015)

Lang, Andrew, 'A History of Cricket', *Imperial Cricket* ed. P.F. Warner (London: The London & Counties Press Association, 1912)

Langland, William, *The Vision of Piers Plowman* (London: Everyman, 1978)

Lansdown, Richard, ed., *Byron's Letters and Journals: A New Selection* (Oxford: Oxford University Press, 2015)

Larwood, Harold and Perkins, Kevin, *The Larwood Story* (London: W.H. Allen, 1965)

Leamon, Nathan, *The Test* (London: Constable, 2018)

Le Genre, Kevin, *Don't Stop the Carnival: Black Music in Britain Vol. 1* (Leeds: Peepal Tree Press, 2018)

Lessing, Gottfried, *Hamburg Dramaturgy*, tr. Helen Zimmern (New York: Dover, 1962)

Light, Rob, 'Cricket in the Eighteenth Century', *The Cambridge Companion to Cricket* (Cambridge: Cambridge University Press) 26-39

Love, James, *Cricket: An Heroic Poem, illustrated with the Critical Observations of Scriblerus Maximus* (London: W. Bickerton, 1744)

Love, James, *Pamela: A Comedy As it is Perform'd, Gratis, at the Late Theatre in Goodman's Fields* (London: J. Robinson, 1742)

Lubbock, Alfred, *Memories of Eton and Etonians* (London: John Murray, 1899)

MacCarthy, Fiona, *Byron: Life and Legend* (London: John Murray, 2002)

Major, John, *More Than A Game: The Story of Cricket's Early Years* (London: HarperCollins, 2007)

Malings, Ron, 'Cricketers at the Wake', *James Joyce Quarterly* 7:4 (Summer, 1970) 333-49

Matthew, H. G. C. and Harrison, Brian, eds, *The Oxford Dictionary of National Biography* Vol. 15 (Oxford: Oxford University Press)

McEwen, John, *John Bellany* (Edinburgh; London: Mainstream Publishing, 1994)

McKinstry, Leo, *Jack Hobbs: England's Greatest Cricketer* (London: Yellow Jersey, 2011)

Meredith, George, *The Adventures of Harry Richmond* (London: Chapman & Hall, 1889)

Midwinter, Eric, *Quill on Willow: Cricket in Literature* (Chichester: Aeneas Press, 2001)

Mitford, Mary, *Our Village: Sketches of Rural Character and Scenery* (London: Geo B. Whittaker, 1828)

Mortimer, Gavin, *A History of Cricket in 100 Objects* (London: Serpent's Tail, 2013)

Morton, Thomas, *Speed the Plough: A Comedy in Five Acts* (London: A. Strahan, 1800)

Mote, Ashley, *The Glory Days of Cricket: The Extraordinary Story of Broadhalfpenny Down* (London: Robson Books, 1997)

Murdoch, Iris, *The Sandcastle* (London: Vintage, 2003)

Nyren, John, *The Cricketers of My Time*, ed. Ashley Mote (London: Robson Books, 1998)

O'Neill, Joseph, *Netherland* (London: Fourth Estate, 2009)

Osborne, Richard, 'Neville Cardus: A Writer for All Seasons', *Oldie* (June 2020) 69-70

Park, Jihang, 'Sport, Dress Reform and the Emancipation of Women in Victorian England', *International Journal of the History of Sport* 6:1 (1989) 10-30

Phillips, Edward, *The Mysteries of Love & Eloquence, Or, the Arts of Wooing and Complementing; As they are Manag'd in the Spring Garden, Hide Park, the New Exchange, and Other Eminent Places* (London: N. Brooks, 1658)

Pinter, Harold, *Collected Poems and Prose* (London: Methuen, 1986)

Pinter, Harold, *Plays: 3* (London: Faber and Faber, 1997)

Pinter, Harold, *The Birthday Party* (London: Eyre Methuen, 1975)

Pipe, Jim, *Cricket: A Very Peculiar History* (Brighton: Salariya Book Company, 2022)

Pope, Alexander, *The Poetical Works of Alexander Pope*, ed. Sir Adolphus William Ward (London; New York: Macmillan & Co, 1956)

P-T, H., *Early Cricket: A Description of the first known Match; and some comments on Creag, Cricket, Cricce, and Shakespeare's Clue* (Nottingham: C. H. Richards, 1923)

Pycroft, James, *The Cricket-Field, or, the History and the Science of Cricket* (Boston: Mayhew & Baker, 1859)

Pynchon, Thomas, *The Crying of Lot 49* (London: Penguin, 1996)

Rae, Simon, *W. G. Grace* (London: Faber and Faber, 1998)

Rajan, Amol, *Twirlymen: The Unlikely History of Cricket's Greatest Spin Bowlers* (London: Yellow Jersey Press, 2011)

Raven, Simon, *Seasons in the Grass* (London: Blond & Briggs, 1982)

Rice, Jonathan, *The Stories of Cricket's Finest Painting: Kent v Lancashire 1906* (Chichester: Pitch Publishing, 2019)

Roebuck, Peter, *It Takes All Sorts: Celebrating Cricket's Colourful Characters* (Crows Nest: Allen & Unwin, 2005)

Rogan, Johnny, *Ray Davies: A Complicated Life* (London: Vintage, 2016)

Rogers, Byron, *The Last Englishman: The Life of J. L. Carr* (London: Aurum Press, 2003)

Rosenwater, Irving, 'Charles Dickens and Cricket', *London Magazine* 10:3 (June 1970) 46-56

Rosenwater, Irving, *A Portfolio of Cricket Prints: A Nineteenth Century Miscellany* (London: Holland Press and Neville Spearman, 1962)

Rousseau, Jean-Jacques, *Emile* (Mineola; New York: Dover Publications, 2013)

Sandiford, Keith A. P., 'Amateurs and Professionals in Victorian County Cricket', *Albion: A Quarterly Journal Concerned with British Studies*, Vol. 15, No. 1 (Spring 1983) 32-51

Sandiford, Keith A. P., 'Cricket and the Victorians: A Historiographical Essay' in *Historical Reflections/Réflexions Historiques*, Vol. 9, No. 3 (Fall 1982) 421-436

Sassoon, Siegfried, *Collected Poems* (London: Faber and Faber, 2002)

Sassoon, Siegfried, *Memoirs of a Fox-Hunting Man* (London: Faber and Faber, 1928)

Sassoon, Siegfried, *The Weald of Youth* (London: Faber and Faber, 1942)

Shakespeare, William, *The Norton Shakespeare*, ed. Stephen Greenblatt (New York; London: W. W. Norton, 1997)

Silver, Brenda R., ed., *Virginia Woolf's Reading Notebooks* (Princeton: Princeton University Press, 1983)

Simpson, M. J., *Hitchhiker: A Biography of Douglas Adams* (London: Hodder & Stoughton, 2003)

Smith, David, '"A little more play": Cricket in Dickens's Fiction', *Dickensian* 86:1 (Spring 1990) 41-52

Smyth, Ethel, *Impressions that Remained* Vol. II (London: Longmans, Green & Co., 1923)

Sontag, Susan, *On Photography* (London: Penguin, 1979)

Stevens, Mark and Swan, Annalyn, *Francis Bacon: Revelations* (London: HarperCollins, 2021)

Strutt, Joseph, *The Sports and Pastimes of the People of England* (London: William Tegg, 1867)

Sylvester, David, *Interviews with Francis Bacon* (New York: Thames & Hudson, 1987)

Taylor, Alfred, D., *Annals of Lord's and the History of the MCC* (Bristol: J.W. Arrowsmith, 1903)

Thompson, A. A., *Cricketers of My Times* (London: Stanley Paul, 1967)

Tomlinson, Richard, *Amazing Grace: The Man who was W. G.* (London: Abacus, 2015)

Trollope, Anthony, ed., *British Sports and Pastimes* (London: Virtue & Co., 1868)

Trollope, Anthony, *The Fixed Period* (Leipzig: Bernhard Tauchniz, 1882)

Trueman, Fred, *As It Was: The Memoirs of Fred Trueman* (London: Macmillan, 2004)

Truffaut, Francois, *Hitchcock* (New York: Simon and Schuster, 1967)

Underdown, David, *Start of Play: Cricket and Culture in Eighteenth-Century England* (London: Penguin, 2000)

Various, *Cricket: A Weekly Record of the Game*, Vol. V, May 13 1886

Waghorn, H. T., *Cricket Scores, Notes, &c. Form 1730–1773* (Edinburgh; London: William Blackwood and Sons, 1899)

Walker, Jennie, *24 for 3* (London: Bloomsbury, 2008)

Wanostrocht, Nicholas 'Felix', *Felix on the Bat*, 2nd edition (London: Baily Brothers, 1850)

Ward, Edward, *The World Bewitch'd: a Dialogue between two Astrologers and the Author, with Infallible Predictions of what will Happen in this Present Year, 1699, from the Vices and Villanies Practis'd in Court, City and Country* (London, 1699)

Webb, J. F., tr., 'Bede: Life of Cuthbert', *Lives of the Saints* (London: Penguin, 1965)

Wells, H. G., *Certain Personal Matters* (London: T. Fisher Unwin, 1897)

Wells, H. G., *The War of the Worlds* (Richmond: Alma Classics, 2017)

Wertheim, Lucy Carrington, *Adventure in Art* (London; Brussels: Nicholson and Watson, 1947)

Whitman, Walt, *Leaves of Grass* (New York; London: Penguin, 1959)

Wilford, J., *Priestcraft: or, the Way to Promotion: a Poem Address'd to the Inferior Clergy of England being Wholesome Advice, how to behave at the approaching election* (London, 1734)

Wodehouse, P. G., *Mike and Psmith* (London: Everyman, 2012)

Wodehouse, P. G., *Psmith in the City* (London: Everyman, 2000)

Wodehouse, P. G., *Tales of St Austin's* (London: Adam & Charles Black, 1903)

Woolf, Virginia, *A Writer's Diary*, ed. Leonard Woolf (London: Hogarth Press, 1953)

Woolf, Virginia, *Jacob's Room* (Oxford: Oxford University Press, 1992)

Woolf, Virginia, *Mrs Dalloway* (London: Vintage, 2000)

Woolf, Virginia, *The Waves* (London: Vintage, 2000)

Woolf, Virginia, *To the Lighthouse* (London: Penguin, 2020)

Wordsworth, William, *Lyrical Ballads and other Poems 1797–1800*, ed. James Butler and Karen Green (Ithaca; London: Cornell University Press, 1992)

Wordsworth, William, *Poetical Works*, ed. Thomas Hutchinson (London; Oxford; New York: Oxford University Press, 1969)

Wynne-Thomas, Peter, *'Give Me Arthur': A Biography of Arthur Shrewsbury* (London: Arthur Baker Ltd, 1985)

Online Sources

breakingcharacter.com/stumped-catching-up-with-playwright-shomit-dutta/

cricmash.com/other-2/neville-cardus-the-charming-charlatan-of-cricket-writing

cristianolovatelliravarinonews.com/talking-with-edward-lucie-smith/

fadmagazine.com/2017/01/04/padding-pauls-art-stuff-train-197/

historyofenglishpodcast.com/2019/02/28/episode-122-the-name-of-the-game/

londondailydigital.com/2022/09/26/sacha-jafri-focuses-on-the-process-of-creation/

luxurylondon.co.uk/culture/art/sacha-jafri-artist-interview/

scroll.in/field/965869/i-received-death-threats-hate-letters-former-england-cricketer-defreitas-on-experiencing-racism

talksport.com/sport/cricket/1485882/footage-australia-jonny-bairstow-ashes-england-long-room-lords/

winstonchurchill.org/publications/finest-hour/finest-hour-194/royal-academy-between-tradition-and-innovation/

wisden.com/almanack/almanack-herbert-sutcliffe-obituary-tribute

wisden.com/almanack/bernard-bosanquet-the-man-who-changed-spin-bowling-forever-almanack

wisden.com/series-stories/ashes-2023/rishi-sunak-backs-ben-stokes-comments-on-the-controversial-jonny-bairstow-stumping

www.bfi.org.uk/features/praise-forest-whitaker-jim-jarmusch-ghost-dog-way-samurai

www.countrylife.co.uk/luxury/art-and-antiques/favourite-painting-robert-sandelson-204908

www.dailymail.co.uk/sport/cricket/article-1344861/ASHES-2011-Welcome-new-era-English-dominance.html

www.dailymail.co.uk/sport/cricket/article-8358849/From-boundaries-singles-Former-England-batting-star-Mark-Butcher-singer-songwriter.html

www.espncricinfo.com/story/ashes-2023-ben-stokes-on-jonny-bairstow-dismissal-i-wouldn-t-want-to-win-a-game-in-that-manner-1385437

www.espncricinfo.com/wisdenalmanack/content/story/150180.html

www.forbes.com/sites/kalevleetaru/2016/04/30/in-an-era-of-unlimited-photos-what-are-we-really-capturing-about-the-world/?sh=4fdf84e95b4f

www.gaieties.net/newpage

www.gedlingeye.co.uk/news/tragic-tale-of-england-cricket-legend-arthur-shrewsbury-who-shot-himself-in-gedling/

www.haroldpinter.org/cricket/wellard.shtml

www.huffingtonpost.co.uk/robert-upstone/david-inshaw-the-greatest_b_3076024.html

www.independent.co.uk/sport/cricket/alex-carey-geoffrey-boycott-jonny-bairstow-ben-stokes-australia-b2368465.html

www.likethesound.com/2011/01/english-corner-video-short-by-mike.html

www.lordbyron.org/monograph.php?doc=ThMoore.1830&select=AD1821

www.lords.org/lords/news-stories/mcc-committee-confirms-five-year-extension-to-oxfo

www.lords.org/mcc/heritage-collections/lowry-exhibition

www.medievalists.net/2010/02/on-the-origin-and-diffusion-of-european-ball-games-a-linguistic-analysis/

https://www.news18.com/cricketnext/news/guys-are-still-trying-to-make-sense-of-world-cup-final-kane-williamson-2304903.html

www.npg.org.uk/collections/search/portrait/mw07127/Ian-Botham

www.nzherald.co.nz/lifestyle/the-streets-mike-skinner-the-poet-of-british-suburbia/5SDVYFKGMN7FGTXFSEFRRHQTOA/

www.oldbaileyonline.org/static/Population-history-of-london.jsp

www.royharper.co.uk/hq-cd.html

www.smh.com.au/culture/music/getting-shot-being-grumpy-ray-davies-is-still-ironing-out-the-kinks-20191010-p52zes.html

www.smith.edu/woolf/vanessawithtranscript.php

www.standard.co.uk/sport/cricket/ashes-australia-england-spirit-of-cricket-ben-stokes-b1109777.html

www.tate.org.uk/tate-etc/issue-14-autumn-2008/homage-bacon

www.telegraph.co.uk/art/artists/pandemic-art-beauty-arose-tragedy/

www.telegraph.co.uk/cricket/2021/08/20/forgotten-ashes-miracle-mark-butcher-flayed-greatest-bowling/

www.telegraph.co.uk/cricket/2022/06/29/eton-v-harrow-match-lords-replaced-national-school-final/

www.telegraph.co.uk/cricket/2022/07/08/eton/

www.telegraph.co.uk/cricket/2023/06/20/ashes-2023-england-vs-australia-first-test-day-5-live/

www.telegraph.co.uk/culture/art/art-features/10191131/The-art-of-cricket-Enough-to-leave-you-stumped.html

www.telegraph.co.uk/sport/cricket/4746173/Maidens-in-demand.html

www.thecricketer.com/Topics/news/stephen_fry_backs_removal_eton_v_
harrow_fixture_ahead_of_mcc_member_vote.html

www.thecricketmonthly.com/story/1179657/how-much-have-odis-changed-in
-the-last-20-years

www.theguardian.com/artanddesign/2015/oct/02/david-inshaw-changed-
landscape-of-art

www.theguardian.com/artanddesign/2019/may/12/howzat-ls-lowrys-cricket-
match-painting-may-sell-for-1m

www.theguardian.com/artanddesign/2019/sep/14/francis-bacon-naked-crick-
eter-barry-joule-reveals-all

www.theguardian.com/culture/2009/mar/08/samuel-beckett-waiting-for-
godot#:~:text=They%27re%20waiting%20for%20Godot,happening%2C%
20twice%20%2D%20twice%20over.

www.theguardian.com/film/filmblog/2012/jul/24/my-favourite-hitchcock-
lady-vanishes

www.theguardian.com/sport/2007/oct/09/cricket.sport1

www.theguardian.com/sport/2011/jan/07/the-ashes-2010-11-england-australia

www.theguardian.com/sport/2021/sep/04/i-just-sat-there-thinking-im-a-crick-
eter-what-makes-me-different

www.theguardian.com/sport/2023/jul/03/cricket-ashes-england-australia-
jonny-bairstow

www.theguardian.com/sport/blog/2013/jun/24/20-great-ashes-moments-
andrew-flintoff

www.theguardian.com/theguardian/2001/jul/21/weekend7.weekend6

www.thehindu.com/sport/cricket/pujara-the-key-says-kapil/article6167172.
ece

www.thesun.co.uk/sport/22909067/australia-ashes-jonny-bairstow-cheating/

www.thetimes.co.uk/article/as-a-patriot-im-going-in-to-bat-for-my-beliefs
-wrt3crgqr

www.thetimes.co.uk/article/focus-britains-new-bard-h8ow9kg7txn;   inews.
co.uk/culture/music/the-streets-earth-review-hackney-mike-skinner-some-
thing-to-say-lockdown-574402

www.thetimes.co.uk/article/no-clear-path-through-fog-of-depression
-3nr7ffc7mzm

www.thetimes.co.uk/article/stumped-review-beckett-pinter-and-the-fine-art-of
-cricket-378dx637x

IMAGES

INDEX

Page references in *italics* refer to images.